D1452570

ALONG ANCIENT TRAILS

ALONG ANCIENT TRAILS

The Mallet Expedition of 1739

Donald J. Blakeslee

UNIVERSITY PRESS OF COLORADO

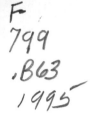

The University Press of Colorado is a cooperative publishing enterprise supported, in part, by Adams State College, Colorado State University, Fort Lewis College, Mesa State College, Metropolitan State College of Denver, University of Colorado, University of Northern Colorado, University of Southern Colorado, and Western State College of Colorado.

Library of Congress Cataloging-in-Publication Data

Blakeslee, Donald J., 1943–
    Along ancient trails: the Mallet expedition of 1739 / Donald J.
  Blakeslee.
      p.   cm.
  Includes bibliographical references (p.   ) and index.
  ISBN 0-87081-410-9 (alk. paper)
    1. Mallet Expedition (1739–1740)   2. Mallet, Paul.   3. Mallet,
  Pierre. I. Title.
  F799.B63   1995
  978'.01—dc20   95-38262
                                                  CIP

This book was set in Adobe Caslon and Adobe AG Oldface.

10 9 8 7 6 5 4 3 2 1

To Joy

CONTENTS

ILLUSTRATIONS

PREFACE

In June 1740, four French Canadians arrived in New Orleans, the capital of the colony of Louisiana. Another three showed up at Fort des Chartres, the center of French Illinois. They brought word of the first successful expedition from the east to Santa Fe. Led by the brothers Pierre and Paul Mallet, eight or nine men had left Illinois the previous spring, found their way to Santa Fe, spent the winter there, and returned by separate routes to French territory.

Jean-Baptiste LeMoyne de Bienville, governor of French Louisiana, was delighted by the news. The French had attempted to reach Santa Fe previously, but all officially sanctioned expeditions had fallen short of the mark. There had been rumors that voyageurs had reached the vicinity of New Mexico, but the truth is that no one in the French colonies knew how to get to Santa Fe. The governor recognized the importance of the Mallet trip and wrote to the king of the opportunity for profitable trade that New Mexico seemed to offer.

His optimism was based on the friendly reception the Spanish government had offered the Mallets. The brothers had dined at the table of the alcalde mayor and had been sent back to New Orleans with the request that, next time, they should bring a passport and an official decree permitting them to trade with the Spanish. The Mallets also carried a letter from a Spanish vicar to a French priest in New Orleans. The vicar begged the priest to send some goods on account, promising to pay in silver currency. Although he received his salary in cash, the Spaniard noted, there was little that he could purchase with it in New Mexico. The desire of New Mexicans for trade with Louisiana was obvious.

The optimism gradually faded. A return expedition in 1741–1742 under the direction of André Fabry de la Bruyère foundered on the lower reaches of the Canadian River. The French authorities attempted no other government-sponsored expeditions. This was just as well, because Spanish policy had changed. After reviewing the Mallet entrada, the Spanish government decided to pursue a hard line to protect its northern marches in North America from French intrusion and possible invasion. The few independent entrepreneurs who reached Santa Fe in the ensuing decades faced arrest and confiscation of all their goods. It was not until 1821, in the aftermath of the Mexican revolution, that William Becknell arrived in Santa Fe to initiate regular trade.

As a result, the Mallet expedition has always appeared to be an isolated event, separated from Becknell's creation of the Santa Fe Trail by eighty-two years of frustration. Scanty documentation also has discouraged historical interest in the expedition. The Mallets kept a journal, but it has been lost. Only a brief abstract of the journal that Bienville provided to the French court has survived, and it provides minimal evidence regarding the route taken. The journey from Illinois up the Missouri River to South Dakota and thence overland through Nebraska, Kansas, Oklahoma, and New Mexico is recorded in a scant five handwritten pages, and the return route is covered in three.

French historian Pierre Margry published the abstract and some related documents in his monumental Découvertes et Etablissements des Francais dans L'Amérique Septentrionale at the end of the nineteenth century. Henri

Folmer (1939a, 1939b) translated the Margry version and attempted to trace the route of the expedition. Despite the fact that his version of the route depends on a series of unverified assumptions, no other historian has challenged it seriously. This lack of interest may derive in part from the apparently isolated nature of the Mallet achievement, but surely it results primarily from the lack of related documents. Without the context provided by other sources, the details in Bienville's abstract of the original journal are too few and too vague to allow a forceful critique of Folmer's analysis.

This book is the result of a discovery that revealed connections between the Mallet route and those of many other expeditions across the Plains. Seen from this new perspective, their trip was not an isolated event but was tied to both earlier and later expeditions. Some of these other expeditions generated documents that help to illuminate the Bienville abstract of the Mallet journal.

The connecting links are Indian trails. Most early explorers of the Plains, beginning with Francisco Vásquez de Coronado in 1541, had Indian guides who led them along Indian trails. Traders followed the explorers, and trading posts sprang up along the trails. In later years, armies erected military posts along them, and many battles in the Indian wars took place on the trails. Emigrants followed the traders, and the Santa Fe Trail, the Oregon Trail, and the California Trail all followed aboriginal routes.

The journals, maps, and letters created by the explorers, traders, military men, and emigrants all help to document the precise location of the Indian trails. Few of them provide complete information for the full extent of a trail, but many describe a particular landmark or otherwise allow a segment of a trail to be pinpointed. When all of the accounts of travel along an individual trail are collated, the result is often a precise delineation of its route.

Such is the case with the trails the Mallet brothers used. The Bienville abstract omits much of the detail that must have been in the original journal. It does, however, provide direct evidence of the use of Indian trails. Additional clues to specific locations are present, and when read in the light of documents from other expeditions along the same trails, such as that of Zebulon Pike or Nathaniel Boone, I found that it was possible to trace the Mallet route. Still, it took over 7,000 miles of travel back and forth across the Plains and the help of many scholars and local informants to unravel all of the puzzles involved.

This book is the story of the Mallet expedition, and it is a drama filled with adventure, tragedy, and mystery. In the presentation here, two stories are intertwined. One is the tale of the Mallet expedition and its aftermath. The other is the story of the investigation that uncovered their adventure. All too often, history is presented as a just-so story. It is not "just so." Accurate history is created through scholarship, and the investigative process can be an adventure in itself.

Trying to follow the route of any early expedition is a wonderful puzzle. The delights it offers are twofold. One comes in solving part or all of the question of where people went. This can be as rewarding as solving any other historical or scientific question, but the product is only a line on a map. The other and deeper reward comes from what one learns along the way. The investigator cannot merely study the records of a single trip, determine its starting point, and try to match comments in a diary with features of the landscape. Often he or she must detour into other topics and the events of other times.

There is no way this kind of research can be completed within a limited time or by searching for the sorts of documents that deal with the subject directly. All I could do was to define the goal and learn what might apply. The rest was indirect vision, reading around the subject rather than in it. Few have written about Indian trails, fewer still about the Mallet expedition. The lode of primary documents is meager indeed. Nevertheless, the landmarks are there, hidden in reports of other expeditions, in family traditions about grandfather's farm, in archaeological site files. It is the adventure of piecing together this sprawling puzzle, the hard work and hot days, the hidden clues, the kind-hearted help of strangers, and the blind luck that I want to share with you.

ACKNOWLEDGMENTS

An enormous number of people contributed to the research that went into this book. I am especially indebted to my colleagues Mildred Wedel, Waldo Wedel, David Weber, David Lyon, Bill Unrau, John Ludwickson, Tom Witty, Douglas Parks, John Koontz, and Bob Blasing. Many people provided help with the translations, including Lorna Batterson, Joyce Scott, Janie Riles, Françoise Brodier, Cathy Culot, and Hector García. Kent Wilkinson drafted the maps.

More valuable assistance came from the librarians and research staff at the University of New Mexico, the History Library and Laboratory of Anthropology in Santa Fe, the Kansas State Historical Society, the State Library and Historical Society in Oklahoma City, the National Archives and the Library of Congress, the Division of Archives, Record Management and History of the Louisiana Secretary of State, Historic New Orleans, the Chancery Archives of the Archdiocese of New Orleans, and the Louisiana State Museum Library. Special thanks are due to Cathy Moore-Jansen and Mike Kelley of the Ablah Library at Wichita State University.

The Faculty Support Committee at Wichita State University helped underwrite some of the research with a summer faculty fellowship, for which I am very grateful. The speakers' bureau of the Kansas Humanities Council provided the means by which I was able to visit many places across Kansas and to meet the multitude of local historians who gave me valuable leads.

Finally, to my sons, Sam and John, who accompanied me on those long, hot field trips, thanks for your help.

ALONG ANCIENT TRAILS

1.

THE SETTING

The Great Plains

The Great Plains of North America nearly bisect the continent from south to north, stretching from southern Texas to the boreal forest of Canada. To anyone entering them from east or west, the change in environment is obvious. In 1739, the West was Spanish territory, a land of forested mountains and desert valleys. Perennial streams flowing from the mountains made life possible for the Spanish colonists and their Pueblo subjects. To their east lay the High Plains—treeless, arid, and in some areas totally lacking in landmarks by which inexperienced travelers might steer their course.

East of the Plains were the French colonies of Canada and Louisiana. In these lands of great rivers, people normally traveled by canoe or boat. Rainfall was sufficient to support enormous forests even on level ground, and the French and their subject tribes were able to cultivate their fields without irrigation.

West from French territory, the landscape changed gradually from almost continuous forest to apparently endless grass. The Plains were then essentially treeless except for gallery forests along streams and the isolated groves that Nicollet, the great French-born mapper of the prairies, called oases in the sea of grass. Here there was often no wood for fuel, and buffalo chips had to be substituted. The farther west one traveled, the more arid the land became. Streams were too shallow for boats, water holes were widely spaced, and timber became scarce. What water was available was often made unpalatable by salt and other minerals.

It took intimate knowledge of the land to live here. There were plentiful herds of game—bison, elk, antelope and deer—but the hunters had to know where to find them in different seasons and in the dry years that came all too often. What made travel possible—especially in the western regions, where both water and landmarks were scarce—were Indian trails. These traditional routes, marked with cairns of stone or sod, were known to all of the tribes and used to hunt, to make war, to make pilgrimages, and to trade. The trails provided optimal routes that were based on generations of observation; they connected major fords and featured water holes, groves of trees, and other resources for the end of each day's journey at named campsites.

The trails provided the easiest routes of travel. They sometimes followed stream valleys where there were not too many tributaries to cross but otherwise ran along divides between drainages. Routes along high ground minimized the time travelers had to spend climbing hills or beating their way through brush, and they provided excellent visibility for hunting and defense. Charles Augustus Murray, who crossed part of the Plains in 1843, stated this clearly:

> [T]o keep along the dividing ridge [is] an advantage so great, and so well understood by all prairie travellers, that it is worth making a circuit of several miles a day to keep it; and the Indian trails which we have crossed since our residence in the wilderness, convince me that the savages pay the greatest attention to this matter. . . .

I have sometimes observed that an Indian trail wound through a country in a course perfectly serpentine, and it appeared to me to travel three miles when only one was necessary. It was not till my own practical experience had made me attend more closely to this matter, that I learnt to appreciate its importance (Murray 1841 Vol II: 29–30).

These trails were part of the culturally created landscape of the Plains Indians. Two common misperceptions are that the Plains Indians never modified their environment and that they lived in isolated groups and hence were ignorant of events that occurred at a distance. To the contrary, these people were in more or less constant contact with one another and exchanged information about the hunt, war and peace, theology, and the white strangers who had begun to appear. When Pierre Gaultier de Varennes, Sieur de la Vérendrye, left some men in a Mandan village in North Dakota, they met there a native trader from the southern Plains who could speak both Spanish and Mandan (Smith 1980: 99). He had learned Spanish in New Mexico and Mandan apparently during regular visits to North Dakota. Similarly, as we shall see, in 1749 a Comanche somewhere on the plains of Colorado mimicked for a visiting Spaniard the actions of a sentry he had seen at an English or French post that had to have been as far east as Illinois or as far north as Canada.

Other features of the Plains Indian cultural landscape were named places known to all of the tribes, ports of call in the sea of grass. In spite of the many mutually unintelligible languages spoken on the Plains, many place-names had identical meanings in the various tongues. For example, the Pawnee called the Platte River *Kíckatus* and the Omaha called it *Nibtháckake*, but both words meant "flat water." Thus, we can be sure that when the Mallets called this stream the Platte ("flat" in French), they were translating an Indian name, although we have no means of saying which language their informant spoke.

The various Indian names for this and other streams were neither cognates (words with a common origin in an ancestral language) nor loan words. If they were, they would be similar in sound as well as in meaning. Instead, the sounds are very different, whereas the meanings are the same. This situation probably resulted from the widespread use of the Plains Indian sign language, which allowed monolingual speakers of mutually unintelligible tongues to communicate freely. Gestures in the sign language, including those for place-names, could be understood by speakers of the Caddoan, Siouan, Kiowan, Athabascan, Algonkian, and Uto-Aztecan languages, all of which were used on the Plains.

The abstract of the Mallet journal gives many stream names, all of which are probably derived from Plains Indian names (although direct proof of origin is lacking in several instances). They are: Missoury, Panimaha, Plate, Padoucas, Cotes, Cotes Blanches, Aimable, Soucis, Cancés, a la Fleche, Arkansas, Rouge, and Jument. The Missouri, Platte, Kansas, and Arkansas of today are easily identified. The Rouge, or Red, River of the Pawnee (kícpahat), Cheyenne (ma'ome), and Kiowa (Gu'adal p'a) is our Canadian River. Early explorers from the East, such as Zebulon Pike and Stephen Long, confused this with the stream that *we* call the Red River (Marcy 1937: 9), which was known to the Indians as the Great Sand River (Mooney 1898: 417).

Some streams in the Mallet journal, such as the Arkansas, Panimaha, and Padouca, were named for tribes that lived on their banks. According to Mildred Wedel, "Those who are familiar with documentation of this period know it was not unusual for Indians to name a stream for another Indian people who could be reached by following its course" (1981: 25–26). The name Padouca, applied to the Loup River by the Mallets, is a somewhat confusing example of this naming practice. The modern name, Loup, is French for "wolf," and the Skiri Pawnee who lived on its banks were known as the Wolf Pawnee. Thus, the modern name is derived from the name of the tribe. The Pawnee themselves called the Loup ickari?, "many potatoes," and the Omaha name, Nuto^mke, had the same meaning. Apparently, the Mallets called this stream Padouca because they learned from the Pawnees that some Padoucas (Apaches) lived on its upper courses. In 1804, Lewis and Clark labeled the

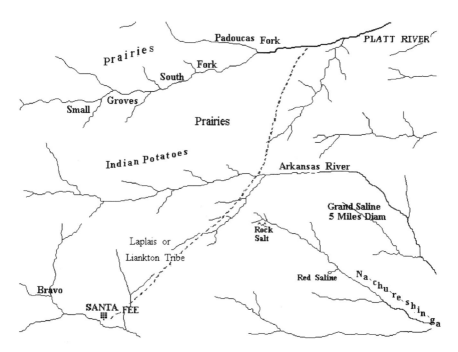

Section of the 1805 Lewis and Clark map. This map shows the Mountain Branch of the Santa Fe Trail and the use of the name Padoueas (sic: Padoucas) Fork for the North Platte. (Redrawn from Moulton 1983: Map 32c.)

North Platte the "Padoueas" River on a map they were drawing, apparently for the same reason (Moulton 1983 I: Figs. 32a-c).

The name a la Fleche, or River of the Arrow, is a rendition into French of the common Indian name for the Arkansas River. In 1739 the French of Louisiana were already calling it the Arkansas, a version of the term for the Indian group that includes the Quapaw, who lived near the mouth of this river. The Indians called it "flint river" for the flint quarries near its course in southern Kansas and northern Oklahoma. In Pawnee, flint is *tahu:ru'*, which also means arrow, arrowhead, and meteor (Parks cited in Chamberlain 1982: 255).

This may seem like an odd congeries of meanings, but arrowheads were fashioned from flint, and when you knap flint, the sparks that fly off look very similar to meteors. The Mallets' name for the river, a la Fleche, is thus a translation of *tahu:ru'*.

The name Rivière a la Jument means "River of the Mare." The Mallets applied this name to the Gallinas River, the first stream they encountered on their return journey after they left the Pecos River; whether or not it is a rendition of a native name is not clear, as the portion of the journal that covers their return trip mentions only this stream and the Arkansas. The modern name, Gallinas, derives from the word the Spanish of New Mexico used for wild turkeys, *gallinas de la tierra*, "native chickens."

The identities of all of these streams are important in tracing the route of the Mallet expedition. Unfortunately, the Indian names for the Cotes, Cotes Blanches, Aimable, and Soucis Rivers have not survived, although we can (and will) make educated guesses about which modern rivers they might be and why they were so named.

This leaves the Panimaha River, the identity of which is a real problem. As we will see, Panimaha is a Siouan term for the Skiri Pawnee, so this river should be one on which the Skiri lived. The Mallets, however, called the latter the Padouca. The unraveling of this puzzle will have to be postponed until we have discussed tribal names and locations, as it appears that there were Panimahas in several places in 1739.

The Spanish Frontier

Organized Spanish exploration of the American Southwest and the Great Plains began with the Coronado expedition of 1540–1542. Following tantalizing hints of what might have been another Aztec or Inca empire, Coronado led an army northward, first to the Zuni pueblos and later to the Rio Grande and the plains of Texas, Oklahoma, and Kansas. The reported riches turned out to be as ephemeral as a mirage, and the fabulous cities were nothing more than villages of adobe and hamlets of grass dwellings. Furthermore, the sheer size of his army (more than a thousand men) and its demands on the local food supply generated conflicts with the native peoples whenever Coronado left a large contingent in one place for an extended time. Injured in a fall and thoroughly discouraged by his failure to find another empire, Coronado led his disintegrating army back to Mexico.

Although participants in the expedition wrote fairly clear and truthful accounts of what they found, these did not find their way into public awareness. Instead, highly distorted geographical images and rumors of fabulous wealth persisted. Indeed, some survived the colonization of New Mexico, and the Mallet brothers were told of white men wearing silk clothing who lived in cities along the coast to the west, illusory descendants of the chimerical Quivirans of Coronado's day.

Two generations passed before more Spaniards entered the country of the Pueblo Indians. In the meantime, the area of Spanish settlement in Mexico expanded to the northeast as fabulous lodes of silver were found and mined. As the Spanish border moved northward and the need for men to work the mines expanded, slave raiders fanned out beyond the frontier. Captives occasionally told of towns to the north where people grew crops and had woven clothing. In 1580, Francisco Sánchez Chamuscado and Fray Augustín Rodríguez led an expedition northward. They were followed in 1582 by Antonio de Espejo and in 1590 by Gaspar Castaño de Sosa. Castaño's expedition was not authorized by the viceroy, nor was another led by Francisco Leyva de Bonilla and Antonio Gutiérrez de Humaña in 1593. Humaña and Leyva de Bonilla persisted in their exploration beyond the pueblos and into the Great Plains. Far in the interior, violence erupted. First Humaña killed Leyva de Bonilla. Then the natives attacked the rest, leaving a single survivor to be found by Juan de Oñate in 1598 (Hammond and Rey 1966: 323–326).

King Philip II authorized establishment of a New Mexican colony in 1583, but various delays prevented Oñate, the man selected as *adelantado*, from leading his expedition northward until 1598. On January 26 of that year, he headed a caravan of settlers, soldiers, and missionaries with their many *car-retas* and thousands of head of stock north to the valley of the Rio Grande. There he established what were to be temporary capitals, first at a pueblo he named San Juan and later at one called San Gabriel.

In 1601 Oñate himself led an exploring party onto the Great Plains. His guide, the single survivor of the Leyva-Humaña expedition, was an Indian from Mexico that Oñate had found living at the Pueblo of San Juan. The expedition set out along a route that later became a major channel of commerce, past Pecos and east to the Canadian River. Downstream, it left the river and struck out to the northeast, eventually reaching the Wichita settlements on the Arkansas River in southern Kansas. Like Coronado before him, Oñate found no riches and returned to New Mexico (Hammond and Rey 1953).

While he was on the Plains, Oñate picked up an Indian named Miguel, who had been a captive among the group that the Spanish called Escanjaques. A native of one of the Wichita settlements, Miguel was taken back to Mexico City. In 1602 he was asked to draw a map of his region. On it he drew Oñate's route from San Gabriel to the Arkansas River, the locations and names of various native settlements, and some native trails. One of these routes, running north-south between two *salinas*, or salt marshes, appears to be one of the trails used by the Mallets in 1739. The map was first published by Newcomb and Campbell (1982), and the proper orientation was demonstrated by Vehik (1986). The identification of the streams and salinas is based on the recognition by Bob Blasing (personal communication, 1986) that the proportions in the map are the same as in the modern landscape.

The colony of New Mexico grew slowly after 1598. In 1609, Oñate's successor, Governor Pedro de Peralta, founded a new capital, the Villa de Santa Fe. It remained the only official town in the province until 1695. The religious capital of the province, however, was established elsewhere, in the Pueblo of Santo Domingo. This placement symbolized a division between the secular and religious centers of power that was to have enormous implications.

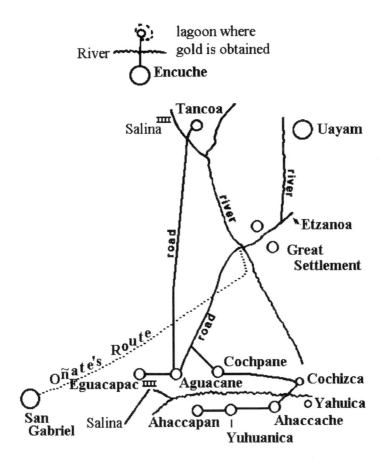

The 1602 Miguel map. Miguel was a Plains Indian who drew this informative map for the Spanish. (Oriented per Vehik [1986] and redrawn for clarity with English captions where appropriate.)

The colony remained weak for decades. Two major factors contributed to New Mexico's slow development. One was its isolation from Mexico City, more than 1,200 miles away. This distance generated slow communication, a sense of isolation, and military weakness. When the Mallets visited Santa Fe in the winter of 1739–1740, they reported that their long stay was necessitated by the time it took communications to flow to and from the viceregal capital. Further, they reported the garrison at Santa Fe as comprising only eighty men, "a bad gang and poorly armed." This military weakness contributed to the longstanding Spanish policy of not allowing outsiders in and preventing most of those who did arrive from returning to their homes (cf. Loomis and Nasatir 1967).

The other reason for New Mexico's slow growth was a deep and abiding conflict between the secular and religious authorities. Each was jealous of its prerogatives and vigilant lest the other should encroach upon them. The conflict appeared almost as soon as the colony was created, when the second governor of the province, Pedro de Peralta, was both excommunicated and arrested by Fray Isidro Ordóñez (Sánchez 1987: 75–86). It continued during two subsequent governorships, peaking in 1641 with the arrest and assassination of Governor Luis de Rosas and again in the 1660s with accusations of heresy against Governors Bernardo López de Mendizábal and Diego de Peñalosa (Scholes 1937, 1942).

The Franciscan Order had been given the colony as its exclusive field for missionary efforts. Funded by the crown to the sum of a million pesos between 1609 and 1680 (John 1975: 65) and with native workshops in some of the missions, the Franciscans had a power base independent of the governor. They had also both the immense prestige of the church itself and the threat of the Inquisition on their side. Franciscans were the officers of the Inquisition in the colony after 1626, and it was only in 1730 that the secular clergy gained a toehold in the province when Bishop Benito Crespo toured it and left Santiago Roybal as vicar of Santa Fe and ecclesiastical judge for all of New Mexico (Kessell 1979: 302).

Some of the conflict was rooted in economics. Oñate's title of adelantado included the right to award his followers *encomiendas*, originally the right to tribute from the natives of various pueblos. The governor also had the right to tribute from the natives, and if they could not supply it in goods, he could take it in the form of labor. But the friars, who lived among the natives and depended on their labor, were quick to dispute any case where they thought the civil authorities had overstepped their bounds. As a large part of the colonial economy was based on Indian labor, conflicts over its allocation were numerous and noisy.

Another element of the nascent economy was made up of trading expeditions to the Apache country. Most of these are undocumented, judging from the spottiness of the records that do exist. For instance, in 1634 one Gaspar Pérez led an expedition onto the Plains and traded with Apaches. We know this only because his son, Diego Romero, who led a similar expedition in 1660, was charged with heresy during the struggle between Governor Bernardo López de Mendizábal and the missionaries (Blakeslee 1981; Kessell 1979: 138, 194–196; Scholes 1942). Accounts of both expeditions survive only in the records of the Inquisition. Both were undertaken at the behest of governors in order to obtain skins and hides to ship to Mexico in the annual caravan, and both appear to have followed the route from Pecos to the Canadian River that Spaniards and Pueblo Indians had used at least since the time of Oñate. These travelers were the literal and figurative ancestors of the infamous Comancheros. Though portrayed as villains in many a Hollywood Western, the Comancheros were in fact peaceful traders who ventured far out onto the Plains to trade with Comanches and Kiowas (Kenner 1969: 78–97).

The Indians from the Plains used the same trails to bring goods to trade at the pueblos. Fray Andrés Juárez, missionary to Pecos Pueblo, described the Apache trade there as essential both to the colonists and to the people of Pecos (cited in Kessell 1979: 137). The most important goods they brought to barter were skins and hides, jerked meat and pemmican, tallow, and slaves. Many of the hides and skins obtained by the Pueblo Indians were passed on to the Spanish as part of their annual tribute. From New Mexico, they were carried on the squealing carretas in the annual caravan southward to Parral and Chihuahua. In the same fashion, many of the Indian slaves were shipped south.

Slave raids into New Mexico had begun prior to the establishment of the colony (Sánchez 1987: 41) and continued afterward. Governor Luis de Rosas was accused of sending raiders against the Apache allies of Pecos, keeping some of the resulting captives as his own slaves and sending others for sale in Nueva Viscaya (Kessell 1979: 158–159). The Apaches in turn raided their neighbors for captives in order to sell them at the trade fairs in the pueblos. Some may have been kept by the Pueblo inhabitants, but the main demand came from among the colonists, who used the captives as household servants or sold them in the slave marts in the mining country.

Forced labor, tribute, slavery, and the repression of native religions fueled resentment of the Spaniards in the Pueblo world. Repeated tremors unsettled the colony prior to the main shock in 1680. Plans for revolution had been uncovered and stifled during the governorship of Fernando de Argüello (1644–1647), again in 1650, and during the governorships of Fernando de Villanueva (1665–1668) and Juan Francisco de Treviño (1675–1677) (Sánchez 1987: 130–132). One of the Pueblo headmen punished in the aftermath of the last plot was Popé, the mastermind of the great uprising.

Popé's revolt finally erupted in August 1680. Natives surrounded and besieged Santa Fe, demanding that certain Spaniards be turned over to them. Most of those caught in the northern half of the colony were put to death. Those killed amounted to about a quarter of the colony's Spanish population. The rest, including the population of Santa Fe, fled to El Paso, which became the northernmost Spanish colonial outpost for a dozen years.

Attempts to regain the lost colony began soon after the revolt. Several times the Spanish probed northward from their refuge at El Paso, but it was not until 1692 that the true reconquest began. The new governor, Diego de Vargas, led soldiers, missionaries, and colonists in the campaign. Fighting continued sporadically until 1696, when an unsuccessful uprising at Picuris caused some of the inhabitants to flee to El Cuartelejo, a region of the High Plains occupied by Apaches.

One Indian threat was replaced by another when a new tribe appeared on the northern marches (Thomas 1935: 26–28). In 1705 there was a report that Comanches and Utes were trading at Taos. The very next year saw the first Comanche raids, and in subsequent years these came to be directed against Spaniards, Pueblos, and friendly Apaches alike.

At first, the Apaches bore the brunt of the invasion. In 1706, Juan de Ulibarrí found Apache groups in southern Colorado banding together for defense against Comanches and Utes. By 1719, when Governor Antonio Valverde y Cosío led an expedition against the Comanches, numerous Apache settlements lay in ruins. In 1723, Governor Juan Domingo de Bustamente reported that Comanches had burned Jicarilla Apache villages, taking women and children and killing all but sixty-nine men, two women, and three boys (Athearn 1989: 400). Bustamente proposed locating a presidio among the Apaches, but it was too late. By the latter half of the decade, the Comanches had overwhelmed all of the Apache settlements, driving some refugees into New Mexico and others south and east. This exodus left the passes into New Mexico open to Comanche raids, which continued with only brief periods of respite until Governor Juan Bautista de Anza accomplished a lasting peace in 1786 (John 1975).

At the same time, a more distant threat began to loom. As early as 1695, the government at Santa Fe began to hear rumors that Frenchmen were approaching the Spanish dominions (Hodge 1929). One early report told of white men trading with the natives at Pecos, but an investigation could not substantiate the rumor. The others proved inaccurate as well. Elizabeth John (1975: 156) thinks the 1695 report may have been a distorted version of the Spanish visit to Quivira. An account of cannons, carbines, and powder flasks being taken from Frenchmen by Navajos during attacks on Pawnee settlements (Thomas 1935: 14) is probably a similar echo from the massacre of René-Robert Cavelier, Sieur de La Salle's colony on the Texas coast by the local tribes. For a time, New Mexico remained distant from the sphere of French operations.

The same was not true of Texas. The Spanish moved to occupy the area after the collapse of La Salle colony at Matagorda Bay. When a Spanish expedition to remove the French finally reached the site of the colony, they found that it had already been destroyed by Indians. To counter any future French threat, the Spanish established missions among the Tejas in 1690 and 1691 (John 1975: 186–191). These did not last beyond 1693, however. The French threat seemed to revive in 1713 when Louis Jouchereau de Saint-Denis established a post on the Red River. In the following year, he set out into Spanish territory in an attempt to establish trade. Teja guides took him to the presidio at San Juan Bautista on the Rio Grande. The Spanish responded by colonizing Texas and revitalizing the abandoned Teja missions.

But there was a more immediate danger. By 1719, Comanches had begun to attack New Mexican pueblos as well as Apache camps. When they killed people near both Taos and Cochiti, Valverde y Cosío led an expedition against them (John 1975: 243–247). Moving north into eastern Colorado, he learned of the destruction of some Apache rancherias and the flight of half of the Sierra Blanca band from its traditional lands. On the Arkansas River in eastern Colorado he met with Cuartelejo and Paloma Apaches, who told of other horrors. One Paloma man was suffering from a gunshot wound given him by a Kansa. (The two accounts of the expedition—the official diary and Valverde's letter to the viceroy—differ in important details, including who attacked the Paloma man [Thomas 1935: 99–132]. I have taken Valverde's letter as the more authoritative source.) The Paloma also told him of two new settlements of Jumanos, Pawnees, and Frenchmen located along a large river.

In response to this new threat, the lieutenant governor, Pedro de Villasur, was sent in 1720 to reconnoiter in force. Heading north and east with forty-two Spanish troops, a priest, three settlers, and sixty Indian allies, he passed through El Cuartelejo, where he picked up some Apache guides and warriors. With this combined force, he appears to have headed east down the Smoky Hill River to a north-south trail that the Mallet brothers would later use. After he reached the forks of the Platte and Loup, his command was attacked, the majority wiped out by a combined Pawnee and Oto force. A single page of the official expedition journal survives. Given by an Indian to the French commander at Fort des Chartres a few months later (Villiers 1923), it tells of the last days leading up to the battle and of how the Spanish force traveled up an Indian trail, across the Loup, and down the north bank of that stream before retreating the day prior to the massacre.

The debacle ended Spain's plans to extend its influence across the Plains to counter the French. There was some talk of erecting a new presidio among the Jicarillas or even at El Cuartelejo, but it was not to be; New Mexico had lost nearly a third of its military strength. As we shall see, Etienne Véniard de Bourgmont was able to take advantage of the blow to Spanish prestige. All the New Mexicans could do was to investigate reports of Frenchmen on their very borders.

In 1724, Governor Bustamente heard rumors that Frenchmen were trading at Taos but could find nobody who had actually seen a Frenchman. Athearn (1989: 37) thinks the rumors arose when the New Mexicans obtained French trade goods from Apaches, who had gotten them in intertribal trade. Indeed, some of the enormous load of goods carried by Bourgmont to the Apaches in that year probably did find its way into Spanish hands, given that the Apaches told Bourgmont that Spaniards came every spring to trade with them at their villages (Norall 1988: 73).

Three years later, Governor Bustamente informed the viceroy that Frenchmen had been seen at El Cuartelejo and on the river called Chinali (Athearn 1989: 39). Perhaps the El Cuartelejo report was of Bourgmont's man, Gaillard, who may have visited there in 1724 (Norall 1988: 68–70). In any case, the treaty Bourgmont made with the Apaches certainly would have opened the way for French traders to penetrate that far. It was true that Frenchmen were coming ever closer.

The French Colonies

Permanent French settlement on the North American continent did not begin until 1608, when Samuel de Champlain established a post at Quebec. In the beginning, French activities in the New World were focused on trade rather than on settlement. As a result, French influence, if not French authority, expanded rapidly over wide regions through the medium of the fur trade. By 1622 Etienne Brulé had reached Lake Superior, and in 1634 Jean Nicolet explored Green Bay. French penetration of the eastern half of the continent neared completion in 1673, when Louis Joliet and Jacques Marquette journeyed down the Mississippi to Quapaw villages near the mouth of the Arkansas River.

In contrast to the rate of exploration, economic development of the French colony was slow. When Canada was overrun by the English in the early 1630s, its permanent population was only 100, the same as the number of investors in the Company of New France, which ran the colony. After 1634 the company granted fiefs to individuals who would bring in settlers. As a result, the population reached 2,500 by the 1660s.

Most of the settlers were concentrated in a narrow strip along the St. Lawrence River. A scarcity of arable land and the continuing threat of Iroquois raids kept them there (Eccles 1972: 35). Continual subdivision of properties and need for river frontage created long, narrow holdings and prevented the formation of villages. This settlement pattern was one of the factors that generated a new kind of person, dramatically different from the peasants of France. The lack of villages meant reduced control by seigniorial, religious, and royal authorities (Eccles 1972: 50). Furthermore, a person who cleared four arpents of land and declared the intent to settle permanently was given the appellation *habitant* and acquired the right to participate in the fur trade, as long as he sold the furs to the Company of New France.

Colonists could profit by trading goods for furs at Indian settlements and then selling the furs to the company. Many tried their hand at it, with or without permission from the authorities. Much of the trade was carried on by coureurs de bois, fiercely independent men who spent much of their time far from the French settlements and took native women as wives. They came to know the native languages and customs, to understand native politics and warfare, and to know the Indian portages and trails. In 1744, Charlevoix said of them:

> They love to breathe a free air, they are early accustomed to a wandering life; it has charms for them, which make them forget past dangers and fatigues, and they place their glory in encountering them often. I know not whether I ought to reckon amongst the defects of our Canadians the good opinion they entertain of themselves. It is at least certain that it inspires them with a confidence, which leads them to undertake and execute what would appear impossible to many others (cited in Eccles 1987: 58).

The Mallets and their companions were such men.

Rapid development came to Canada only when Louis XIV made it a royal province in 1663. The crown subsidized the colony, and for a period new settlers arrived every year. The population reached about 10,000 by 1680 and was 43,382 in 1739, the year of the Mallet journey (Eccles 1972: 120). The colony was nearly self-sufficient in food and generated variable profits from the fur trade.

In Canada, relationships between secular and religious authorities were not as fractious as in New Mexico. Canadian clerics published the *Jesuit Relations* as a public relations scheme that benefited both the colony and the Society of Jesus. The Jesuits were also deeply involved in generating support for the establishment of the settlement at Montreal (Eccles 1969: 39). Missionary activities began as early as 1604. Unlike their New Mexican counterparts, the Canadian missionaries scattered among the Indian villages did not hold the threat of military power over the natives; instead they had to depend on their powers of persuasion. Although resentments and conflicts arose between natives and missionaries, they never approached the ferocity of the Pueblo Revolt.

The French colony in Illinois had its tentative beginning in 1674 when Father Marquette founded a mission in a Kaskaskia village on the Illinois River. The mission ceased operation for a few years and shifted its location whenever the village moved, ultimately reaching the location of present-day Kaskaskia on the banks of the Mississippi in 1703. In 1680 La Salle built Fort Crèvecour where Peoria now stands, but it was destroyed in a mutiny that winter. In 1682 he constructed Fort St. Louis at Starved Rock, and this proved more permanent. La Salle placed Henri de Tonty in charge of Illinois, and the outpost grew under his guidance. In 1691–1692 he moved Fort St. Louis 80 miles downstream, and in 1699 the Cahokia mission was founded. As the center of French Illinois moved to the Mississippi River, the pace of activities increased. In 1702 Charles Juchereau de Saint-Denis led an expedition overland, then down the Ohio River and established a short-lived tannery. *Coureurs de bois* gathered near the missions because of restrictions in Canada (Howard 1972: 39).

In 1717, even though the bulk of the population was Canadian in origin, the French crown placed Illinois under the jurisdiction of Louisiana. In 1720 Fort des Chartres was founded on the east bank of the Mississippi and became the center of both military and civil authority. Prairie du Rocher was founded nearby in 1723, and by 1752 the population included 1,536 Frenchmen, 890 blacks, and 147 Indian slaves (Eccles 1972: 167). It was here that Pierre and Paul Mallet came in about 1734.

Louisiana was long the weakest of the French outposts on the continent. It was founded by Pierre LeMoyne d'Iberville under orders from Louis XIV in 1699, as Europe prepared for the War of the Spanish Succession. The French intended to control the Mississippi River mouth and to establish a base for a possible invasion of Mexico in case the Spanish crown should go to a Hapsburg (Eccles 1972: 102). Created for political rather than economic reasons, it remained economically dependent on France, costing the crown 80,000 livres a year by 1707 (Eccles 1972: 158–159).

Biloxi was founded in 1699 and Mobile in 1702, but by 1711 the population of Louisiana was still less than 200 people. The crown tried a variety of administrative schemes to reduce the drain on the treasury. In 1712 Antoine Crozat, a wealthy financier, accepted responsibility for development of the colony in return for a fifteen-year monopoly over trade, but he lost money so rapidly that in 1717 he abandoned his privileges, and Louisiana reverted to the crown (Eccles 1972: 161–164). The colony was then placed under the supervision of companies directed by John Law, the minister of finance, with Jean-Baptiste LeMoyne de Bienville as governor. The latter founded New Orleans in 1718 and moved the capital there in 1722. In 1719 the Company of the Indies was formed by a merger of two previous firms. It held a monopoly on trade with all of the New World colonies, and for a brief period John Law's company had the resources to develop Louisiana.

Those who purchased shares regretted their investment. Between 1717 and 1720, more than 1,800 people were shipped to the colony, including Swiss and Germans, along with French convicts, vagrants, deserters, and prostitutes. Many died en route, and even more expired after they arrived. These factors gave the colony an unenviable reputation as both a penal colony and a charnel house (Eccles 1972: 164–165). At home, the creation of the Company of the Indies created a speculative frenzy among French investors, and the inevitable collapse came in 1720. John Law had to flee France, and support for the Louisiana colony disappeared. The newly arrived settlers were abandoned to their fate, desertions were common, and starvation was widespread. After 1721, immigration was suspended temporarily, and Governor Bienville was recalled to France in 1723, only to be reinstated in 1732.

The rapid influx of people and the collapse of the planned economy led some to make their living as hunters. When this happened, the furthest outposts of the colony came to be important (Faye 1943). From Natchitoches on the Red River and from the Arkansas Post near the mouth of the Arkansas

River, dried and salted meat of deer and bison was shipped to the colonists down the Mississippi. By 1718 French hunters were involved with commercial-scale bison hunting among the Wichita Indians at their new settlements on the Arkansas River in northern Oklahoma (Wedel 1981: 39).

As in New Mexico, the Indian slave trade was formally banned by the French government, but it remained widespread nonetheless. The tribes at the borders of the French sphere raided the Plains for captives. Pawnee and Wichita slaves were so common that *pani* (a term applied to both tribes) became synonymous with *slave* in Illinois and Canada (Eccles 1972: 78; Wedel 1973). Apache slaves were also common. In 1724, when Bourgmont was in a Kansa village, his hosts brought thirty Apache slaves to dance before him (Norall 1988: 128). He also learned that the Illinois had come to the Kansa village the previous year and had purchased fifteen slaves (Norall 1988: 131).

The population of Canada never depended on native labor to any extent after the first years, but a slave trade did exist. Sixty to eighty Indian slaves were purchased each year from the Crees and Assiniboines at Michilimacinac (Eccles 1972: 78). Indian slaves were also present in Louisiana, but their importance was reduced by the fact that black slaves made up about half of the population. The same was not true in Illinois, where Indian slaves made up about 10 percent of the population in 1754. Illinois was both close to the supply source for captive Plains Indians and far from New Orleans, the source of black slaves, where a would-be slaveowner had to compete in the bidding with large landholders.

The French equivalent of the Pueblo Revolt came in 1729, when the Natchez Indians turned against the French colonists who were oppressing them (Giraud 1991: 388–439). At the time, some 400 Frenchmen and 280 slaves lived in the vicinity of the Natchez. They were supposedly defended by Fort Rosalie, a decrepit post housing some twenty to twenty-five men and three officers. It was the actions of the commandant, one Detchéparre, that triggered the revolt, which left about 200 people killed. Fortunately for the

French, only two other tribes, both small in number, joined the uprising, and after two years of rather desultory fighting the rebellion sputtered out.

The eventual French penetration of the Great Plains came from all three of its colonial centers: Canada, Illinois, and Louisiana. In 1702 Pierre Charles LeSueur established a post in Minnesota. There he obtained information about Omaha and Oto villages near the Missouri River. In 1714 Saint-Denis crossed Texas to the Rio Grande in an attempt to open trade. In the same year, Etienne Véniard de Bourgmont journeyed up the Missouri to the mouth of the Platte River. In about 1718 the Wichita founded villages on the Arkansas River in northern Oklahoma, perhaps with French involvement (Wedel 1981). This was reported to Governor Valverde by his Cuartelejo and Paloma Apache informants the following year (Thomas 1935: 132). In 1719, Jean-Baptiste Bénard de La Harpe traveled from his new post on the Red River to a rendezvous of various Wichita bands near present Tulsa, Oklahoma (Wedel 1971), and Claude-Charles Du Tisné went overland from Illinois through the Osage villages of western Missouri to some other Wichita settlements in southeastern Kansas (Wedel 1973).

All of this activity took place immediately prior to Villasur's devastating defeat at the hands of Pawnees and Otos in 1720. Then, in 1723, Bourgmont established a new outpost, Fort d'Orleans, on the Missouri River. He capped this achievement in 1724 by forging an alliance among all of the tribes of the southeastern Plains border and the Apaches (Norall 1988). To accomplish this end, he journeyed about halfway across the present state of Kansas to the eastern edge of the Apache country. His generous gifts, the promise of peace with the eastern tribes, and the recent Spanish defeat made the Apaches enthusiastic about their new white friends. The road to New Mexico seemed to be open.

The French, however, did not exploit their advantage. The only officially sanctioned exploration after 1724 was undertaken by Vérendrye, who ranged from Canada into North Dakota (Smith 1980). Individual coureurs de bois probably came to Plains Indian villages with increasing frequency, but the

Apaches never received the guns that might have helped them fight off the Comanches. By the late 1720s the Apaches were gone, replaced by Comanches, who felt no particular friendship toward Frenchmen. The road to Santa Fe, open only for a moment, had closed again.

2.

THE CHARACTERS

Frenchmen

Alarie, Jean-Baptiste: a member of the expedition of 1739. There was an Alary family in Canada by 1678 (Alvord 1907: 631 n. 89), and an Illinois branch (that spelled the name Alarie) shows up in the Cahokia census of 1787 (Alvord 1907: 631). Thus, it is likely that Alarie, like all but one of the other men in the expedition, was a French Canadian.

Alarie chose to stay in Santa Fe, where he married María Francisca Fernández de la Pedrera, a widow, on March 24, 1741 (Chávez 1954: 122). They had five children before she died, and he had another by a second wife. María Francisca owned a house on the lot where the Hotel La Fonda now stands in downtown Santa Fe, and various records indicate that Alarie made his living there sometimes as a surgeon/barber and sometimes as a soldier. Alarie died in 1772, "a man of substance."

In New Mexico the surname Alarie was Hispanicized to *Alarid* to sound like *Madrid*, and Jean-Baptiste Alarie appears in one of the documents of the 1750 expedition as Juan Alarido (misread as *Marido* in Hackett 1941 III: 348).

A fundamental mystery of the Mallet expedition is that none of the documents shown to the governor of Louisiana in 1740 mention Alarie. Indeed, all but one of them are consistent in saying that only eight men went to Santa Fe. Three separate documents provide names for all eight, but none of the lists includes Alarie. Furthermore, the 1740 documents explicitly assert that only one Frenchman, Louis Moreau, stayed in Santa Fe. The single exception (a letter by Santiago Roybal, vicar of Santa Fe) says nine men entered the province but lists only the eight names that are common to the other documents.

Later Spanish documents, however, are consistent in indicating that nine men reached Santa Fe in 1739. Indeed, two documents state specifically that two Frenchmen remained in Santa Fe. These are letters by Fray Menchero in 1744 and by Governor Joaquín Codallos y Raball in 1748. Why did the Mallets and the Spanish officials who wrote to Bienville and others in 1740 not mention Alarie? Was he a deserter from the French colony, someone who might have sullied the Mallets' reputation? If so, the Spanish authorities cooperated with the other Frenchmen in a plot to keep his presence a secret from Governor Bienville. Could he have arrived in New Mexico on his own after the Mallets had started home? This is possible but would be an unlikely coincidence. Alarie remains a man of mystery.

Beaubois, Pere Nicolas Ignace de: born in Orléans, France, in 1689. Beaubois entered the Jesuit Order in 1706 and was assigned to Canada in 1719 to work among the Indians. He later was named the first superior of the Jesuit mission in New Orleans, where he became an important and powerful figure (Conrad 1988 Vol. I: 53). The Mallet brothers gave his name to Santiago Roybal in Santa Fe in 1739, and the latter wrote to Beaubois asking his help in obtaining a line of credit. Apparently the Mallets did not know that Beaubois had been recalled to France in 1735. Their ignorance of this fact suggests that they spent most of their time on the frontier, far from New Orleans.

Bellecourt, Joseph: a French-Canadian member of the 1739–1740 expedition. Bellecourt was one of three who returned to Illinois from the Canadian River rather than going with the Mallets to New Orleans. Governor Bienville reported to the king that he had received notice from Illinois that all three men had returned safely.

Beslot or Beleau, Michel: a member of the expedition of 1739–1740 and another French Canadian. Bienville lists him by his nickname, La Rose. He returned with the Mallets to New Orleans and was a member of the Fabry de la Bruyère expedition in 1741–1742. The documents of the latter expedition list him both as Beleau and as La Rose.

Bienville, Jean-Baptiste LeMoyne de: governor of the French colony of Louisiana, with three interruptions, from 1701–1743. Founder of the city of New Orleans and the younger brother of the founder of the colony, he was responsible for what success the colony had in its early years.

Brin-d'amour: a Canadian hunter with a camp below the forks of the Arkansas in 1742. He was hired by Corporal Grappe of the Fabry de la Bruyère expedition to hunt for his men during their return from the forks to their camp on the Canadian River. His name translates roughly as "hunk o' burnin' love."

Bruyère, André Fabry de la: a clerk in the Marines. Fabry volunteered to lead the return expedition of 1741–1742. In spite of previous successes on expeditions within Louisiana, he failed to reach Santa Fe.

Champart: a sergeant in the Marines and second in command to Fabry de la Bruyère on the 1741–1742 expedition. I have found no documents that give his Christian name.

David, Jean: also known as Petit-Jean. The only member of the 1739–1740 expedition to have been born in France, he went to Illinois with Galien and Bellecourt in 1740.

Galien or Gallien, Emanuel: another of the three members of the Mallet expedition who returned by land to Illinois in 1740, and another French Canadian.

La Grandeur: a hired hand, or engagé, on the 1741–1742 expedition led by Fabry de la Bruyère. This is obviously a nickname.

Grappe, Alexis: a corporal in the Marines and member of the 1741–1742 expedition.

Mallet, Pierre and Paul: French-Canadian fur traders. They were the sons of Pierre Mallet and Madelaine Tuvée DuFresne, both of Montreal. Pierre was born in 1704. He and his brother moved to Illinois in 1734, and ten years later Pierre married Louise Dupré. She was a native of Natchez, the daughter of Jacques Dupré Terrebonne and Marie Bienvenu. The couple had two sons, Pierre and Antoine.

Paul was the younger Mallet brother, yet one of the documents of the expedition indicates that he did the talking for the Frenchmen during their initial interview with the lieutenant governor of New Mexico. Paul married Marie Jeanne Barre prior to 1747, and by 1749 he was the father of three daughters.

Marcelle: a trader and a friend of the Mallets. He accompanied the 1741–1742 expedition and left with the Mallets from Fabry's camp in a last attempt to reach Santa Fe.

Michel, Honoré. Commissaire ordonnateur of Louisiana in 1750 and critic of Governor Pierre-François de Rigaud, Marquis de Vaudreuil. In the French system of government in the Louisiana colony, the commissaire ordonnateur was the equal of the governor. The governor was the military and administrative official, the commissaire ordonnateur the fiscal and administrative officer.

Michel suspected that Governor Vaudreuil had a monetary interest in the 1750 expedition.

Moreau, Louis Maria: A French Canadian and the only villain in this play. In 1740 Moreau chose to remain in Santa Fe rather than to return to French territory because he was engaged to a Spanish woman, Juana Muñoz, whom he married on October 12, 1740 (Chávez 1954: 239).

In 1742 Moreau was accused of fomenting rebellion among the Indians, and for this he was executed. In 1743, Governor Gaspar Domingo de Mendoza wrote that he had been sentenced to having his heart taken out through the back. Fray Juan Miguel de Menchero said in 1744 that he had been hanged, and in 1748 Governor Codallos y Raball claimed Moreau had been shot (all of these documents are translated in Folmer 1939a: 168). No details of his trial have been found in the archives.

Pantalon: a black man who accompanied the Fabry de la Bruyère expedition of 1741–1742. The records do not indicate whether he was a freedman or a slave.

Robitaille, Philippe: A member of the expedition of 1739–1740. Bienville describes him as a French Canadian. One of the two men who accompanied the Mallet brothers to New Orleans during the return trip, he also was a member of the Fabry de la Bruyère expedition of 1741–1742, on which he served as interpreter with the Osages.

Salmon, Édmé Gatien: Commissaire ordonnateur of Louisiana in 1740. With Bienville, Salmon wrote to the crown about the Mallet expedition.

Vaudreuil, Pierre-François de Rigaud, Marquis de: governor of Louisiana from 1743 to 1753. He was the most successful of the early governors. Under his guidance, the colony finally began to thrive. It was during his administration that Pierre Mallet returned to New Orleans to propose the expedition of 1750.

Spaniards

Cachupín, Tomas Vélez: governor of New Mexico for two terms, 1749–1754 and 1761–1767. He was in office when Pierre Mallet made his second trip in 1750. He deplored the previous governor's decision to let the Mallets return to French territory, blaming this choice for the trickle of Frenchmen who washed up on his doorstep in the 1750s.

Hurtado, Juan Paëz: alcalde major and military commander of Santa Fe, lieutenant governor and captain general of the province of New Mexico. He welcomed the Mallets in 1739.

Hurtado, in his capacity as captain general, led a punitive expedition against Faraone Apaches in 1715 (Thomas 1935: 80–98). It is noteworthy here because the expedition followed the same trail east of Picuris that the Mallets would use nearly two decades later (see Chapter 6). Hurtado was governor *ad interim* in 1704–1705 after the death of Vargas (Twitchell 1911: 421) and acting governor in 1717 after the ouster of Governor Don Félix Martínez (John 1975: 242). In 1724 he was one of the witnesses who testified regarding rumored illegal trade with the French (Thomas 1935: 245–256). At that time, he stated that he had been a resident of New Mexico for thirty-four years.

Mendoza, Gaspar Domingo de: governor of New Mexico in 1739. He was appointed to the office in 1737 but did not arrive in Santa Fe until January 1739 (Twitchell 1911: 438). He served until 1743. His friendly reception of the Mallets encouraged the French to think they might be able to open trade with New Mexico.

Roybal, Santiago: vicar of Santa Fe and ecclesiastical judge for New Mexico. Roybal gave the Mallets a letter to carry to a priest in New Orleans asking for trade goods and indicating that he could pay in silver, as he received a regular salary. He asserted that there were no goods available in New Mexico. Native to New Mexico, he was made vicar and ecclesiastical judge by the bishop of Durango in 1730. In this capacity he was the "opening wedge for the secular clergy" in its struggle with the Franciscans in New Mexico (Kessell 1979: 327).

Sandoval, Félipe de: a native of El Puerto de Santa María in Spain. Félipe de Sandoval had wide-ranging adventures in the New World: He was held prisoner in Jamaica from 1742 to 1744, made a living as a hunter in French Louisiana from 1744 to 1749, and served as a soldier in New Mexico after 1750. Sandoval surfaces in the records of the 1750 expedition as a guard at the prison in Mexico City where Pierre Mallet was held.

Native Americans

The individual natives who participated in facets of the Mallet expedition are anonymous. None are named in any of the documents in the French and Spanish archives, yet Indians made the whole affair possible. Indians put the Mallets on the right track when they were woefully lost; Indian trails made up most of the route; and for one section of the journey the Mallets had an Arikara guide. They may have had guides elsewhere as well, as they somehow came to know the native names for streams all the way from northern Nebraska to central Kansas and, in 1740, were able to recognize the trail in western Oklahoma that led to Illinois.

In lieu of individual roles, the Native Americans must be assigned to the chorus. They are as follows:

Village Siouans: The first tribes the Mallets listed in their trip were the Missouri, Kansa, and Oto. Another Siouan-speaking tribe, the Omaha, figured prominently in considerations of the route taken, although their presence in the records of the trip is not immediately apparent. The Osage played a role in the 1750 expedition. All of these tribes spoke dialects of the Chiwere and Dhegiha divisions of the Siouan language family. Chiwere speakers included the Ioway, Oto, and Missouri tribes; the Dhegihan tribes were the Omaha, Ponca, Kansa, Osage, and Quapaw.

In 1739 the Missouri and Oto were living separately from one another, although they have become closely affiliated in recent years (today they are a single legal polity, the Otoe-Missouria tribe). The Missouri were situated on the Missouri River upstream from the mouth of the Grand River; the Oto lived much higher upstream, in the vicinity of the Platte. Neither tribe was ever very large. Mooney (1928) estimates, conservatively, that there were about 900 Otos and 1,000 Missouris in 1780. Both tribes occupied fairly compact villages, consisting primarily of bark-covered lodges. Their economy was based on a combination of gardening and hunting. Both made long-distance hunts to obtain buffalo, but closer to home deer was the main game species.

The Kansa, Osage, Omaha, and Ponca share a common origin and as a group are distantly related to the Quapaw. These Dhegihan-speaking tribes originally occupied some of the Ohio River valley. The names of the various tribes in this group are derived both from clan names and from geographic references. Thus, the Kansa clan is found not only among the Kansa proper but also among the Omaha, Ponca and Osage. Similarly, Ponca and Osage are also clan names. The tribal names of the Omaha and Quapaw refer to locations. Quapaw translates as "with the current" or "downstream," referring to the tribe's traditional location as the southernmost of the Dhegihan groups. Omaha translates as "against the current" or "upstream," and the Omaha (and the Ponca who later split from them) are the northernmost of the Dhegiha speakers.

The aboriginal population of the Omaha seems to have been around 3,000 (Smith 1974: 198–201), the Osages numbered about 6,200 in 1780 (Mooney 1928), and the Ponca consisted of about 800 people. The Omahas normally lived in a single large village, and their houses included Plains-style earth lodges, tipis, and bark longhouses and wigwams. The Dhegihan-speaking tribes lived by a combination of horticulture and hunting. They raised maize, beans, squash, and sunflowers in the bottomlands near their villages. In summer and winter they hunted bison communally, with whole tribes or villages moving long distances to find the herds. Elk, deer, and other game were sought when the tribe was at the village.

In the mid-eighteenth century, the Kansa lived in northeastern Kansas, and the Omaha and Ponca were in northeastern Nebraska. The Osage lived in western Missouri along the river that bears their name, but later some of them began moving south and west into Kansas and Oklahoma. In 1739 the Mallets followed one of the old trails the Osage used to take into the bison country. As the easternmost of the Plains tribes, these Siouan speakers provided the French with some of their first information about other Plains Indians. Their names for tribes such as the Pawnees, Wichitas, Apaches, and Comanches often were used by the French or translated into French. Sometimes both things happened, yielding alternative names for the same tribe. For example, various Wichita bands were called Mentos, a Quapaw term for one band; Paniasa, a term applied to the Wichita and meaning "Black Pawnee"; and Pani Noir, the French translation of Paniasa. In the accounts of the Fabry de la Bruyère expedition of 1741–1742, both Mentos and Panis Noirs are used, apparently to distinguish among several Wichita bands.

Plains Caddoans: Three tribes that speak Northern Caddoan languages (Parks 1979), the Wichita, Pawnee, and Arikara, are actors in the Mallet drama. The Wichita, residents of Kansas when white men first encountered them, were in Oklahoma by 1739. The Pawnee lived north of them in northern Kansas and central Nebraska, and the Arikara occupied central South Dakota. In each tribe's territory, protohistoric archaeological complexes have been identified as ancestral remains. In South Dakota, the Coalescent Tradition preceded the Arikara; in Nebraska, the Lower Loup Focus gave rise to the Pawnee; and in Kansas, the Wichita derive from the Great Bend Aspect.

All three of the Plains Caddoan tribes lived in horticultural villages. The Arikara and Pawnees built circular earth lodges, whereas the Wichitas constructed grass lodges (Dorsey 1904: 4–5). All three tribes were composed of at least semiautonomous, if not fully autonomous, bands. There are oral traditions, for instance, of the South Band Pawnees having fought the Skiri Pawnees (Hyde 1951: 2). The archaeological remains of the Wichita imply that at least three independent bands existed within the tribe, each with its own territory (Blakeslee 1988a), just as the Skiri and South Band Pawnees had individual hunting territories (Holen 1983).

Each of these tribes grew corn, beans, squash, sunflowers, and tobacco, and all three also depended heavily on bison hunting. Two communal hunts were undertaken each year—a summer hunt primarily for meat and a winter hunt for robes and luxurious pelts. Whole bands cooperated in these hunts, the large number of hunters helping to ensure a good kill. The tribes traveled to the hunting grounds along marked trails (Weltfish 1965: 171–174), some of which the Mallets followed in 1739.

The Plains Caddoans also used established trails for intervillage, inter-band, and intertribal visits of varying duration (Blaine 1982: 116; Wood 1955). Most visits were for brief intervals, but others were lengthy. In 1772, for instance, some 600 Skiri warriors and their families settled near the Wichita on the Red River of Oklahoma and Texas and remained there until 1778 (Bolton 1914: 96–97, 115; John 1975: 518). One such lengthy sojourn is critical to the interpretation of the Mallet route. In 1734, Governor Bienville wrote that he had learned that Panimahas (Skiris) had moved to the Missouri River near the Arikaras (Nasatir 1952 I: 25). In 1723 Philippe de La Renaudière, on the basis of accounts by voyageurs, placed the Arikaras 10 leagues above the Omaha village. As the Omaha were then occupying a village on Bow Creek (Ludwickson et al 1987: 71–74), the Arikaras and presumably the Skiris would have been in the vicinity of Weigand Creek in present-day Knox County, Nebraska.

There is a major archaeological site at the mouth of Weigand Creek (Blakeslee and O'Shea 1983: 227–237), but none of the material from it is consistent with either an Arikara or a Pawnee occupation. Distances given in the Mallet journal abstract suggest that the problem lies in a transcription error in the La Renaudière manuscript. If we assume 70 leagues instead of 10 (a handwritten French 7 looks very much like a 1), the Arikaras and Skiris would have been in central South Dakota. Indeed, about 70 leagues above the Omaha village on Bow Creek there are two archaeological sites, Oacoma and Oldham, which yield pottery that is essentially identical to Lower Loup (Pawnee) ceramics of the first half of the eighteenth century.

Before concluding that the Skiris were living on the Missouri River in South Dakota, however, it is important to note that other archaeological information indicates that the majority of the Skiris were still living in their homeland on the Loup River during the time period in question (Grange 1968). Apparently, only some of the Skiris moved to the Missouri; the majority of the band remained in central Nebraska.

In 1803–1804, Tabeau described a Pawnee-like dialect among the Arikaras (Parks 1979: 202–203), and a Lewis and Clark map indicates one Arikara village that claimed descent from the Pawnees (Moulton 1983: Plate 25). These were probably the descendants of the Skiris mentioned by Bienville and La Renaudière. The Mallets visited the Skiris living among the Arikara in South Dakota in 1739, and this tribe put the Frenchmen on the road to Santa Fe.

The origin of the tribal name, Pawnee, is shrouded in mystery. The modern version is of Siouan origin and appears to have been applied to all of the Plains Caddoans as an inclusive term. It was Ppádi, Ppáyi, or Ppáni in Dhegiha, Pháni in Chiwere, and Paaní in Winnebago (Koontz, personal communication, 1987). None of these terms can be analyzed in Siouan, and they may derive from a word borrowed from some other language. Various divisions of the Plains Caddoans were sometimes indicated by adjectives attached to the base term. Thus, the Wichita bands were often Paniasa, or "Black Pawnee," (Panis Noirs in French) probably because of their habit of tattooing the body. The Skiri Pawnee were the Pani Maha, literally "upstream Pawnee," with the secondary meaning of North Pawnee. The similarity of Pani Maha for Skiri and Maha for Omaha often led to confusion among early writers (cf. Ludwickson et al 1987: 75–76). Indeed, Governor

Bienville probably was confused by the Mallet journal. If my interpretation is correct, he encountered in it references to two widely separated Panimaha villages with a Maha village between them.

The abstract of the Mallet journal makes repeated references to a Panimaha village on a Panimaha River. By rights, this should be a Skiri Pawnee village on the Loup River in central Nebraska. Skiri means "wolf" in Pawnee, and the French sometimes referred to the Skiris as the Pani Loup, or "Wolf Pawnee." As we have seen, however, there appear to have been at least two Skiri villages in the period in question, one on the Loup River and another in South Dakota. The abstract refers sometimes to one, sometimes to the other, and sometimes merely to the Pani. Furthermore, it probably confuses both Skiri villages with a Maha village on the Maha River.

Poor Governor Bienville had to deal with a document that first mentioned a Panimaha village on the Missouri River, then described how the Mallets traveled to a Maha village at the mouth of the Maha River (an Omaha village at the mouth of Bow Creek), and continued overland to a Panimaha village on the Panimaha River (a Skiri village on the Loup River). It should not be too surprising that he became confused.

The Padoucas: Before discussing the tribes of the southwestern Plains that figure in the Mallet narratives, it is necessary to deal with the Padoucas. In French texts of the seventeenth and eighteenth centuries, this term is used to name a tribe that occupied the High Plains from South Dakota to Texas. The ethnic identity of this tribe has been the subject of controversy among historians and anthropologists for decades.

Only the Apaches and Comanches are serious candidates; no other Plains tribes were in the appropriate region at the right time. The belief that the Padoucas were Comanches is based on linguistic and ethnohistoric evidence. For instance, Fletcher and La Flesche (1911: 102) recorded the Omaha word for Comanche as *pa' du^n ka* (Padouca). Clearly, then, Padouca meant Comanche to Siouan speakers in the nineteenth century. It also is clear that the French usage was derived from this Siouan term, but at an earlier time. The French, coming onto the Plains from the east, heard of the Padoucas before they met these Indians, and they continued to use the Siouan-derived term afterwards.

Others argue that the Padoucas were Apaches and that the term became applied to the Comanches after the latter dislodged the Apaches from most of the High Plains. At first blush, such a change in meaning might not appear likely, but there is a good deal of evidence to support it. Numerous early French documents either use Apache and Padouca synonymously or distinguish Comanche from Padouca.

The Mallet abstract is one of the latter. En route to Santa Fe, the Mallets encountered Laitanes (Comanches; see below) on the Cimarron and Canadian Rivers. On the return journey they happened on two more groups of Laitanes, both on the Canadian River in Oklahoma. But the day after seeing the last of the Laitanes, they met two men and three women of the "Padokas." To the Mallets, then, the Padoucas were distinct from the Comanches.

In spite of this particular piece of evidence, the ethnic identity of the Padoucas has continued to spark debate. Some fine historians (e.g., John 1975: 219–220) have followed the lead of A. B. Thomas in identifying the Padoucas as Comanches and in assuming that Laitane and Padouca referred to two different divisions of the tribe. Most anthropologists and archaeologists, however, not only regard the Padoucas as Apaches but also consider the archaeological complex called the Dismal River Aspect to be remains of the Plains Apaches, circa A.D. 1675–1725 (Champe 1949; Hyde 1959: 28–35; Secoy 1951; Wedel 1959: 77–78). (A notable exception is Morris Opler [1982], who argues vigorously that the Apaches could not have created the Dismal River Aspect and is inclined to doubt any substantial Apache presence on the High Plains beyond the immediate vicinity of the mountains.)

As Wedel (1959: 77–78) has pointed out, the journal of Bourgmont's 1724 expedition describes the Padoucas as horticultural, something the Comanche were not. In it, the Padoucas are described as growing a little maize and squash, as having pots, and as trading with the Spaniards who came to their camps every spring (Norall 1988: 125–161). Bourgmont had extensive discussions with the Padoucas, and one of his men stayed among them for a matter of months, so there can be no doubt about this description. The Comanches, however, grew no crops and made no pottery, and there is no mention of trade expeditions to their camps in Spanish records of this period. Later such trade would be carried on by the Comancheros, but this did not flourish until around 1786 (Kenner 1969: 78–97). As will be seen, the Apaches of the period grew crops and made pottery, and Spanish trading expeditions into their territory began as early as 1630 (Blakeslee 1981). The Bourgmont journal also indicates that the Padoucas had been at war with the Kansas, and Valverde's letter to the Viceroy, written in 1719, mentions an Apache who had been shot by a musket-bearing Kansa (Thomas 1935: 143).

Thus, it seems clear that the Padoucas who made the treaty with Bourgmont were Apaches, not Comanches. The Padoucas of the Mallet journey are also not Comanches, and the most reasonable assumption that can be made is that they are Apaches as well.

Apaches: Just prior to the time of our story, Apaches controlled the High Plains of Nebraska, Colorado, and eastern New Mexico. They lived in rather fluid groupings, with old groups sometimes merging and new ones sometimes splitting off from parent bands. As a result, the historical records apply a plethora of names to them, many of which cannot be verified with confidence today (Opler 1983: 385–392). Of these groups, several are important here.

The Jicarillas lived in northeastern New Mexico, on the headwaters of the Canadian River. North of them, the Carlanas inhabited southern Colorado (Opler 1983: 389). The Cuartelejos were in western Kansas, and the Palomas lived still farther out on the Plains. Down the Canadian River from the Jicarillas, in eastern New Mexico, was a group sometimes referred to as the Faraones (Kessell 1979: 361). A possibly separate Apache band that lived in the Sandia Mountains east of Albuquerque also was called Faraones.

The name is of Spanish, not Apache, origin and means "wandering Egyptian-like hordes."

Most non-Indians think of Apache groups (with the exception of the Kiowa-Apaches) as typically southwestern, but the archaeological record, certain biological traits, and early historical documents show that they originally came from western Canada and that many lived on the Great Plains before entering the Southwest. Linguistically, they are related to the Athabascan tribes of western Canada (Hoijer 1971). The linguistic technique called glottochronology indicates both that the Apache language differentiated from that of the northern group at around A.D. 950–1000 and that Jicarilla and Lipan did not become separate until about 200 years ago (Hoijer 1956; Hymes 1957).

The linguistic evidence also demonstrates clearly that the Athabascan languages are older in the north than in the south. Thus, the ancestors of the Apaches and Navajos must have migrated south, either at the time of the divergence of their ancestral language from the northern Athabascan languages or at some later time. There is a lively controversy over when they arrived in the southwestern Plains and what route(s) they took. Estimates of their time of arrival range from circa A.D. 1000 to after A.D. 1500. Some scholars have them drifting south along the High Plains; others trace them to certain archaeological complexes in the Great Basin or in the mountainous reaches of the Continental Divide.

Regardless of how and when they got there, Apaches were living in the southwestern Plains at the very beginning of the historical period. Coronado found them there when he made his foray to Quivira in 1541. On the Canadian River, he encountered a people called Querechos in the records of his expedition. Coronado was being led by Indian guides from Pecos, so it is not surprising to learn that Querechos is a rendition of the Pecos word for Apaches (Opler 1983: 386–387).

At that time the Apaches led a nomadic life, moving camp frequently as they followed the buffalo herds. They depended on the meat of this animal for most of their subsistence and sometimes drank the water from the bellies of the animals they slew. They ate the meat fresh, dried in strips to make jerky, or pounded into powder (pemmican). They lived in tipis, conical skin tents of bison hide supported by long poles. The Querechos used the Plains Indian sign language, and dogs were their beasts of burden (Hammond and Rey 1940).

In the winter they moved near settled tribes, either in the Southwest or on the Plains, to trade products of the hunt for vegetable foods. Later documents indicate that individual Apache bands were allied with different pueblos. The Jicarilla were allied with Taos, while the Faraones of the Canadian River traded at Pecos. The latter bond was so close that when the Spanish planned to move against the Faraones in 1715, they were warned not to let the Pecos Indians know lest they warn their Apache trading partners (Kessell 1979: 364). Judging from where refugees from the Pueblo Revolt ended up, the Cuartelejos may have been allied with Picuris. So were the Apaches of the Canadian River in 1601 (Hammond and Rey 1953: 292–293).

Later in time, the Apache way of life changed, and at least some of them became horticultural. They did not stop hunting the bison or trading with the Pueblos, but they added crop growing and pottery making to their former way of life. Corn and squash were grown in small plots in well-protected locations near creeks. This form of horticulture did not require season-long care, allowing the Apaches to continue going on their bison hunts. Bourgmont's expedition recorded this pattern in 1724 (Norall 1988: 159).

The archaeological remains of the horticultural Plains Apaches are known as the Dismal River Aspect (Gunnerson 1960). Two sites investigated so far have yielded remains of substantial houses with five-post foundations. Dismal River pottery consists of thin-walled jars, globular to somewhat elongated, with simple-stamped or smooth surfaces. Tools include arrow points, end scrapers, and other hunt-related items, but some horticultural tools, such as bison-scapula hoes, are present. Bison dominate the faunal assemblages, although corn and squash are found on occasion. Trade goods include a few European items along with obsidian and turquoise and southwestern-style pottery, pipes, and arrow-shaft smoothers.

The distribution of Dismal River sites, from South Dakota to Kansas, fits the documented distribution of Padouca villages. Related material in eastern New Mexico and Texas appears to derive from the Jicarillas and other Apaches (Gunnerson 1984). The dates for Dismal River sites, from about A.D. 1675 to 1725, also fit the dates for reports of horticulture among the Apaches and for their expulsion by the Comanches. Finally, at the site of El Cuartelejo, in Scott County, Kansas, there is a seven-room pueblo that probably once housed Picuris Indians who fled to this area (Wedel 1959: 466).

These Apache groups bore the brunt of attacks by the newly arrived Comanches in the early eighteenth century. The Cuartelejos, Palomas, Faraones, and Carlanas retreated south, first to the vicinity of Pecos, then onto the plains of Texas. Some remained with the Lipan Apaches of southwestern Texas, but the rest returned north in the nineteenth century to become amalgamated with the Jicarillas. The latter were also attacked by the Comanches and moved their farming communities west of the Sangre de Cristo Mountains, but they continued to use their traditional homeland for hunting until the reservation period (Gunnerson 1969: 162–164; Opler 1983: 389–392). Some of the Palomas may have remained on the Plains to become the Kiowa-Apaches, but this is not as certain as a reading of the literature might imply. Most of the others were gone by the time the Mallets traveled across what had been their territory in 1739.

Comanches: Comanches call themselves *nemena,* "people." The name Comanche is derived from a Ute word, *komantcia,* "enemy" (Opler 1943). The Ute term came to be applied to them in great part because the Comanches first visited the Spanish Southwest in the company of Utes, with whom they were temporarily at peace (Twitchell 1914 II: 301). Other names for the Comanche include Snake, Ietan, and Tetau. The name *Snake* is derived from the gesture denoting the Comanches in the Plains Indian sign language, a wriggling motion made with the right hand and arm. They shared this appellation with the Shoshones, for reasons that are discussed below. *Ietan* is the name given the Comanches by the Plains Caddoans. When the Mallet brothers encountered the Comanches, an Arikara captive among the Comanches served as interpreter. The Mallets used a variant of this name, Laitane (i.e., *l'Ietan*) to designate them.

The name Tetau shows up in Zebulon Pike's journal and on the Antoine Nau map of his 1806 expedition (Jackson 1966: Map 3). It is readily confused with Teton, a division of the Sioux, but Tetau is actually the result of a mistranscription of the name Ietan. Pike had written Ietan several times in his abominable penmanship on a sketch map, and neither he nor his cartographer was able to read it correctly at the conclusion of the expedition.

The Comanches speak a Uto-Aztecan language. As is the case with the Apaches, the language relationships of the Comanches indicate clearly that they migrated to the southern Plains from a northerly homeland. Comanche is mutually intelligible with Shoshone, a language spoken from Nevada to Idaho and western Wyoming. The Comanche have to be derived from this group, and they most likely lived in the Green River region of southwestern Wyoming before the migration (Miller 1986: 98–99). It is because they were once contiguous with and essentially the same as the other Shoshone speakers that, like the Shoshone, they were called Snake in the Plains Indian sign language.

Comanches first showed up in Spanish records for New Mexico in 1705, and within a decade they had begun to press on the Apache bands northeast of Taos. The 1705 visit was friendly, but as early as 1706 the Utes and Comanches were at war with the Apaches. In that year, the Ulibarrí expedition to El Cuartelejo came upon Apaches in the vicinity of Two Buttes, in southeastern Colorado (Gunnerson 1984: 55), who were preparing to defend themselves against these combined forces (Thomas 1935: 65). When the Valverde expedition traversed the same general region in 1719, the situation was much worse. Jicarilla Apaches as close as two days' travel from Taos lived in fear of the Comanches and Utes (Thomas 1935: 112–114; Gunnerson 1984: 62–63). These enemies were attacking the little Apache settlements in force, killing all of the men and carrying the women and children into captivity. Such an attack had been made at Ponil Creek, where the Apaches suffered sixty deaths and sixty-four women and children captured (Thomas 1935: 115–116; Gunnerson 1984: 63). Valverde wrote of seeing many abandoned Apache settlements, already in ruins (Thomas 1935: 142). This pattern of total war was typical of the "Snakes." Valverde recorded it in the Southwest, and the Vérendrye brothers described it in the northern Plains (Smith 1980: 104–110).

In the southern Plains, the slaughter continued. By 1723, when Bustamente visited the Jicarillas, he found that the Comanches were still attacking Apache *rancherias* (Thomas 1935: 197–199). By this time some Carlana Apaches may have taken refuge among the Jicarillas (Gunnerson 1984: 66). The Apaches begged Bustamente for relief, and he recommended that a presidio be built for their defense, but this was never done.

In 1726 Pedro de Rivera, sent by the viceroy to inspect the defenses of the province, described the Comanches as follows:

> Their origin is unknown, because they are always on the move and in battle array, for they war with all tribes. They halt at any camp site and set up their campaign tents, which are made of buffalo hide and transported by large dogs which they raise for this purpose. . . . As soon as they conclude the trade which brings them there, which is confined to tanned skins, buffalo hides, and the Indian children they capture (because they kill the adults), they withdraw, continuing their wandering until another time (Rivera cited in Kessell 1979: 371).

By the 1730s Jicarilla refugees were living in the vicinity of Pecos, and their presence may have drawn Comanche attacks on that place. Jicarilla war casualties were buried in the Pecos cemetery as early as 1734, and in 1739 the first Pecos Indian victims of the Comanches were recorded (Kessell 1979: 371–372). This alone explains why the Mallet brothers ended up at Picuris rather than at Pecos; the Comanches, with whom their guide had lived, were at war with the people of the Pecos area.

The Comanches made their living primarily by the hunt. They took the bison, antelope, and elk of the southern Plains, hunting primarily from horseback with short bows and lances (Richardson 1933). They also killed and ate horses and mules. This dietary practice may have been an adaptation to the southern Plains, which were not always plentifully supplied with bison; the Apaches and Navajos ate horses as well.

Comanches did not live by meat alone. They also gathered wild plant foods such as mesquite beans, prickly-pear fruit, berries, nuts, and acorns. Like the Apaches before them, they also traded with horticultural tribes for corn, squash, and tobacco. The Comanche adaptation to the southern Plains was thus similar to the earlier pattern for the Plains Apaches.

The Pueblos: The term *pueblo* refers both to the Indian communities of the American Southwest and to the architecture that helps make their settlements distinctive. The villages consist of several multiroom buildings situated around a central plaza. Upper stories were often stepped back, creating a terraced effect, and the spaces so created were sometimes used as subsidiary plazas. Each family occupied a suite of rooms that included living space, storage rooms, and work spaces. Residents gained access to the interior of the buildings via doorways above ground level and reached the roof by ladders, which could be pulled up in case of attack.

Like miniature city-states, each of the pueblos of the Southwest was an independent political entity. Two of the pueblos important to this story, Taos and Picuris, were related by language, with the two populations speaking mutually intelligible dialects of the Tiwa group. Other Tiwa speakers lived at Isleta and Sandia, in the vicinity of present-day Albuquerque (Bodine 1979: 255). The people of Pecos, who also played a part in the Mallet expedition, spoke a more distantly related Towa language shared by the inhabitants of Jemez Pueblo, west of the Rio Grande (Schroeder 1979: 430).

These were agricultural people who grew corn, beans, and squash in irrigated fields near their pueblos. All three groups also hunted in the mountains and in the bison territory to the east. Their social organization was tightly controlled but lacked the kind of hierarchy to which we are accustomed. Leaders included war chiefs, who dealt with external relationships, and officers for internal affairs, whom the Spaniards called *caciques*. Religious fellowships that used underground structures called kivas for secret rites and plazas for public dances dominated spiritual life.

Taos, Picuris, and Pecos were the northeasternmost of the pueblos and were important points of contact with the Great Plains in both the prehistoric and historic periods. Each pueblo was situated adjacent to a pass that connected the Plains with the Rio Grande Valley. Pecos lay at the east end of Glorietta Pass, near the head of a valley that stretched toward the Plains. This pass was the most open of the three and hence the most appropriate for wagon traffic. As a result, it was on the main route of the Santa Fe Trail after 1821.

Picuris Pueblo lies west of the Sangre de Cristo Mountains, where the Rio Pueblo cuts through the foothills, some 45 miles north of Pecos. Its pass lies at the headwaters of the river, which nearly meets head to head with a branch of the Mora River. In fact, the name of the pueblo is a rendition of a term meaning "at the mountain gap," referring to the pass and indicative of its importance (Brown 1979: 276).

Taos lies about 18 miles north of Picuris by trail on a plateau at the western base of the mountains. It is blessed with two passes across the mountains. Both are reached by ascending the Rio San Fernando de Taos. After heading that stream, travelers could take either of two routes east from the intermontaine valley. A northerly route ran east through Fowler Pass, reaching the Plains near Cimarron. The Ulibarrí expedition took this route in 1706 (Gunnerson 1984: 49–52). A southerly route struck the Plains at the place called Rayado; it was taken by Valverde in 1719 (Gunnerson 1984: 57).

The three Pueblos were much reduced from their aboriginal state by the time of the Mallet expedition. Estimates of their populations in A.D. 1630 are 2,000 for Picuris, somewhat more than that for Pecos, and 2,500 for Taos. By 1749 the populations were 400, 1,000, and 540, respectively (Simmons 1979:

185). The population declined as a result both of the pueblo revolts of A.D. 1680 to 1696 and repeated epidemics of introduced diseases. Episodic Apache attacks also added to the toll. Attacks from the Plains had occurred prior to the arrival of the Spanish conquistadors, but in later years the Apaches and Comanches acquired horses, making them more formidable foes.

Relationships between the border pueblos and the Plains nomads were complex, involving both peaceful trade and warfare (Ford 1972). As mentioned, each pueblo was allied with one or more Apache bands. The Jicarillas were the allies of Taos, the Faraones of the Canadian River traded at Pecos, and the Chipaynes and perhaps Cuartelejos were allied with Picuris. The plainsmen traded with their allies at periodic fairs in the individual pueblos. In historic times the largest fair was at Taos, but Picuris and Pecos also held them (Simmons 1979: 189). This was a pattern of some antiquity. Oñate's men found evidence of trade between the Apaches of the Canadian River and Picuris (Hammond and Rey 1953: 292–293), whereas Coronado's men learned of similar trade in 1541. By 1739, Comanche bands had replaced most of the Apaches as trading partners, and an Arikara who had lived as a captive among some Comanches led the Mallets to Picuris.

3.

THE JOURNAL

The Mallets kept a journal of their expedition, but it has been lost. Surviving documents make it clear that they turned it over to Governor Bienville, but what became of it after that is not known. Fortunately, the governor sent a summary of the journal to Paris, and a copy of this document has survived (AN, Col. F3 24: 387–391vo; photocopy in Library of Congress, Manuscript Division). It is extremely brief and at times confused, but it is the most important record of the expedition.

Folmer (1939a) translated the summary, but he used Margry's (1876–1886 VI: 455–462) published version, which contains some errors of transcription. Only one of these is critical to interpretation of the route. In a section describing the return of the Mallets from Santa Fe, Margry transformed "a la Fourche" ("at the fork") into "a la Source" ("at the source") of the River of the Arkansas. Folmer (1939a: 170) translated this as "on the upper Arkansas" but did not seem to recognize the distortion of the route that this implied. The Forks of the Arkansas are in eastern Oklahoma, but its source is in central

Colorado, hundreds of miles to the west. Because the mention of the spot in question occurs after the Mallets had traveled down the river in question for many days, it is unlikely that they would have thought they were anywhere near the source. Rather, Folmer's vague translation was a good stab at making sense of what was otherwise an incomprehensible passage.

An English translation of the abstract follows. The original French version can be found in Appendix A.

Extract of the Journal of the Expedition of the Mallet Brothers to Santa Fe, May 29, 1739, to June 24, 1740

Abstract of the journal of the expedition made to Santa Fe, capital of the province of New Mexico by the two brothers, Pierre and Paul Mallet, Canadians, along with those named La Rose, Philippes, Bellecourt, Petit Jean, Galien, and Moreau.

In order to understand the route which these Canadians explored to New Mexico, it is well to know that it is 100 leagues from Illinois to the villages of the Missouris on the river of the same name, 80 leagues from there to that of the Kansas, 100 leagues from the Kansas to the Oto, and 60 from there to the mouth of the river of the Panis Maha on the Missouri. That nation is settled at the mouth of the river that bears their name, and it is from this point that the explorers made their departure on May 29, 1739.

Up till now, all of those who tried to travel to New Mexico thought they would find it at the sources of the Missouri, and to accomplish this, they ascended as far as the Arikaras, who are more than 150 leagues from the Pawnees. On the advice of some natives, the explorers took an entirely different route, and leaving the Pawnees, they traveled overland, retracing their steps roughly parallel to the Missouri.

On the 2nd of June, they came upon a river that they called the Platte, and seeing that it did not deviate from the route they had in mind, they followed it upstream along the right bank for a distance of 28 leagues, and at that point, they found that it made a fork with the River of the Padoucas which empties into the Platte.

Three days after reaching the River of the Padoucas, that is to say on the 13th of June, they turned left across said river and crossed a tongue of land. They camped on the 14th on the other side of the River of the Hills which also feeds into the Platte.

On the 15th and 16th they continued to travel overland, and on the 17th they came upon another river which they named the White Hills. During these three days, they crossed a region of plains in which they did not find enough wood to make a fire, and they relate in their journal that these plains extend to the mountains in the vicinity of Santa Fe.

On the 18th they camped on the banks of another river that they crossed and which they named the Friendly River.

On the 19th they found and crossed another stream which they called the River of Worries.

On the 20th, they reached the River of the Kansas, which shows the approximate route they took from the Pawnees. They crossed it and in so doing lost seven horses loaded with merchandise. This river is deep and has a strong current.

The 22nd, they crossed another river, which they called the River of the Arrow.

On the 23rd, they again found the great prairies where one finds nothing to make a fire save buffalo dung.

On the 24th, they crossed another river, and from the 26th to the 30th they encountered some streams every day. Finally, on the 30th, they found Spanish markings on some rocks on the banks of the last river.

They had made, in their estimation, 155 leagues overland from the Pawnees, travelling almost always to the west. They believe that this river is a branch of the Arkansas River and is the river that they encountered lower down on their return journey the tenth day after leaving Santa Fe.

They ascended the left bank of this river until the fifth of July, when they found a village of the Laitane [Comanche] nation. They made a present to these people and received some venison in return. They made their camp at a distance of 1 league from the Laitanes, as they noticed that these people had some evil purpose in mind.

On the 6th, they left the banks of this stream and upon their leaving, an Arikara Indian who was a captive among the Laitanes, told them that this tribe wanted to attack them. They sent him back saying that the natives could come and that the French would wait for them. The Laitanes did not make any move, and the slave returned to the French. They asked him if he knew the road to the Spaniards, and he answered that he did, as he had been a slave among them and had been baptized there. They hired him as a guide with the promise to procure his liberty. He consented to this, and that day they made 10 leagues in order to put distance between themselves and the Laitanes.

On the 10th they saw the Spanish mountains at a distance of over 10 leagues, and on the 12th they camped at the first mountain. On the 13th they stayed at three Laitane lodges, and they made a small present to them.

On the 14th they once again encountered a river, which they named the Red River, but which very likely is another branch of the Arkansas. Twenty-one leagues from here, they found the first Spanish post, which is a mission called Picuris.

On the 15th they encountered three Indians to whom they gave a letter for the commandant of Taos who the next day sent them some mutton and a beautiful loaf of wheat bread.

When they arrived at a league from the first post, the commandant and the padre came out to meet them along with the whole population and received them very graciously, even with the ringing of bells, according to their account.

The 21st, they left Picuris and arrived at noon at another mission called Sainte Croix, and after dinner they passed another called La Cañada, and they spent the night at a town called Sainte Marie, where they were pleasantly received by the Spaniards.

On the 22nd of July, they arrived in Santa Fe after having travelled 265 leagues from the river of the Panis Maha. One can see in the certificate enclosed herein the manner in which they were received and how they lived there nine months while they awaited the response from the Viceroy of Mexico. It is not surprising that they had to wait for so long because it is 500 leagues by land from Santa Fe to Old Mexico and no more than one caravan makes the journey each year.

The response of the viceroy, according to the report of the Canadians, was to have them stay in New Mexico. They thought that they would be hired to make the discovery of a country that, according to a tradition of the Indians, whether true or false, lay three months journey overland toward the western coast and where it was said that white men dressed in silk lived in great cities along the edge of the sea. Whatever might be so, they preferred to return and they were allowed to depart with the letters, copies of which are attached.

Santa Fe, according to their account, is a village built of wood and without any fortification. There are about 800 families, Spanish or mulatto, and in the region roundabout are a number of villages of Indians. Residing in each of them is a priest who runs the mission. There are only eighty soldiers in the garrison, a bad gang and poorly armed. There are mines very close by which are not worked at all. There are others in the province which are worked for the royal treasury, the silver from which is transported every year to Old Mexico by caravan.

It would seem, from one of the enclosed letters, that the governors seize for themselves all the merchandise that they desire and do the little trading that goes on, which the priests and others would like to do.

The Laitane nation, which is mentioned in this journal, is not a Christian tribe like the others in the region, but it is at peace with the Spaniards. The Canadians assert that the little merchandise that they distributed among them had a great effect, and that this tribe would be entirely on our side if we had some sort of post in their country.

The Return

On the first of May, the explorers, now numbering seven, as Moreau had married in that country, left Santa Fe to find their way to the Mississippi and to New Orleans by a route other than the one they had taken on the outward journey. On the 2nd of May, they arrived at a mission named Pecos, where they stayed two days.

They left on the 4th and camped on a river of the same name, and they think that this river might be a branch of the Red River or of the Arkansas. They followed it on the 5th and left it on the 6th. On the 7th, they encountered another that flowed in the same direction that they named the River of the Mare. They left this stream to cross overland, following the route they had in mind, and on the 10th they encountered a third river, which they believe flows into the Red River or into the Arkansas, and which they think is the same branch on which they found higher up the Spanish inscriptions when they were en route to Santa Fe. They were then 35 or 40 leagues from that capital and they estimate that one could ascend to that place and then return in order to perfect their exploration.

On the 11th, 12th, and 13th, they followed this river and on the last day, three of the seven men quit their comrades to retake the road of the Pawnees to go to Illinois, which they accomplished according to letters sent later from that post. The other four continued in their resolution to come here. The same day, they encountered eight Laitane men with whom they camped.

On the 15th, continuing along the same river, they found a Laitane village where they said they saw a quantity of horses. They spent the night there. The Indians provided them a feast, and they traded horses for some knives and other trinkets.

They continued to follow this river until the 22nd, and on that night they lost six horses. From the 22nd until the 30th, they kept at a distance from the river. That day, they encountered two men and three women of the Padoucas to whom they offered their hand, but after a bit fear seized the Indians who abandoned the meat they had been carrying and fled with their wives, and it was not possible to make them return.

On the 8th of June, the Canadians returned to the bank of the river which they followed until the 14th. On the 15th through the 19th, they camped and having carefully discussed the course of the river, they resolved to abandon the eighteen horses they had and to make elm bark canoes. They did this although they had but two knives among the four of them. At this point, they had come about 220 leagues by land from Santa Fe.

On the 20th, they embarked in two small canoes and made 6 leagues, as this river does not have a strong current.

The 21st, they made the same distance. The 22nd, they saw two beautiful river mouths which likely could be the Pecos and Mare Rivers, which they had crossed near Santa Fe. Finally, on the 24th, they were agreeably surprised to find themselves at the forks of the Arkansas River. They had made about 42 leagues by canoe. Below the forks, they found an encampment of Canadians who were hunting in order to make salted meat. Because they had nothing left save their arms and a little ammunition, they went hunting with the others and packed a pirogue with salt meat with which they returned to our post on the Arkansas and from there to New Orleans on   1741.

4.

NEBRASKA

The Missouri River, Spring 1739

In order to understand the route which these Canadians explored to
New Mexico, it is well to know that it is 100 leagues from Illinois to
the villages of the Missouris on the river of the same name, 80 leagues
from there to that of the Kansas, 100 leagues from the Kansas to the
Oto, and 60 from there to the mouth of the river of the Panis Maha
on the Missouri. That nation is settled at the mouth of the river that
bears their name, and it is from this point that the explorers made
their departure on May 29, 1739.

Up till now, all of those who tried to travel to New Mexico thought
they would find it at the sources of the Missouri, and to accomplish
this, they ascended as far as the Arikaras, who are more than 150
leagues from the Pawnees.

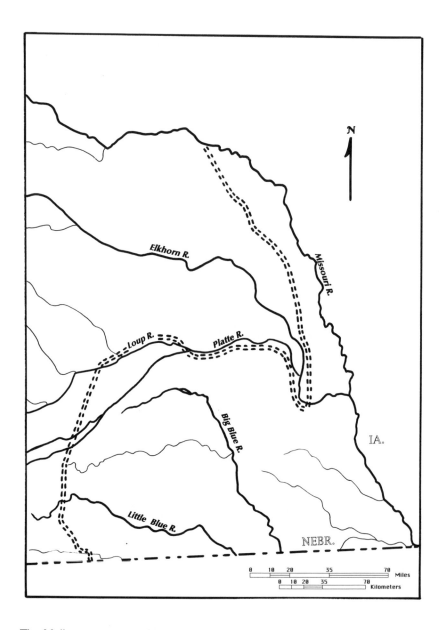

The Mallet route across Nebraska.

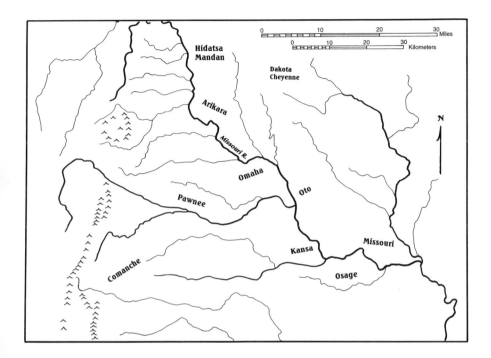

Tribal locations in the Great Plains, 1739.

This description of the early portion of the Mallet route seems straight-forward until one tries to connect it with known tribal locations in 1739. The critical questions involve the location of the Panimaha River, with a village at its mouth, and whether the Mallets actually went up the Missouri as far as the Arikaras in South Dakota. Taken at face value, the manuscript is very confusing; it says they went as far as the Arikaras (which should be in South Dakota) but, after ascending the Missouri River, traveled overland from a Panimaha village 60 leagues above the Oto village (which would be in Nebraska).

It is clear from modern measurements between known points that the Mallets were using the common French land league, equivalent to about 2.75 English miles. They were very good at estimating distances traveled, making interpretation of this abstract far easier than is the case with other early travel documents. Their estimates of the distances between villages along the Missouri River, however, are obviously general assessments, as the very round intervals of 100, 100, 100 and 60 leagues make abundantly clear.

Their starting point was the French colony in Illinois, probably Fort des Chartres, 20 leagues from the mouth of the Missouri River. The little expedition must first have moved up the Mississippi to the mouth of the Missouri, then westward along the latter's lower course. The first tribe they encountered would have been the Missouri. In 1739 the Missouris lived in a village on the right (south) bank of the Missouri River above the mouth of the Grand River, in the present state of Missouri. Other sources place this village at 80 leagues from the mouth of the Missouri, indicating that the Mallets were counting from their starting point at Fort des Chartres. Guillaume Delisle, the famous French cartographer, mapped the Missouri village based on information from Bourgmont, and this map eventually was discovered in the French archives by Mildred Wedel (Wood 1983: Plate 1).

The Missouris were living in the vicinity of the mouth of the Grand River at the time of the earliest clear historic references to their location, and they remained there until 1750. Their first village in this location is identifiable today as the Utz site, a large, early-contact-period archaeological site (Chapman 1959: 2). By about 1714, the Missouris moved their village about 7 miles upstream to a spot now known as Gumbo Point (Bray 1978: 12–13).

The abstract places the Kansa tribe 100 leagues by water above the Missouri villages. There are two possibilities for the location of this tribe in 1739. The more likely one is the Doniphan site, which is located near the mouth of Independence Creek in northeastern Kansas. The Kansas lived here when they were contacted by Bourgmont in 1714, and the site is shown on the Delisle map of 1718 (Wedel 1959: 51). They were still there in 1724, when

Bourgmont used the village as his jumping-off place for his expedition to the Apaches (Norall 1988: 63).

The other possibility is a location near the mouth of Salt Creek in the vicinity of present-day Leavenworth, Kansas. Wedel (1959: 51) notes that the earliest documentation of this second village comes from the 1740s and that the last reference to the Doniphan village is from the 1720s. Other documents do not indicate precisely where the Kansa were in the 1730s.

The Mallets placed the Otos 100 leagues upstream from the Kansas. In 1714 the Otos were living near the mouth of Salt Creek, a tributary of the Platte (Norall 1988: 109). They had moved by 1739 to a village on the right (west) bank of the Missouri River, about 20 miles above the mouth of the Platte. Sources that place them in this spot range in date from 1721 to 1757 (Mott 1938: 260–261). Lewis and Clark recorded the ruins of this village in 1804.

The abstract says it is 60 leagues from the Oto village to the mouth of the Panimaha River and the Panimaha village. Locating this settlement is one of the most difficult interpretive problems in the Mallet documents. As we have already seen, the Skiri Pawnees, or Panimahas, were living in two separate places in 1739—on the Loup River in central Nebraska and on the Missouri River in south-central South Dakota. The Omahas, or Maha, lived at the mouth of Bow Creek (sometimes called the Maha River), between the two Skiri groups (Court of Claims 1914: 42, 51–52, 102).

The Panimaha River in question obviously could not have been the Platte, as the mouth of the Platte is below the Oto village, opposite from the direction indicated in the abstract. The Loup River is another candidate, but the distances are wrong. To go from the Oto village to the mouth of the Loup, one must follow the Missouri downstream about 20 miles, then go up the Platte some 51 miles, for a total of 71 miles, or about 26, not 60, leagues.

The remaining possible interpretation is that the reference is to a spot farther up the Missouri River. Sixty leagues above the Oto village would be about 185 miles above the mouth of the Platte. The second Panimaha location, however, is farther away than that. The distance from the Oto village to the Oacoma and Oldham sites in South Dakota is on the order of 402 river miles, or 146 leagues.

Folmer (1939a) guessed that the Mallets referred to a Skiri village at the mouth of the Niobrara, but there is no archaeological evidence to show that a Skiri village once existed there. Furthermore, the next few sentences of the abstract indicate that the Mallets traveled with pack horses from this spot to the Platte River in four days, an unlikely feat if they started at the Niobrara. Frontiersmen typically traveled about 20 miles per day when on long journeys; anything more would weaken their horses dangerously. If the Mallets had gone from the mouth of the Niobrara to the Platte in four days, they would have been covering 44 miles per day.

If the Panimaha village at the mouth of the Panimaha River does not match either location occupied by the Skiris, then where was it, and who were the Panimahas in question? The answer is maddeningly simple: The Mallets were referring not to the Panimaha River but to a stream they knew as the Maha—today called Bow Creek. Likewise, they meant not the Panimaha tribe but the Maha, or Omaha. In compiling the abstract, Governor Bienville mistakenly changed Maha to Panimaha. As a result, I (and others before me) had been searching for the wrong Indians and the wrong river.

I began to untangle this case of mistaken identity when I was working on another project. Along with a large number of other scholars, I participated in the study of some human skeletal remains from the Over Museum in South Dakota prior to their reburial. My job was to review the archaeological evidence so that the physical anthropologists in the project would know what cultural traditions they were encountering. Among the sites that yielded the materials in question was one called Oacoma, located in South Dakota. This site is one of two in South Dakota that has yielded pottery of the Lower Loup Focus. Lower Loup is the cultural antecedent of the Pawnee tribe, and the Oacoma and Oldham sites had always been something of an anomaly in South Dakota.

The background material I had written up on Oacoma remained in the back of my mind when I returned to my work on the Mallet route. I had extracted all of the distances reported in the journal and was trying to make sense of them. Working backwards from the mouth of the Loup River in central Nebraska, I was trying to match the Mallet route with known features. I had on the table not only these figures but also every other scrap of information I could get on known village locations, including La Renaudière's description of a Skiri village 10 leagues above the Omahas. An Omaha village at the mouth of Bow Creek was one of the known points, and as I was looking at the map, the Oacoma site bubbled up from the depths of my subconscious. How far was it from the Omaha village to Oacoma? The map said about 70 leagues, versus the 10 leagues in the published version of the La Renaudière report.

The similarity between the French numerals 1 and 7 suggested that La Renaudière had been referring to the Oacoma site, *70* leagues above the Omaha, when he said in 1723 that Panimahas had gone to live among the Arikara *10* leagues upstream. Then it struck me that perhaps this was the place where the Mallets had been told they were on the wrong trail if they wanted to go to Santa Fe. I checked the distance they gave from the Pawnees to the Arikaras (more than 150 leagues). It matched the distance (by their route of travel) from the known Pawnee villages in central Nebraska to the Oacoma site. By comparison, if the Skiri Pawnees had been at the mouth of the Niobrara (as Folmer had them), 150 leagues would have put the Arikaras in central North Dakota, whereas every account of the period places them in South Dakota. Furthermore, the estimate of 60 leagues from the Oto site to the Panimahas fits well the distance from the Omaha village on Bow Creek to the Oacoma site.

This interpretation of the location of the Panimaha village seemed pretty good, but it got better when I sent a version of the argument to a friend. John Ludwickson, who works for the Nebraska State Historical Society, is a careful scholar and very knowledgeable regarding the region. His response, even though he had previously made different interpretations of the La Renaudière

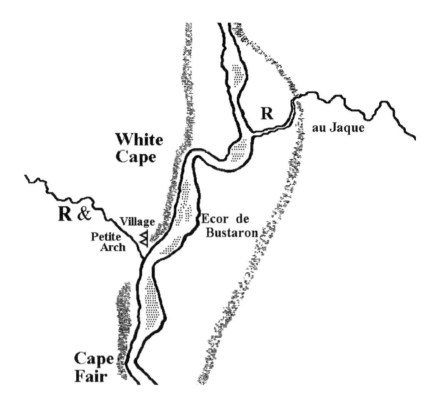

Portion of the Evans map. Lewis and Clark used the Evans map during their ascent of the Missouri River. This detail shows the location of the Omaha village site at the mouth of Bow Creek (Maha River). (Redrawn for clarity; the original is reproduced by Moulton 1983: Map 7.)

reference, was that my hypothesis was likely true. His main reason for saying so was based on a point I had missed; it explained why the Omahas were not mentioned in the abstract.

The Omahas had lived in the region of northeastern Nebraska and southern South Dakota since about the beginning of the century. A 1723 report by

La Renaudière mentioned an Omaha village, probably the one at the mouth of Bow Creek (cf. Ludwickson et al 1987: 71). They remained in this spot until sometime before 1758, when they established villages downstream on the Missouri River (Court of Claims 1914: 145). When the Omaha tribe sued the U.S. government in 1912, several witnesses said the Omaha residence on Bow Creek existed prior to the creation of a village near Homer, Nebraska, and after a village on the Niobrara River, which in turn followed a village on the White River. Therefore, the Mallets must have passed an Omaha village en route to the Arikaras.

Why were the Omahas not mentioned when all of the other tribes along the river were named? Simply because Governor Bienville or the clerk who drew up the abstract had mistaken Maha for Panimaha. The Mallets visited Panimahas among the Arikaras in South Dakota and then met more in Nebraska, stopping in the Maha village on the way. There were Panimahas to the north and Panimahas to the south, with Mahas in the middle. To make matters worse, the Mahas were living at the mouth of a stream called Maha River. This was a name applied to Bow Creek because of the Omaha residence there (Court of Claims 1914: 42, 102). No wonder the governor was confused.

Everything else we know about the trip is consistent with the hypothesis that Bow Creek—the Maha River—was the Panimaha River mentioned in the abstract. From the Omaha (Maha) village at the mouth of that waterway, the Mallets must have continued up the Missouri to the Arikaras and the Skiris living in South Dakota. This is clear from the portion of the abstract that reads: "Up till now, all of those who tried to travel to New Mexico thought they would find it at the sources of the Missouri, and to accomplish this, they ascended as far as the Arikaras, who are more than 150 leagues from the Pawnee."

The idea that Santa Fe was near the sources of the Missouri had been around for quite a while. It seems to have been derived from La Salle, who probably misunderstood his Pana slave boy. The youth, probably a Wichita (Wedel 1973), told La Salle that his people lived "more than 200 leagues to

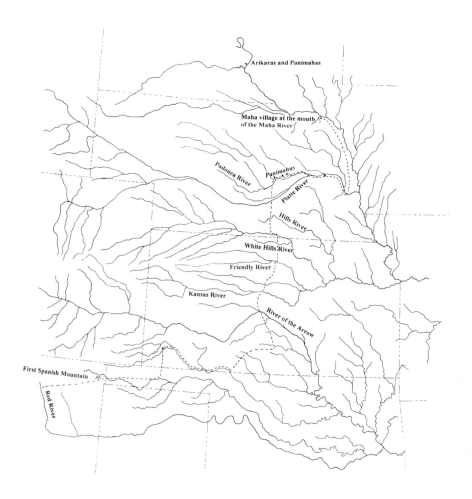

Places visited by the Mallets en route to Santa Fe. The villages of Panimahas (Skidis) on the Padouca River are not mentioned in the abstract presumably because of the confusion created by the presence of other Panimahas among the Arikaras and by the Maha (Omaha) village at the mouth of the Maha River.

the west [of Starved Rock], on a tributary of the Mississippi, and there it has two villages near together" (Wedel 1973: 57). In 1683, La Salle wrote that the Panas could be reached by way of the Missouri, which is navigable for a great distance from its mouth (Wedel 1973: 57). La Salle did not state directly that the Panas lived *on* the Missouri River, but he drew a map that showed them living on a southerly tributary of the Missouri, which he depicted as having its source fairly close to Santa Fe (Delanglez 1943: 29). This information became codified in the Franquelin maps of 1684–1687 and was still believed in 1739. As Wedel has shown, however, the Panas known to La Salle were probably the Wichitas living on the Arkansas River, the headwaters of which are close to those of the Rio Grande.

In 1751, while being held prisoner in New Mexico, Pierre Mallet testified that he and his brother decided to try for Santa Fe on the word of a companion who had lived among the Comanches. This unnamed man must have been one of the intrepid voyageurs who went among the Comanches in the aftermath of Bourgmont's expedition. Mallet claimed that this man told the brothers that Santa Fe lay only eight days beyond the Missouri, which is clearly incorrect. Presumably, his informant was not along on the expedition or he would have taken them by a more direct route to the Comanche country.

Folmer (1939a) noted that the rather vague wording in the French original of the abstract leaves open the question of whether it was previous explorers or the Mallets who traveled as far as the Arikaras before learning of their error. He did not resolve this question to his satisfaction, but the answer is simple. If previous explorers had learned that Santa Fe lay far west of the Missouri, the Mallets certainly would not have gone as far upstream as the Arikaras before retracing part of their route back to the Platte River. Clearly, then, the intent of the sentence is that since 1684 voyageurs had thought that the way to Santa Fe lay near the source of the Missouri and that, acting on this misinformation, the Mallets had proceeded upriver to the Arikaras. There, among the Arikaras and some Skiris, someone set them straight, and the Mallets returned downstream to the Omaha village on Bow Creek to purchase horses and to begin their overland journey. This is the spot described in the abstract as "the mooth of the Panis Maha on the Missouri."

The Old Ponca Trail, May 29–June 1, 1739

On the advice of some natives, the explorers took an entirely different route, and leaving the Pawnees, they travelled overland, retracing their steps roughly parallel to the Missouri.

I visited the spot where the Mallets spent the first night of the overland journey even before I had begun to investigate their route. It lies at the headwaters of Daily Creek in western Dixon County, Nebraska. This area of beautiful loess hills bordering the last free-flowing section of the Missouri River below Montana is filled with prehistoric archaeological remains.

My interest in the area began when I was in a graduate seminar and opted to study some of the archaeological material from northeastern Nebraska. It might have ended there except for a letter forwarded to me years later from a farm woman in Dixon County. She had written to the Nebraska State Historical Society for advice on how to excavate a site on her land. Because they knew of my interest, the archaeologists at the historical society passed the letter on to me, and it led to unexpected results.

The woman, Annie Lamprecht, has been interested in the Indian remains near her home for most of her life. In response to her inquiry, I sent her a how-to book and offered some long-distance advice. In return, she and her friends plotted the locations of the sites they knew on maps for me. When other work took me to northeastern Nebraska, I visited her and was awed by the beauty of the region and by the preservation of the archaeological remains there.

I returned in the years 1983 to 1985, with funding from the Nebraska State Historical Society, Earthwatch, and Wichita State University. In 1983 we surveyed the area around Annie's farm and found twenty-five sites. The next year we excavated one lodge that dated to the early fifteenth century, and

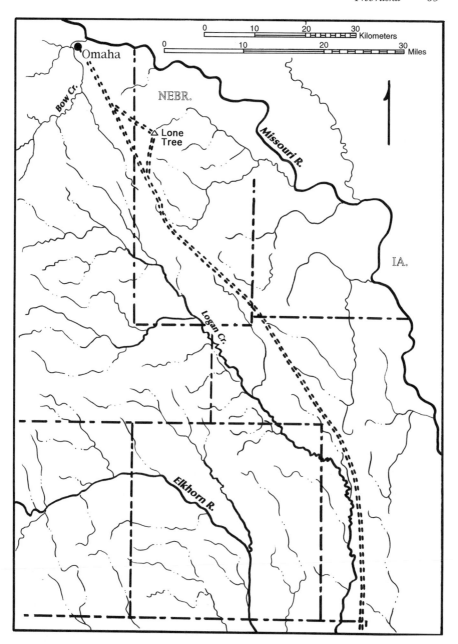

The Mallet route, May 29–June 1, 1739.

in 1985 we surveyed various parts of the county in an attempt to determine why sites were located in some spots but not in others.

During that last expedition, we reviewed all of the available historical records, and these yielded information about the first part of the Mallet route. An old history of the county (Huse 1896) made several references to archaeological materials in the vicinity of the "Lone Tree." We visited the spot but did not find much, as dense forest had grown up around what had been an isolated tree, burying artifacts under leaves and humus.

The Lone Tree had been quite a landmark in the early days. Standing near the springs that feed Daily Creek, it was easily seen from the high ground to the west. The county history said that Indians traveling from the west used it to guide them to the clear water at its base. Euro-Americans also noticed it. Mike Addison, with whom we visited in 1985, said that his grandfather had homesteaded that property and that, when he was a child, classrooms would make field trips to it. It was so large that it took twenty children to link hands and form a ring around the trunk.

Mr. Addison warned us that it was much changed. Not only had many other trees grown up where once there was only a single great cottonwood, but the Lone Tree itself had fallen in the 1960s. We beat our way through the underbrush anyway and were rewarded by what we saw. Although the original tree was gone, the twigs that had sprouted from its stump had grown to massive size.

The historical record indicates that the Lone Tree was a landmark for Indians traveling through that part of Nebraska. The archaeological materials found near it demonstrate that they camped under its branches. By themselves, however, these facts do not prove that the Mallets camped there. That conclusion is drawn from the Lone Tree's location with respect to the Omaha village and the trail that the Mallets followed. The tree stood about 19 miles from the Omaha village near the mouth of Bow Creek, one day's travel on a long overland journey. It is also the last spot for a considerable distance where good water is available. It also turns out to be on a branch of an old Indian trail.

The Lone Tree. This photograph shows the site of the first Mallet camp in 1739, as it looked in 1988. The original tree had blown down a generation before, but these massive trunks had grown up from the stump. (Photograph by the author.)

When we were looking through the historic records of Dixon County in 1985, searching for clues to what the environment was like before the advent of modern farming, we looked at the original records of the General Land Office surveys. The General Land Office was in charge of laying out the range, township, and section lines according to which homesteaders could stake their claims. The surveyors were private contractors who followed strict government regulations regarding the nature of their notes and map making. Because the basic intent of the survey was to enable homesteading, the contractors were asked to keep careful records of the nature of the soils, kinds of vegetation, and sources of water. Their notes, therefore, are a valuable source of information about the environment prior to homesteading. The surveyors also were supposed to keep notes on cultural features of the landscape such as Indian villages, roads, and the like. Many ignored this part of the regulations, but a few were conscientious about them.

One of the surveyors of Dixon County recorded the existence of an Indian trail in the areas he surveyed, plotting its location and describing its general route in his notes. He called it "the Old Puncas Trail" and said that it ran along the divide between the waters of the Platte and those of the Missouri all the way from the vicinity of Omaha. It is fortunate he did so, because the surveyors who worked further south did not bother to record so much information, and only one even noted the existence of a trail.

His "Puncas" are the Poncas, a tribe closely related to the Omahas. In fact, the Omahas and Poncas were a single group when they first came to northeastern Nebraska. Then, some time around 1700, the people who became known as the Omaha formed their tribal organization (Fletcher and La Flesche 1911). Some people refused to join the new political entity, most of them from the clan called Ponca. So today there is both a Ponca tribe (actually, there are two of them, the result of the forcible removal of some Poncas to Oklahoma) and a Ponca clan within the Omaha tribe.

After the political split, the two tribes gradually drifted apart. The Poncas occupied the area around the mouth of Ponca Creek, and the Omahas moved downstream to the vicinity of Homer, Nebraska. In 1857 the old trail across Dixon County would still take one toward the territory of the Poncas but not to that of the Omahas, who had moved to the east. This explains why the surveyor would name a trail leading to an old Omaha village for the Poncas.

Near the western edge of Dixon County, according to the General Land Office map, the trail forks from the point of view of someone heading northwest. The southernmost branch seems to head west around the Bow Creek valley. The middle fork is shown as continuing from the southeast toward the site of the Omaha village at the mouth of the creek. The third fork heads north, straight toward the Lone Tree. Here, then, is the evidence that the Mallets camped at the Lone Tree. It is one day's travel from the Omaha village from which they started, and a branch of the trail they followed ran directly to the tree. That they followed this trail, there can be no doubt. It fits perfectly the description of their route in the abstract—parallel to the course of the Missouri but inland from it.

The Land Office surveyors did not record trail along the divide all the way across Dixon County, and most of those who surveyed adjacent counties did not record it at all. There are, nevertheless, several clues regarding its location. When we were surveying in Dixon County in 1985, we did not have the time or personnel to survey the whole county. We did try to obtain information about site locations in the areas we could not visit, but for the most part such information was scanty. Several informants, however, mentioned that friends had found archaeological remains in the southeastern corner of the county, near the town of Emerson. This is one day's travel along the divide trail from the Lone Tree and near a tributary of Logan Creek. The Mallets probably camped here on the second night after leaving the Omaha village.

Between this spot and the Platte River, the Indian trail was mapped at only one location, just east of the little town of Craig. Here it ran almost due north-south, as the General Land Office surveyors found that it crossed the line between Ranges 9 and 10 East three times in less than 3 miles. The trail presumably continued south along the divide, which means it must have struck the Platte downstream from the mouth of the Elkhorn River. The Mallets estimated that they reached the Platte 28 leagues below the mouth of the Loup River. This point lies about 12 miles below the mouth of the Elkhorn River.

In 1846, the famous missionary Father Pierre De Smet almost lost his life on this trail. Traveling up the Missouri River from Bellevue, he accompanied a wagon load of goods being taken up the trail for one of the fur companies. Upon reaching the vicinity of the Ponca settlements, they had a close call with warriors of that tribe. The latter, seeing them coming up that trail, assumed that they were associated with the Pawnees because the trail came from Pawnee territory. Because the Poncas were at war with the Pawnees in 1846, they prepared to attack. Luckily for the good father, they recognized their mistake in time (Chittenden and Richardson 1905 Vol II: 617).

Along the Platte, June 2–10, 1739

> On the 2nd of June, they came upon a river that they called the Platte, and seeing that it did not deviate from the route they had in mind, they followed it upstream along the right bank for a distance of 28 leagues, and at that point, they found that it made a fork with the River of the Padoucas which empties into the Platte.

The abstract of the Mallet journal provides the first recorded use of the modern name for the Platte River. As we have seen, the French term is a translation of the names used by both the Pawnees and the Omahas for this important river. It is not possible to say how the Mallets came to learn it, but it is quite possible that they had one or more guides for this portion of their journey. Whether the guide was Arikara, Pawnee, or Omaha, we cannot say, as any one of them would have used a name for the river that would translate into French as "Platte."

The Mallets estimated that the mouth of the Loup Fork was 28 leagues, or about 77 miles, from where they struck the Platte. The abstract states that the explorers traveled up the right bank of the Platte. The convention for this sort of terminology is to identify banks as seen by an observer facing downstream; as the Platte flows east, the right bank would be the south one. Folmer, however, chose to interpret the phrase as meaning the right (north) bank, given their westward direction of travel on this leg of the journey. He based this interpretation on a later passage, which mentions that the party crossed the Loup River (a northerly tributary of the Platte) before moving

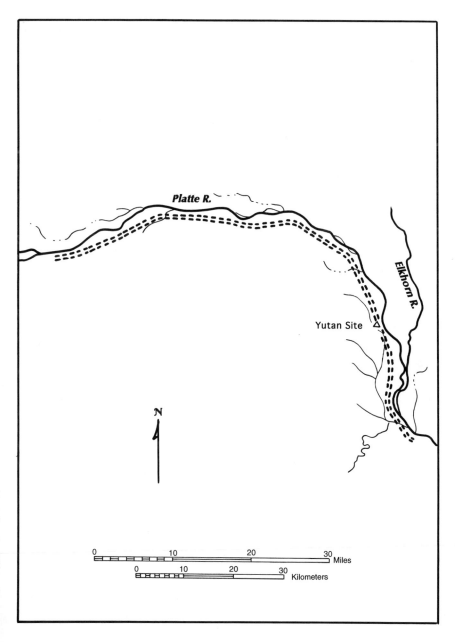

The Mallet route, June 2–10, 1739.

south. Hence, cursory examination of the abstract gives the impression that the Mallets stayed on the north side of the Platte until they reached the Loup River.

The evidence regarding this portion of the route is equivocal. If the Mallets had gone up the north bank of the Platte, they would have had to cross the Elkhorn River, but there is no mention of this stream in the abstract. Neither is there any reference to the party's crossing the Platte to the south side. Thus, mentions of crossings cannot be used to determine which side of the river the Mallets followed. The fact of the matter is that the abstract names only those streams on which the explorers camped; other stream crossings are not mentioned.

Documentation of Indian trails does not help, either; there were trails on both sides of the Platte. The one on the north side is less well documented than that on the south. We do have, however, the testimony of Good Old Man, an Omaha, and Standing Elk, a Ponca, that both tribes sometimes used a trail there (Court of Claims 1914: 85–86, 420). From the vicinity of Fremont onward, it coincided with what was later called the Mormon Trail.

In contrast, there is good evidence of an Indian trail that snaked along the south bank of the Platte. Here, the documentary evidence is buttressed by the presence of Pawnee villages. Both the trail and the village sites are recorded on General Land Office maps. Lt. John C. Frémont also mapped the route.

Given the presence of Indian trails on both sides of the river, and given that the Mallets fail to mention crossing either the Elkhorn or the Platte, it seems reasonable to assume that they went up the south bank, as the abstract says. If so, they would have crossed Salt Creek in the vicinity of Ashland. The only rock-bottomed ford of the creek is in this location, and it attracted Native Americans in both prehistoric and historic times. The Oto village was located here in 1714 (Norall 1988: 109). Going north from there the Mallets would have reached the vicinity of Yutan, where the Otos and Missouris later lived.

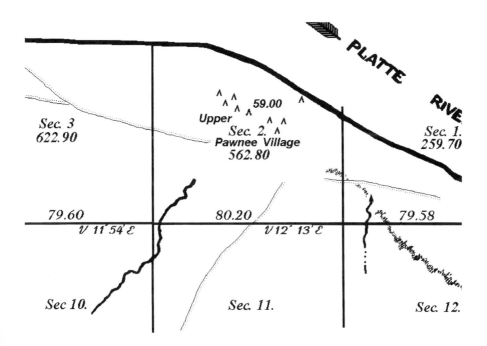

Pawnee village and trails. This is a segment of the General Land Office survey map of Township 16 North, Range 8 East of the Sixth Principal Meridian. (Redrawn from a microfilm print from the Office of the State Engineer, Lincoln, Nebraska.)

In 1823, Paul Wilhelm, Duke of Württemberg, traveled along the trail from this point (Wilhelm 1973: 375–395). Accompanied by Capt. Bennet Riley and some traders from Fort Atkinson, he marched over the prairie to the Elkhorn, crossing it 9 miles above its mouth. From there he headed west to the ford of the Platte at the Oto and Missouri village near present Yutan. The trail along the right bank of the Platte continued for about 30 miles to another Oto village, apparently the Linwood site formerly occupied by the Pawnees. Continuing farther west, Wilhelm reached the Platte at the mouth of the Loup, which he called the Wolf Fork. He crossed the Platte at a ford a few miles upstream from the junction with the Loup and visited the South Band and Skiri villages. There, one of the old men showed him sixteenth-century Spanish weapons that he said had been taken from Spaniards in a great battle long ago.

At the Pawnee Villages, June 10–13, 1739

> At that point, they found that it made a fork with the River of the Padoucas which empties into the Platte.
>
> Three days later, that is to say on the 13th of June, they turned left across said river and crossed a tongue of land.

The Loup River is the major tributary of the Platte from the north. Combining the flow of three branches, it enters the Platte at the modern town of Columbus, Nebraska. Its banks were the protohistoric homeland of the Skiri band of the Pawnee tribe. As discussed previously, its modern name is derived from the French translation for *Skiri*. Nevertheless, the Mallets called it the Padouca, a term that sometimes was applied to the Dismal River fork of the Loup because a Padouca, or Plains Apache, settlement was located on it.

The confluence of the Platte and Loup was the scene of one of the most important early battles in Plains history. Near here, in 1720, a Spanish force under Pedro de Villasur, lieutenant governor of New Mexico, was wiped out by a combined Pawnee and Oto force. A single page of the official expedition journal survives; given to Pierre Dugué de Boisbriant, commandant at Fort des Chartres, by an Indian late in 1720, it tells of the last days leading up to the battle and of how the Spanish force traveled up an Indian trail, across the Loup, and down the north bank of that stream before retreating the day prior to the massacre.

Another entirely different document survives. It is an Indian painting of the battle scene that shows Villasur's demise in dramatic detail. The painting,

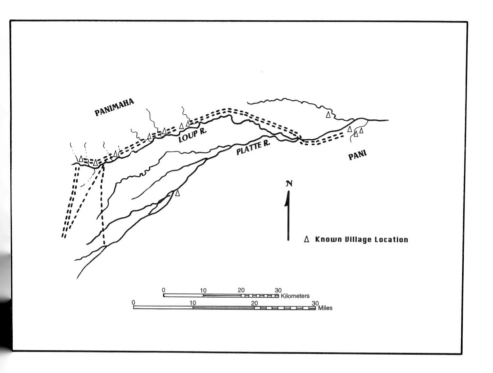

The Mallet route, June 10–13, 1739.

drawn on bison hide, showed up in the possession of a Swiss family, the Sege-ssers, for which it is named (Hotz 1970). It is now in the Palace of the Gover-nors in Santa Fe, and an excellent reproduction is on display in the Nebraska State Historical Society.

Many of the details of the painting are so precise as to suggest that the artist either was at the scene (Villasur had Pueblo and Apache allies) or was guided by an eyewitness. Nevertheless, it also contains errors. The Spanish claimed that the Indians had French help in the battle, and the painting shows uniformed French soldiers armed with guns. But there could not have been French soldiers present. The French commandant in Illinois learned of the battle from the Indians, and he would have known of any soldiers posted to the Pawnee villages. Furthermore, no Frenchman, whether or not he was a soldier, would have shrunk from claiming the glory due him for this terrible blow to Spanish arms. The French and Spanish had been at war just a year earlier. Indeed, although a truce was declared in Europe in 1719, the New World colonies did not learn of it immediately, and France and Spain did not begin peace negotiations until October 1720 (Folmer 1953: 260). Paintings, it seems, are no easier to interpret than other historical documents.

The abstract claims that the Mallets crossed the Loup and a tongue of land on the 13th, three days after reaching its mouth. This statement contains a wealth of implications. First, it means that on the 10th of June, the Frenchmen had reached the mouth of the Loup. Because the abstract places this site 28 leagues from the point where the explorers reached the Platte on the 2nd of the month, they were averaging only 3.5 leagues (9 miles) per day. This is very low compared to other sections of the route, on which they averaged 7.3 leagues (20 miles) per day. The abstract makes no mention of the party's traveling up the Loup; instead, the group spent another three days somewhere on the lower Loup.

Here is indirect evidence that the Mallets encountered Pawnee villages along this part of their route. Pawnee villages were recorded on the Platte and Loup both before and after 1739 (Wedel 1936). The abstract makes no mention of such villages, yet the rates of travel imply the loss of about six days of travel along the two rivers. Three to four days, not coincidentally, was the amount of time required for performance of the Calumet ceremony, the ritual by which the Pawnee created peaceful trading relationships with foreigners (Blakeslee 1975, 1981). In the eighteenth and nineteenth centuries, they and other tribes performed it for all important visitors.

This bit of indirect evidence provides another piece in the puzzle regarding the Panimaha village on the Panimaha River from which the Mallets supposedly started. As we shall see, the abstract states that on the 30th of June, when the Mallets were on the Cimarron River, they estimated that they had come 155 leagues (405 miles) from the Panis. The actual overland distance by the route proposed here is approximately 390 miles from the general vicinity of the South Band (Pani) villages. The abstract also placed the Arikara at "more than 150 leagues" from the Panis. This figure is consistent with the distance between the southern end of Arikara territory in South Dakota and the Pawnee territory in central Nebraska.

The tongue of land mentioned in the abstract is the long narrow strip of low-lying land between the Loup and Platte Rivers. The phrase, "they turned left across this stream," makes it clear that the Mallets left from the north bank of the Loup. Yet, with its usual brevity, the abstract omits any mention of the crossing of the Platte that must have occurred after the tongue of land had been traversed.

Pedro de Villasur had led his doomed expedition across this same piece of ground nineteen years earlier. At this point, it is possible that the Mallets were on the later Mormon Trail, which crossed the Loup in the vicinity of Palmer and ran slightly east of south to reach the Platte near the present town of Chapman. Just south of the river at this point, General Land Office surveyors recorded a north-south Indian trail, and it is clear that there was a traditional ford of the Platte southeast of Chapman. A crossing at that point fits well with the details of the Villasur diary (cf. Shine 1924:85–87). If the Mallets also crossed there, they must have then turned west, as we shall see in the next scene.

It is also possible that they were following a trail that ran a bit more to the west, crossing the Loup at the very west edge of present Merrick County. A glance at a modern map will show the trail's effect on modern political boundaries. Merrick County was once the Pawnee Reservation, which included a mile-wide extension that ran 9 miles north of the regular boundary to provide the Pawnees legal access to the trail; this strip survives as the Merrick County panhandle. North of Grand Island, the trail seems to have joined another that ran down from farther east. Hyde (1951: facing 30) illustrated this route but did not provide his source for this information. From this spot, the combined trail continued to the Platte about 5 miles west of Doniphan, where it crossed the river and connected with the trail that led along the south side of the river. Weltfish (1965: 186–188) records a traditional camping spot of the Pawnees at this spot.

The Hills River, June 14, 1739

> They camped on the 14th on the other side of the River of the Hills which also feeds into the Platte.

The Mallets were south of the Platte and probably following an Indian trail. The pertinent question is which one, as there are several candidates in the region. One continued in use as late as December 1876, when the Omaha tribe made its last winter bison hunt. The bison had grown so scarce that the Omahas were forced to travel to western Kansas before they found any. Gilmore (1932) presents their route as it was described to him by Francis La Flesche, an advance scout for the tribe on this hunt. Their thirteenth camp since leaving their reservation village was opposite Grand Island, near the Hall-Hamilton county line (Gilmore 1932: 28). Here the women gathered enough wood and water for two days, as the trail ran over high, dry prairie, and the Omaha were traveling at a rate of only 12 to 15 miles per day. Their dry camp was about 6 miles north of Hastings, the next one on a small creek a bit northwest of Roseland. If the Mallets were on this trail, this small creek would correspond to the "River of the Hills."

Another north-south trail, 12 miles east of Hastings, was recorded by General Land Office surveyors. It ran from the ford near Chapman slightly east of south, reaching the Clay County line due north of Harvard. It was not recorded south of this point. If the Mallets used *this* trail, then two days'

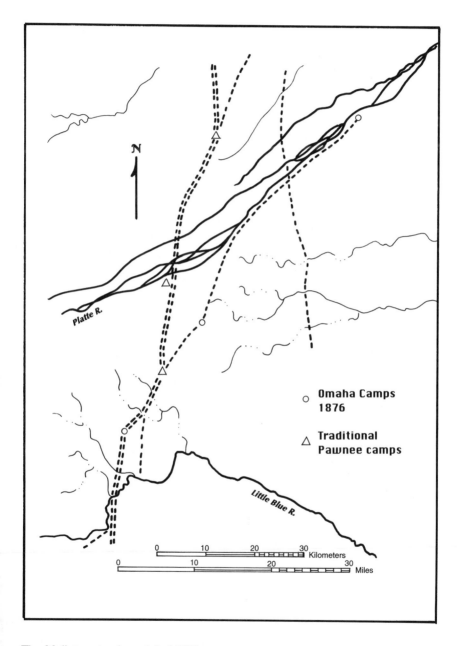

Omaha Camps
1876

Traditional
Pawnee camps

Platte R.

Little Blue R.

0   10   20   30 Kilometers

0   10   20   30 Miles

The Mallet route, June 14, 1739.

travel from the Loup would make their Hills River the West Fork of the Big Blue River.

A third north-south trail lay west of where Hastings is situated. Although I have found no full map of the trail, bits of it are recorded in different places. One is the map of the expedition led by Lt. L. C. Easton in 1849. This party came down the Republican River from Fort Laramie and went on to Fort Leavenworth. East of Red Cloud, the map shows short segments of two trails running down from the north near the modern town of Amboy.

The same trail is mentioned in a history of Adams County. Early immigrants crossing the county noted a heavy north-south Indian trail carved by the dragging travois poles and pony hooves "as the Pawnee passed back and forth from the Platte to the Republican and further south" (Osborne 1972: 1). Unfortunately, the book does not describe the location of the trail.

An 1846 Frémont map shows this trail crossing the Oregon Trail at a point west of the present city of Hastings (Jackson and Spense 1970: Map 4, Section II). Early editions of the *Adams County Weekly Record* (1899) mention two more points, described as regular campsites of the Indians who traveled through the region. One is about 4 miles west of the northern edge of Hastings on the upper portion of Pawnee Creek (this name is another clue), the other about 3 miles east and a little north of Assumption. The latter, which falls at the junction of this route with the one used by the Omahas in 1876, is described as featuring "trails leading from all directions" (*Adams County Weekly Record* 1899). On the trail that connects all of these points, the Hills River of the abstract would be the Little Blue.

Here is an embarrassment of riches: three trails that the expedition might have followed. The clue that allows one to chose among them is a geographical error. The abstract states that the River of the Hills flows into the Platte, but there are no southerly tributaries to the Platte in this region. If one traces the Omaha route of 1876, the only stream crossing south of the Platte is on the upper reaches of the West Fork of the Blue River, in a stretch where its flow is almost due south. It is difficult in the extreme to see how the Mallets could have confused it with a tributary of the Platte.

Along the easterly north-south trail, the Hills River encountered two days south of the Loup would have been the West Fork in the vicinity of the Clay-Hamilton county line. Here the stream flows east-west, away from the trend of the Platte. Again, the explorers would have had no apparent reason to mistake the river for a tributary of the Platte.

On the other north-south trail, the Hills River would be the Little Blue in the vicinity of Ayr. In this vicinity, for about 15 miles, the river flows in a northeasterly direction. It would have been easy for the travelers to conclude from observing the line of trees along it that this stream flowed into the Platte. Hence, it is reasonable to conclude that the Mallets were on the more westerly north-south trail.

On the Barren Prairies, June 15–17, 1739

On the 15th and 16th, they continued to travel overland, and on the 17th they came upon another river which they named the White Hills. During these three days, they crossed a land of plains in which they did not find enough wood even to make a fire, and they relate in their journal that these plains extend to the mountains in the vicinity of Santa Fe.

The high divides south of the Little Blue River between the Republican River and White Rock Creek were originally devoid of trees. In 1739 they would have been covered with short grasses rather than the tall grasses now present, making them remarkable to the Mallets, who certainly had seen the tallgrass prairies previously. Bourgmont found short grasses on the high ground in northeastern Kansas in 1724 (Norall 1988: 137), where tall grasses dominate today. Eugene Ware (1960: 43) noted that tall grasses were replacing short grasses in the Platte River region in the 1860s. The reason, apparently, is

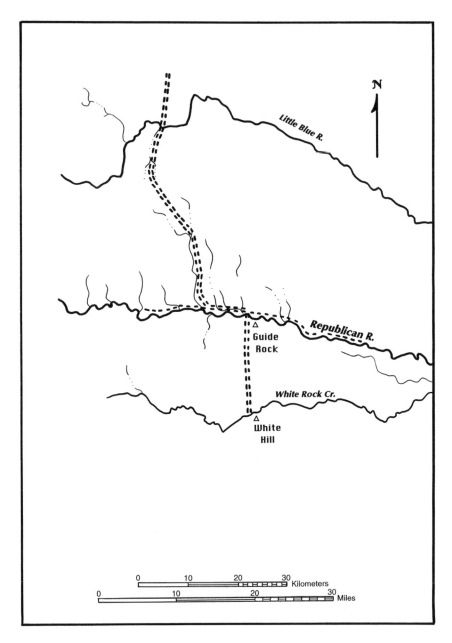

The Mallet route, June 15–17, 1739.

that the destruction of the bison herds gave the tall grasses an ecological advantage over short grasses. An early hunter and trader in Kansas, J. R. Mead (1986: 74), noticed the resulting effect on the distribution of prairie dogs: "In other words, wherever the buffalo ceased to eat, the prairie grass and the rank grass grew up, and the prairie dogs perished."

South of the Little Blue River, the trail continued to the Republican River upstream from the town of Guide Rock. A map drawn during Easton's 1849 army expedition (map photocopy, Kansas State Historical Society Library) recorded two branches of the trail coming to the Republican from the north only a few miles apart, on the divides on either side of Elm Creek. Here the route briefly joined the east-west trail along the north side of the river, resuming its southward course a short distance downstream at a crossing where the Highway 78 bridge now stands. This site boasted a number of attractive features. A grove of trees stood nearby, south of the modern town of Guide Rock. In the same vicinity were University Springs, an important source of clean water. Third and most important was a spot sacred to the Pawnee, the place for which Guide Rock is named: *Pa:hu:ru'*, or "the rock that points the way," one of the animal lodges of Pawnee religion.

The Pawnee, like other Plains tribes, believed that the spirits of various animals resided underground in special places. At such spots, humans could communicate with these important supernatural beings (Parks and Wedel 1985). The Pawnee animal lodges shared certain features, including a cliff or bluff, water, and a small hill or mound shaped like a Pawnee earth lodge. All of these are present at Guide Rock. The earth lodge–shaped hill at this spot was thought to be destroyed, but it was relocated recently by my friend and former student, Bob Blasing, on the south side of the river.

The sacred animal lodge at Guide Rock. Pawnees made pilgrimages to this spot to obtain the power to cure disease from the animal spirits that lived in this earth lodge–shaped mound. (Photograph by the author.)

5.

KANSAS

The White Hills and Friendly Rivers, June 17–18, 1739

[O]n the 17th they came upon another river which they named the White Hills River. . . . On the 18th, they camped on the banks of another river that they crossed and which they named the Friendly River.

From the Republican River, the trail runs south along a high, narrow ridge of land to White Rock Creek in northern Kansas. A glance at the 1:250,000 map of the region shows why. The land here is highly dissected, and the map is a maze of closely spaced brown contour lines. The only feasible route shows up as a narrow white band—the flat high ground along the ridge. The brown lines everywhere else connote steep hillsides that would discourage any traveler.

In the summer of 1987, my sons and I followed this portion of the route as closely as modern roads would allow. The roads led us to White Rock Creek near the town of Burr Oak. The crossing at this spot is mentioned in

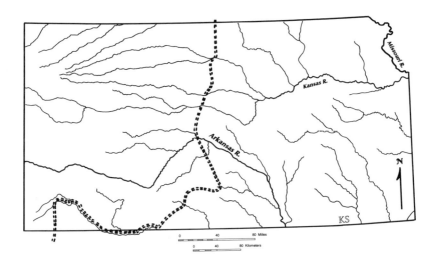

The Mallet route across Kansas.

the History of Webster County, Nebraska (Peters 1915), and a local informant told us of a campsite there. At this place, we noticed what the Mallets must have seen—the prominent white loess hill on the south side of the stream and west of the present town. They called the creek the Cotes Blanches (White Hills); early maps label it White Mound Creek. Although the Pawnee name for this stream has not survived (Parks, personal communication 1989), I would not be surprised to learn that the Mallet name is a translation of it.

The next major stream is the Solomon River. A map drawn by John C. Frémont in 1845 depicts a Pawnee Trail running from Grand Island, Nebraska, across the Solomon to the Smoky Hill River. Close examination of it proved the map to be an interesting mix of detail and conjecture. The well-documented portions of the map lie along routes followed by Frémont

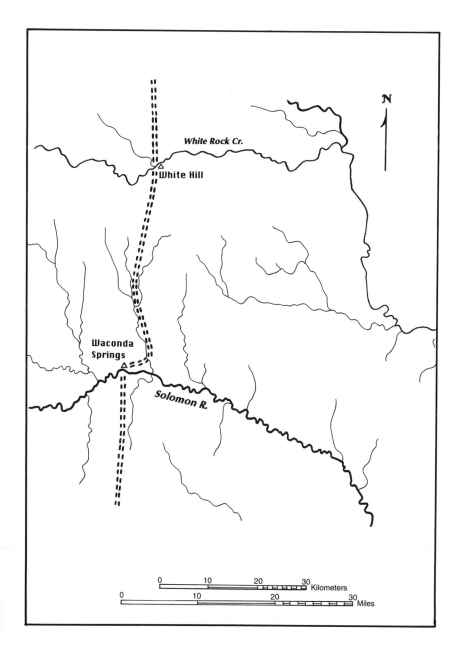

The Mallet route, June 17–18, 1739.

between 1842 and 1844. The detail there made Frémont's version of the trail seem convincing. Then I tried to determine the exact point at which the route reached the Solomon River. To do so, I used a projector to enlarge the Frémont map and superimpose it onto a modern map of Kansas. Not too surprisingly, the Frémont map was not terribly accurate. Frémont compressed the distances between streams significantly, but the detail with which he drew their courses where he crossed them allowed me to identify them anyway.

When I added his version of the trail to a modern map on which I had recorded other trails, it became clear that Frémont had encountered several Indian trails during his various expeditions and, assuming that they were a single route, had simply connected the dots to draw his map. The trail he noted near the Solomon was on Cedar Creek. That trail, rather than connecting with the one coming from Grand Island, actually ran northwest, not northeast as Frémont drew it. The Cedar Creek trail was used by the Omaha on their last bison hunt in 1876 (Gilmore 1932: 28).

An initial cursory examination of the map seemed to show the Pawnee Trail as running down Limestone Creek, a northerly tributary of the Solomon whose mouth sits today at the picturesque little town of Glen Elder. Just upstream is Glen Elder Dam, which creates Waconda Lake. In 1989, when I began surveying the federal land around the lake for the Bureau of Reclamation, I read the General Land Office survey notes for the area. They indicated that Limestone Creek once flowed with clear water and was lined with hardwood groves. It seemed a logical route for the trail.

When I finally interpreted the Frémont map accurately early in 1991, I was left without any direct evidence for the trail on the north side of the Solomon. The General Land Office survey notes showed that Oak Creek, the next major tributary west of Limestone Creek, was also a clear-flowing stream with major hardwood groves along its banks. It was a viable alternative to Limestone Creek. Moreover, Dr. Donald Jackson (Jackson and Spense 1966: 331–332) interpreted the Zebulon Pike documents as indicating that Pike traveled down this stream.

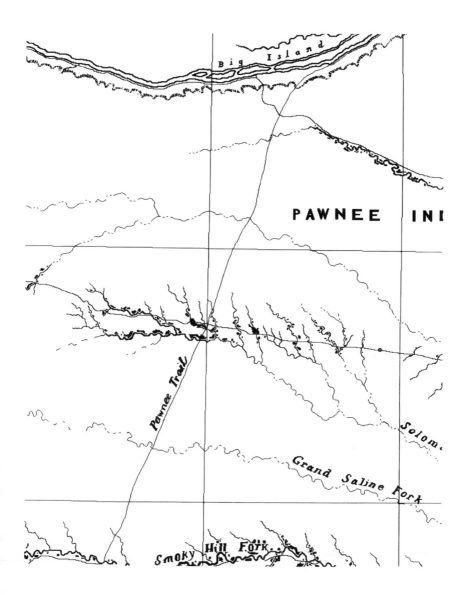

Frémont's map of the Pawnee Trail. This map shows Frémont's interpretation, which is actually based on his observation of segments of three separate trails. (Redrawn from a photocopy of the original.)

The course of the trail north of the river was resolved in the summer of 1991 through what by that time had become a familiar process: If you visit an area and enough people learn of your interest, someone will step forward with the necessary information. In this case, three local residents offered independent but mutually supporting evidence.

The first was Mr. Dale LaDow. My students and I met him on our first evening in the town of Downs in 1991. We had come back to the area for our third year of survey of the federal lands around Waconda Lake and had gone to a store to buy something to drink. The clerk, who remembered us from the previous year, asked us how our work was going and introduced us to Mr. LaDow, the only other customer. Mr. LaDow proceeded to tell us the locations of some archaeological sites.

One of them was on the former family farm on Limestone Creek. As a child, he was told of lodge poles that were still visible at one spot along the creek east of the old highway crossing. The family lore also referred to Sioux traveling along the creek at that point. He drew a little sketch that placed this site east of the Winn homestead.

Later that summer, Mr. Gerald Dubbert told me another story about a trail along Limestone Creek. He said that a Mr. Winn had homesteaded land in the vicinity indicated by Mr. LaDow, having been advised to do so by Black Kettle, the Cheyenne chief. According to this story, Black Kettle told Winn of a major spring that never went dry during the summer nor froze during the winter. The Cheyenne leader told Mr. Winn to travel along the Solomon River to the mouth of Limestone Creek, then go up Limestone Creek to the spring. These directions seemed to imply a trail up the Solomon and another up Limestone Creek. Another version of the same tradition collected later by my student Mark Latham asserted that Black Kettle had given this information to another homesteader, who botched the directions and ended up homesteading north of the most desirable property. Mr. Winn was thus able to claim the beautiful springs at the trail crossing.

My third informant was John McClure, the state representative from the region. I met him in September 1991 after giving a talk at the Chautauqua at Beloit, Kansas. Mr. McClure told me he had grown up on a tributary of Limestone Creek and knew the countryside intimately. He described a major archaeological site near the mouth of Limestone Creek, where the Pawnee Trail would have intersected the one along the north bank of the Solomon, and mentioned many other sites along the Limestone.

The trail reached the Solomon River where the town of Glen Elder now stands. It had to swing around the bluff to which Glen Elder Dam is now anchored. As we shall see, this is not the only place where a dam marks the crossing point of a trail.

Just upstream from where the dam now stands was another of the Pawnee animal lodges, one of the most spectacular. It was Waconda Spring, a natural formation that drew the attention of all of the tribes of the area. Its modern name is derived from a Siouan word meaning "sacred." The Pawnee called it Kicawi:caku, "water on a bank." This description fit the spring, which issued from a hill thirty-five feet high. The hill was composed of deposits laid down by the mineral-rich spring water. Artesian pressure maintained the flow of water from the original spring, and the deposits grew ever higher until the spring issued from the very top of a hill.

The hill was circular and dome-shaped, like a Pawnee earth lodge, and the pool on top formed by the spring corresponded to the smoke hole of an earth lodge. A cut bank nearby provided another feature to be expected at an animal lodge. The Pawnee tossed offerings to the spirits into the water of the pool (some of them were recovered by a diver in the early part of this century). The Pawnee believed they had received a special blessing if the spring began to overflow its banks after their offerings had been made. The waters of the spring did do this on occasion. The Euro-American residents of the area had similar ideas. Some believed that the waters of the spring were somehow connected to the ocean and that they rose and fell with the tides. The question is moot now, as the spring has been covered by the waters of Waconda Lake.

South of the spring, the trail crossed the river. Local traditions assert that in the latter half of the nineteenth century Native Americans visitors to the spring camped across from it on the south bank of the river. In 1990, Wichita State University performed an archaeological survey of the south side of the lake and found what appears to be the place where the trail emerged from the river valley. It is marked by two unusual sites, long linear scatters of lithic debris (the by-products of flint knapping) on the ridges that lined a valley leading up from the river. I have found similar sites adjacent to other trails. They probably reflect the activities of young men who would station themselves on high ground to keep a watchful eye for game and for tribal members who might need some help getting up the trail.

A more spectacular but less concrete piece of evidence also came to light. In 1990 we found what appears to be the figure of an animal carved into a hillside on the south side of the river. Only one other such figure had been known to exist in Kansas—the Serpent Intaglio, near the town of Lyons. That carving has been demonstrated to be of Native American origin; two tiny flint chips were found in a test pit excavated into it. It is associated with a set of villages and sacred sites of the ancestors of the Wichita tribe (Mallam 1983).

The intaglio at Waconda Lake appears to be of a heavy-bodied animal with a prominent tail. Unfortunately, it has been disturbed by a farm road, a salt lick for cattle, and a windbreak. Tests by a geomorphologist, however, indicated that the intaglio probably dates to prehistoric times. It might have been associated with Waconda Spring, the trail, or both.

Bob Blasing has suggested that the intaglio is associated with the spring and the animal lodge (personal communication, 1991). In his research on Pawnee animal lodges, he noticed that certain rituals may have been associated with particular animal lodges. The only ritual known to be associated with Kicawi:caku is the White Beaver ceremony. At first we wondered if the intaglio might represent a beaver, but information gained later suggests strongly that it was a serpent, the tail of which had been destroyed by erosion.

In September 1991 I returned to the intaglio with Bob Blasing, who now works for the Bureau of Reclamation. We were there to discuss what additional archaeological work might be necessary. I took this opportunity to find out what had caused a bluish spot to show up on all of the aerial photos I had taken of the intaglio. The cause turned out to be a dense stand of sage just downslope from the figure. When Bob and I walked the rest of the ridge and examined the two adjacent ridges, we could not find a single sage plant. It is possible that the community of sage at the figure was started accidentally by Native Americans, who traditionally use sage smoke as a purifying agent prior to participating in religious ceremonies. We named it the Sage site for this feature.

In 1993 we returned to both the Sage site and the intaglio at Lyons with Dr. John Weymouth, a retired professor of physics from the University of Nebraska. He brought with him two pieces of equipment, a magnetometer and a resistivity meter. Both machines measure soil disturbances of the sort caused by prehistoric activity. The results indicated that both sites were created by the removal of sod and topsoil from the figure. We also used John's equipment on the site at Lyons. While we were there, one of the students noticed another patch of sage.

In the fall of 1993, a woman named Marty Johnson called our department to report an unusual feature on her property southwest of Wichita. When we investigated it, we found what appeared to be another intaglio. Then, in the spring of 1994, Marty and her husband burned off the prairie grass as part of their range-management plan. This enhanced visibility enormously; instead of a single intaglio, two serpents were exposed, along with paths, embankments, and other features. All are preserved in a patch of native prairie surrounded by cultivated fields. A single plowing would have removed all traces of the complex. At present, the intaglios at Waconda Lake, near Lyons, and near Wichita are the only such features known from all of the Great Plains. How many more might there have been prior to the breaking of the ground by Euro-American farmers?

The River of Worries, June 19, 1739

On the 19th they found and crossed another stream, which they called the River of Worries.

South of the Solomon River, the trail appears to have run a little east of due south to ascend the west bank of Walnut Creek. In the high hills that form the divide between the Solomon and Saline Rivers, water is very scarce. The General Land Office survey notes recorded only a single spring on the headwaters of Salt Creek. The trail very likely led past this important water source in an otherwise dry countryside.

South of the divide, information regarding the trail is plentiful. First, a General Land Office map shows a Pawnee village, with the trail running through it at the forks of Bacon Creek, a tributary of Spillman Creek, which in turn flows into the Saline River. The "village," shown on the map in the same style as a platted town, was actually a campsite.

A second source of information is a nineteenth-century sketch map drawn by J. R. Mead, a hunter who established a ranch in the area. That site is now memorialized by the Meade's Ranch geodetic base point, one of the markers from which the U.S. Geologic Service measures its maps (Mead 1986). In later years, Mead turned to trading with Indians. He was one of the founders of Wichita, Kansas, and late in his very productive life he wrote articles for the Kansas State Historical Society, including one on Indian trails (Mead 1896).

The Mead sketch map is very schematic (Blakeslee, Blasing and Garcia 1986: Figure 2). It shows the trail as a more or less straight line running from a crossing of Salt Creek across a tributary of Spillman Creek, then Spillman Creek itself, and on to the Saline River. The General Land Office map shows that the unnamed tributary of Spillman Creek in Mead's sketch must be Bacon Creek. At that point the trail actually begins to swing to the southwest. It probably crossed Spillman Creek at the fork between the north and south

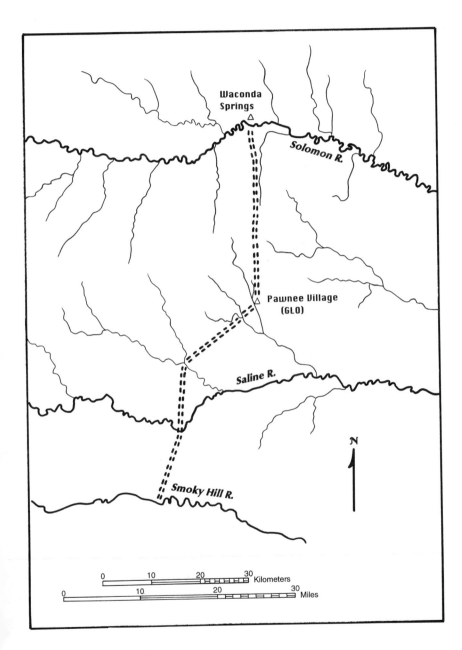

The Mallet route, June 19, 1739.

branches and then continued southwest to cross Wolf Creek at its forks. It reached the Saline River just upstream from the present Wilson Lake Dam.

Another document, the Antoine Nau map of Pike's expedition (Jackson and Spense 1966 I: Map 3), is even more difficult to interpret. In 1806, Pike headed south from the Hill Site Pawnee village on the Republican River. He was following the army of Lt. Facundo Melgares, who had visited the Pawnee village ahead of him. Melgares had been sent from Santa Fe to arrest Lewis and Clark as they returned to St. Louis from their expedition to the Pacific, but the Pawnees refused to cooperate in any such venture (Cook 1973: 446–490).

Pike's map shows the locations of the Spanish camps that he saw, his own camps, and the streams that he crossed. The latter are depicted accurately at the spots where he saw them but are often very inaccurately delineated elsewhere. Frank J. Munday (1927) did a masterful job of deciphering this map. He has Pike camping on Bacon Creek before crossing the forks of the Spillman and moving to the forks of Wolf Creek and then to the Saline. The Pike map shows both Spillman Creek and Wolf Creek, labeled as the Little Saline, as tributaries of the Solomon.

I obtained the General Land Office reference to the spring on the divide in 1989, when I began the research for an archaeological survey of Waconda Lake for the Bureau of Reclamation. The other information derives from a similar survey of Wilson Lake done for the U.S. Army Corps of Engineers, Kansas City District. I did this project in 1985 and 1986, with Bob Blasing working as my field supervisor. Bob was just finishing up his master's degree based on work he had done in the Flint Hills, south of Manhattan. It was during that project that he ran across information on an Indian trail, and we had a long series of discussions of the research potential offered by such trails.

When we made our first trip to Wilson Lake in 1985, we speculated about the possibility of finding an Indian trail there but had no idea that the route we found would dominate our final report (Blakeslee, Blasing and Garcia 1986). When I researched travelers who might have used the trail, I came across the names of the Mallet brothers. Later that summer, when I also found documentation of the Old Ponca Trail in eastern Nebraska, I realized that it might be possible to trace the whole route of that expedition. The seeds for this book were planted.

In 1985 a former landowner showed Bob where the trail ran down to the north side of the Saline River. It was upstream from the dam at a spot now called Rock Town. The trail is no longer visible at that point, but on the south side of the river one can still find trail markers. These are cairns, or piles of stone, placed at the mouths of some of the deep, narrow canyons that dissect the slopes south of the river. Some of these are box canyons, which are difficult to get out of. Hell Creek Canyon, the largest of these, was named by some early travelers who made the mistake of entering it one winter day and spent a miserable night before they could find their way out.

The trail markers we found all stood at the entrances of canyons that provide good access to the upland divide along which the trail runs. All of them have been knocked over, and today you have to look very hard to find them. The canyons are very narrow and twisting, and there are points at which you can almost touch both rock walls with your outstretched hands.

Charles Augustus Murray came down one of these canyons in 1835 (Murray 1841). A Scottish noble who sought excitement on the Great Plains, he ended up accompanying the South Band Pawnees on their summer bison hunt that year. During the course of this adventure, he inadvertently insulted the head chief, who sent him packing. Traveling with a Pawnee guide and three other companions, he headed north along the Pawnee Trail. Eventually they reached the head of one of the canyons that run north to the Saline River.

There the guide began to dally, and Murray smelled a rat. In the "small narrow ravine, full of broken heaps of sandstone," Murray found out why the guide wanted someone else to go first. He wrote, "I never should have believed it possible that so many rattlesnakes could have assembled together as I saw in that ravine. I think there must have been nearly enough to fatten a drove of Missouri hogs" (Murray 1841: 319). Could this explain why the Mallets called this place the River of Worry?

The River of the Kansas, June 20, 1739

> On the 20th, they reached the River of the Kansas, which shows the approximate route they took from the Pawnees. They crossed it and in so doing lost seven horses loaded with merchandise. This river is deep and has a strong current.

South of the Saline River there were at least two branches of the trail. One ran from south of the mouth of Hell Creek Canyon to the mouth of Coal Creek, south of Wilson. Its course is marked at several points by Native American rock art. Some of it survives today, but it was better preserved when it was first recorded early in this century by J. R. Mead (Mead 1986). Mead drew sketches of the rock art at two spots: on the shore of Wilson Lake in Hell Creek Canyon, and at the trail's intersection with the Smoky Hill River (about a mile west of where the road running south from Wilson crosses the river).

There is also some rock art along the western branch of the trail. This fork appears to have run south past the town of Dorrance, reaching the Smoky Hill River near the mouth of Beaver Creek. There, J. R. Mead recorded a very interesting petroglyph in 1863. On the south side of the river, in a small cave, he saw an inscription that read "TRVDO. 1786." This is probably a record of a visit by Jean-Baptiste Truteau, an important figure in the fur trade out of St. Louis. He usually spelled his name "Truteau," but there are two instances where he spelled it "Trudeau." He was the author of an important description of the upper Missouri in which he abbreviated the tribal name Padouca as "Pado." The similarity between the abbreviations of the tribal name and his own are striking. There is evidence indicating that he lived among the Republican Pawnee (one of the South Bands) prior to 1794,

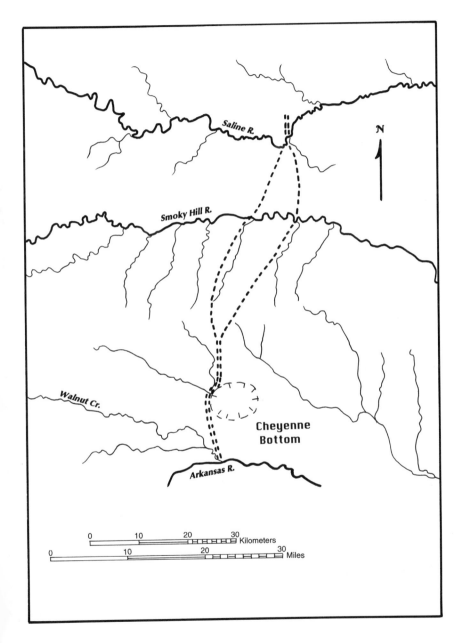

The Mallet route, June 20, 1739.

so it is quite possible that Jean-Baptiste Truteau left his name at the Smoky Hill crossing.

Other candidates for the honor do exist. In 1751, Louis and Laurent Trudeau, along with six other men, went to the Pawnee country. They were in company with Jean Chapuis and Louis Feuilly, who continued on to Santa Fe. The Trudeaus went no further than the Pawnee country (Faye 1943: 702). Though it is possible that one of them returned to carve his name in the cave beside the Smoky Hill River thirty-five years later, it does not seem probable. There were other people in the region who normally spelled their name Trudeau instead of Truteau, and one of them might be responsible for the inscription.

South of the Saline River, the Mallets crossed the Smoky Hill, which they called the River of the Kansas. Governor Bienville recognized the name and commented that it "shows the approximate route they took from the Pawnees." The location of the mouth of the Kansas River had been known since Bourgmont's 1714 exploration. Folmer (1939a: 165), however, thinks the Mallets were referring to the South Solomon, without explaining why they would have called it the River of the Kansas. He also had to assume that there had been heavy rains in order to explain why the Mallets lost seven horses in such a minor stream. No such explanations or assumptions are needed if the stream in question is the Smoky Hill, the major branch of the Kansas River.

South of the crossings of the Smoky Hill, the two branches of the trail joined, probably southwest of the little town of Beaver. My sons and I followed both branches to the extent that this is possible in a car. The section-line roads keep fairly close to the trail routes, and when we followed the eastern branch in 1989 we found that a southwesterly course past Dubuque and Beaver provided a nearly level route. The western branch ascended the Beaver Creek valley on the left-hand (west) side. Again, the landscape provides for easy traveling, and the stream provides a ready source of water.

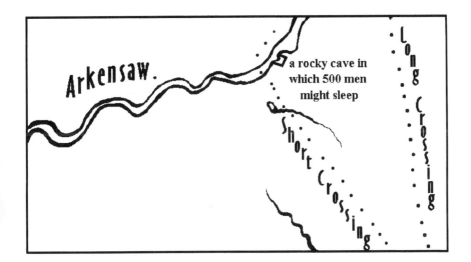

The 1807 Pike sketch map. This segment depicts the Pawnee Trail, labeled "short crossing." The Cheyenne Bottom and Blood Creek make up the snakelike figure. (Redrawn from a photocopy of the original [cf. Wheat 1958 #287].)

From this point the trail looped around the west side of the Cheyenne Bottoms, a marshy basin with no outlet stream. The low ground is about 9 miles across. When George Sibley, the Indian factor at Fort Osage, came down the trail with some Osage guides in 1811, he noted: "From where we crossed the Konsee to the Arkansas, it is about thirty-five miles and the country is much more level and less interesting" (Sibley 1927:210).

We know that the trail came around the west side of the Cheyenne Bottoms because it is shown on two early maps. One is the map drawn by Zebulon Pike (Wheat 1957 Map No. 287) in 1807 in St. Louis. His information came from three French fur traders whose names appear on the map: Polite Cardinal, Jean Marie Cardinal, and Joseph Tibeau. Spence and Jackson (1966

I: 458–459) suggest that the information on the map derives from an expedition the trio made to Santa Fe in 1797.

This map is of considerable interest because it shows several variations of the Santa Fe Trail fifteen years before William Becknell made his first journey. A set of trails from the vicinity of Salt Creek, near present Lincoln, Nebraska, to Santa Fe is depicted. Two routes, shown as dotted lines, appear south of the Smoky Hill River. A "short crossing" runs past the west side of the Cheyenne Bottoms to reach the Arkansas downstream from a "rocky cave." A western "long crossing," indicated to take eighteen travel days, reaches the Arkansas much farther west, crosses it, and continues to what appears to be the Canadian River. The latter part of the route seems to be the Cimarron Cutoff of the Santa Fe Trail.

A Stansbury map of 1850 also shows the trail (Bruce 1932). In this case, however, the Cheyenne Bottoms are not depicted. Nevertheless, the dotted line marking the trail loops to the west around where the Cheyenne Bottoms are located. It would be interesting to know Stansbury's source of information for the course of the trail at this point.

The River of the Arrow, June 21–23, 1739

> The 22nd, they crossed another river, which they called the River of the Arrow. On the 23rd, they again found the great prairies where one finds nothing to make a fire save buffalo chips.

In 1988 my sons, Sam and John, accompanied me on the first of two exploring expeditions we took together to trace portions of the Mallet route. We set out from our home in Wichita and headed first to Great Bend, where the Mallets would have crossed the Arkansas on June 22, 1739. As we saw earlier, "River of the Arrow" is a French translation of the Pawnee name for this river. The spot where the Pawnee Trail spans the river is sometimes

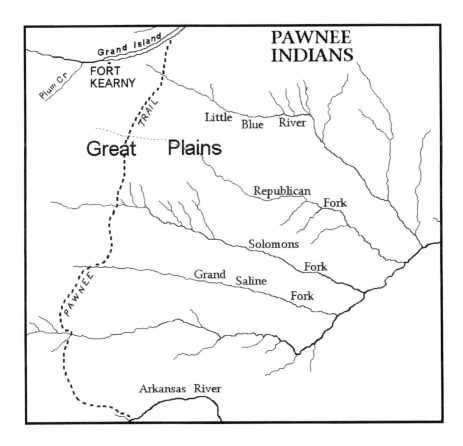

The Pawnee Trail in the vicinity of Cheyenne Bottom. This portion of an 1850 Stans-bury map shows the route of the Pawnee Trail precisely, even though the Cheyenne Bottom is not depicted. (Redrawn from Bruce [1932].)

called the Walnut Creek crossing for the stream that enters the Arkansas at this point.

This was an intersection of two major trails. The Pawnee Trail, running north and south, crossed the east-west trail paralleling the north bank of the

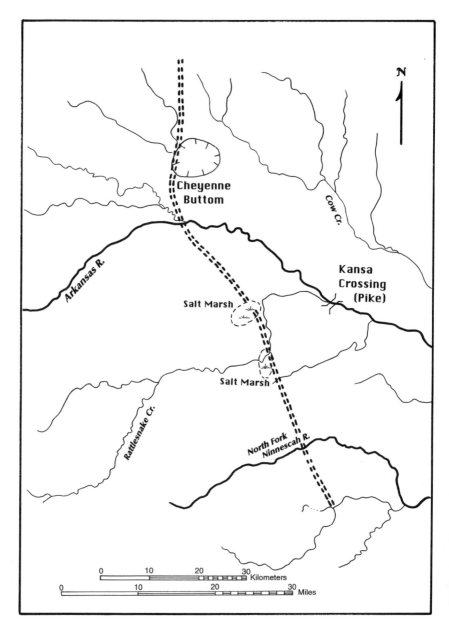

The Mallet route, June 21–23, 1739.

Arkansas River. The latter eventually became the Santa Fe Trail, but it was an Indian trail when Coronado used it in 1541, and it was still in use when Zebulon Pike followed it in 1806. A variety of archaeological sites in the vicinity date from as early as A.D. 100 to as late as circa A.D. 1700, the date of a Dismal River Apache camp (Graves 1964, 1965; Gunnerson 1968).

This intersection was a busy one. Fort Zarah, created in 1864, was designed to protect merchants from Indian depredations, which were especially common here because the Pawnees resented the fact that Santa Fe Trail wagon trains crossed their territory without giving them the appropriate gifts. Other tribes also raided the mule trains, using the north-south trail to gain access to the wagon road. In 1864 some Kiowas attacked a small wagon train at the Walnut Creek crossing. More than a century later, in 1973, the flooded Walnut Creek began to erode the graves of ten men killed in the raid (Topeka Capital-Journal 1973).

In 1988, a park to mark the site of Fort Zarah opened, but it was a disappointment. Though spacious, it contained no sign of the fort, no artifacts, no reconstruction. In fact, experts think the original site of the fort may not even have been in the park. It has since been closed.

The Kiowa, who held their annual sun dance in this vicinity in 1863, called Walnut Creek No Arm's River (Mooney 1898: 283, 313). They named it for William Allison, a trader who ran a post here (Witty 1969). He had lost his right arm in a gunfight in which he shot and killed his father-in-law. History does not record his wife's reaction.

On the first day of our trip in 1988, the boys and I visited the Quivira National Wildlife Refuge south of the Great Bend of the Arkansas River. Rainfall had been good that spring, and the marsh was well watered and full of life. As we approached the refuge on a dirt road, we saw two animals in the road ahead of us. At first I thought they were rabbits, but as we drew closer it became apparent that they were too large for that. "Foxes!" said Sam, but as we got even closer we recognized them as coyote cubs. With none of the cunning attributed to adults of the species, they ran along the road ahead of the

Getting a taste of western history. John Blakeslee sampling the salt flat at the Quivira Wildlife Refuge, Kansas. (Photograph by the author.)

car for quite a distance. We followed slowly behind them until they finally cut to the right and disappeared in the reeds beside the road.

We turned south into the refuge and found other company: great blue herons, terns, a multitude of ducks, American egrets. We got out and walked around, and all of us tasted the salt that covered one of the dry flats. The refuge is a fantastic open space, and we were there on a fine day. There were no other people, only sky, sun, wind, water, and birds—just as when Indian tribes, the Mallets, and other early travelers passed through.

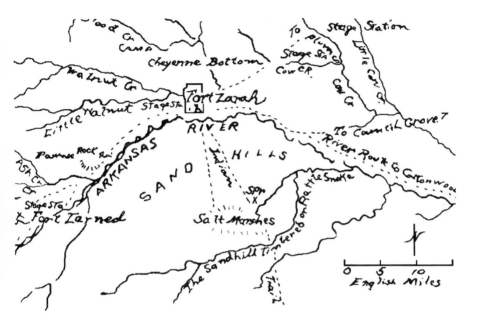

The 1867 Hunnius map. This sketch is titled "Portion of Santa Fé Trail, Section Ft. Zarah and Ft. Larned." It shows the beginning of the lower portion of the Pawnee Trail. (Redrawn from a copy at the Santa Fe Trail Center, Larned, Kansas.)

We had with us a map of the region drawn by Adolph Hunnius in 1867. Hunnius was a member of the Army Corps of Topographic Engineers and an excellent cartographer, although you couldn't prove it by this little sketch map. It does, however, show an Indian trail running south of east from the Walnut Creek crossing, and we followed it as best we could by driving along the back roads. Not too surprisingly, it turned out to follow an excellent route, avoiding the worst of the sand dunes that are scattered all across the region south of the Arkansas.

South of the big marsh we lost our way, and for a long time I was not able to trace with precision the next few days of the Mallets' travel. The reason we got lost is simple enough: We relied on an old USGS base map that didn't show some of the newer roads, and so we ended up to the east of our intended route. The 1:250,000 map also shows vast areas labeled "rocky" in this region, when sand dunes actually occur there. I pointed this out to a geologist friend, but he defended the map makers, claiming that sand is, after all, just very small rocks.

At this point, the Mallets appear to have been following the north-south trail depicted on the Miguel map of 1602. It runs south from a crossing of the Arkansas River toward the Great Salt Flats of the Salt Fork of the Arkansas River in Oklahoma. Apparently the same crossing is labeled "Kansa Crossing" on the Nau map of the Pike expedition (Jackson 1966). In 1602, however, it was most certainly a Wichita crossing. On the 1823 James map of the Long expedition, the crossing shows up again as the northern end of what he labels the Pawnee Trail. We shall encounter it again in the consideration of the return route from Santa Fe. I have proposed that it be called the Rattlesnake Creek Crossing to avoid confusion (Blakeslee 1988b).

The prairie here is barren of trees, as the Mallets noted. It was not until later in our journey, however, that we experienced a fire fueled with the modern equivalent of buffalo chips.

The Osage Trail, June 24–29, 1739

> On the 24th, they crossed another river, and from the 26th to the 30th they encountered some streams every day.

This laconic entry made tracing an important section of the Mallet route very difficult. I managed to compound the problem initially by equating the Spanish inscriptions mentioned in the very next entry (the 30th of June) with a Coronado inscription reported on the Cimarron River in the panhandle of

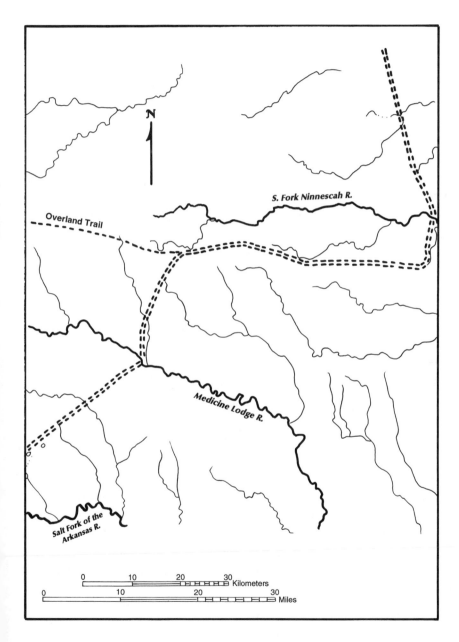

The Mallet route, June 24–29, 1739.

Oklahoma. No matter how thoroughly I searched through county histories, atlases, old maps, and the like, I couldn't come up with a route matching the terrain and the normal rate of travel that would have placed the Mallets at the Coronado inscription on the 30th. Eventually, the Coronado inscription turned out to be a false lead, and I could search a wider region for evidence of the route.

South of the salt marsh, there are streams enough to account for all of those that the Mallets crossed between the 24th and 30th of June. The first is Rattlesnake Creek, which must have been their camping spot on the 24th. The other streams on which they camped are the North Fork of the Ninnescah near the mouth of Silver Creek, Painter Creek, the Medicine Lodge River, and Mule Creek. On the 30th the Mallets camped on the Cimarron at a spot that, as we shall see, can be delineated precisely. In between, the going is more difficult—at least, it was for us. All we had to go on was the suspicion that they might have ended up on the Black Dog, or Osage, Trail.

The Black Dog Trail ran along the southern border of Kansas from the Osage villages to the Arkansas River at Oxford and west from there along the divide between the Ninnescah and Chikaskia Rivers (Kingman County 4-H Council 1977: 2, 159). West of the modern town of Pratt, the trail forked, with one branch (called the Overland Branch of the Santa Fe Trail) leading west to the Arkansas River near Ford and the other southwest to the Cimarron and then west along that stream.

One of the more interesting sidelights associated with this trail has to do with an expedition that did *not* use it. In 1821, Jacob Fowler accompanied Hugh Glen on an expedition from Arkansas to the Rocky Mountains. When they reached the Arkansas River in southern Kansas, they encountered Osage Indians who told them not to follow the river but to take a more southerly route: "[T]he Indeans advise us to Cross the arkensaw and Steer West Corse and strike the arkensaw at the big timber Near the mountains but the Season is late and Want of Wood and Watter Renders it a Hazardous undertaking" (Fowler 1965: 16).

When they received this advice, Fowler's party was at an Osage camp on the Walnut River in the vicinity of present-day Winfield, directly east of the ford of the Arkansas at Oxford. Because the route suggested by the Osages went directly to the Arkansas near the Big Timbers in eastern Colorado, it is clear that they were referring to the Overland Branch of the Santa Fe Trail. It runs nearly in a straight line, especially compared to the huge detour created by the Great Bend of the Arkansas.

Although the Mallets had taken much of the more direct route in 1739, Fowler and Glen decided that because it was late in the year (9th of October) they should follow the Arkansas River in order to be sure of their water supply. Had they followed the advice of their Osage friends, they might have arrived in Santa Fe before William Becknell (he got there in November), and credit for opening the Santa Fe trade might have fallen to them.

The Kingman County history (Kingman County 4-H Council 1977:2, 159) credits an early trader, J. G. Griffith of Wichita, with marking out parts of this trail. The branch credited to him ran southwest from the ford across the Arkansas at the northern edge of present Wichita, merging with the Osage Trail south of Kingman. It is described as being marked all the way to Santa Fe by earthen mounds on the crests of each ridge, "crossing the streams at convenient fording places and by way of the best springs and camping places" (Child cited in Kingman County 4-H Council 1977: 165). However, Griffith could not have created the trail in the 1870s, because Nathan Boone recorded a branch of it in 1843 (Sanders and Sanders 1968: 22). Furthermore, it is far more likely that Indians made the trail markers than that a white trader did. Not only is the amount of labor implied tremendous for one person, but we also have direct documentation of native use of such artificial landmarks in precisely the sort of terrain covered by the Osage Trail.

> On unusually level ground, and also in very rough and difficult country, where the range of vision is restricted, the Indians set up small mounds of stones. On the level mesas overlooking the precipitous

cañons of Lower Kansas, on the Uncompagre, and other (so called) valleys of Colorado, in Utah, in the broken ground of the Laramie Plains, and all over the vast and difficult country north and east of the North Platte River, wherever the sameness of the water-worn steppes presents no natural distinctive mark, such cairns are to be found.

I have heard many ingenious and far-fetched surmises as to their object. It is simply to establish a sequence of landmarks indicating the best route, and this purpose they serve admirably, not only in summer, but in winter, when snow has obliterated every other distinguishing mark. They, of course, only serve their purpose in open ground, where they can be seen, one from the other (Dodge 1886: 557–558).

Where no rocks were to be had, piles of sod or earth sufficed. In 1706, when Juan de Ulibarrí headed across the High Plains of western Kansas to El Cuartelejo, his Apache guides depended on such sod cairns (Thomas 1935: 66).

I learned the details of this trail by consulting the journal of an 1843 expedition led by Nathan Boone, the youngest son of Daniel Boone.An officer in the First U.S. Dragoons stationed at Fort Gibson, Oklahoma, Boone led a company into Kansas, to the vicinity of Great Bend. In several spots south of the Arkansas River he encountered bands of Osage Indians, and I hoped that tracking his movements and theirs might shed some light on the locations of trails.

The manuscript was written in a clear hand and was easy to read. Using it in conjunction with the state base map, I could trace the day-to-day movements of the expedition with some accuracy, although there were spots where this was difficult. One of them was in the Gypsum Hills between Great Bend and the salt plain of the Cimarron River. They met Osage Indians several times in this vicinity, so it was likely that they were on an Indian trail at the time.

The entries in the journal did not differ from those in the published article, but the journal contained a bonus: sketches of the hills that surrounded the expedition's camp on the Medicine Lodge River. These were so detailed that I thought it might be possible to identify them in the field and so to pinpoint the location of the camp. The boys and I had photocopies of the sketches with us in 1988, when we drove up the Medicine Lodge River from Medicine Lodge to Sun City and beyond.

The old trail runs southward to Sun City along Turkey Creek, a tributary of the Medicine Lodge River. Local informants had told me about it in 1987, when I made a brief visit. In its later years, the trail had been a stage road, and some ruts are still visible north of the cemetery. This road appears to be a continuation of the Indian trail shown on the General Land Office maps for the region north of Sun City.

We drove every road in the vicinity of Sun City and finally found the hills we were looking for. They were difficult to spot because they could not be seen from the place where the diarist of the Boone expedition had drawn them. This spot is at the mouth of Elk Creek, but a grove of trees has grown up there since 1843. Kansas has more trees today than it had at the beginning of the historic period, both because of intentional planting and as a result of the suppression of the prairie fires that previously maintained the grassland at its maximum extent.

We were forced to take pictures of the hills from the south side, where they were visible. We used slide film, so it was not difficult to reverse the images to compare them with the sketches in the Boone journal. In any case, the modern road leading south from the west edge of Sun City appears to follow the route that Boone took south toward the Cimarron. It is steep and twisting, and the journal records the difficulty of the passage. The Mallets, however, seem to have taken another trail, one that led up the more gentle Elk Creek valley. We headed in that direction, only to run into trouble.

We followed the highway to Wilmore, stopped for cold drinks at the little town's only store, and asked the owners about old trails and archaeological sites. No luck. South of Wilmore, no luck gave way to bad luck. Miles from town, the front-wheel bearing suddenly went out, and we limped into

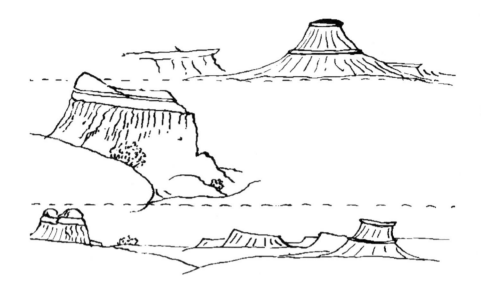

The Red Hills in the vicinity of Sun City, Kansas. From the original journal of the Nathan Boone expedition of 1843. (Courtesy of Special Collections Division, Ablah Library, Wichita State University.)

Coldwater using the four-wheel drive. We had to spend a night and most of a day in Coldwater while mechanics worked on the car, and we used the time to search for informants. But bad luck ended up being good luck. Denneis Andersen, who runs the *Western Star* newspaper, gave us the names of several knowledgeable folks. One of them, Gregg Bramlett, met us at the cafe and took us on a tour of the countryside. He showed us the lay of the land east of Coldwater, where rough country to the south would have hindered east-west travel. North of the line he pointed out, the land is gently rolling and easily traversed. Here an early stage road and then a highway, the Cannonball Trail, ran west-southwest from Sun City.

Gregg also pointed out a series of three mounds that lie more or less in a straight line across the branches of Nescatunga Creek. The easternmost of these appears to be a natural hilltop into which some trenches have been cut in the shape of a square, with a pit at each corner. This does not have the appearance of a Native American site, but no one has excavated it to determine its origin.

The second mound is a prominent natural knoll that would have been a clear landmark in earlier times. Today it is not visible from the first hill, nor can the third (which we did not visit) be seen from the second; trees growing up along the watercourses have blocked the view. Prior to the suppression of prairie fires, however, each mound would have been visible from the preceding one, and the set of three could have guided travelers for a considerable distance. This does not prove that the mounds actually were used in this fashion, nor does the fact that Gregg found arrow points at the easternmost mound. However, the mounds do lie along a line between the camp at the mouth of Elk Creek and the next camp we were able to locate. It was not until we found the Mallets' camp on the Cimarron that I could see that Gregg's landmarks were on the right route.

Colonel Richard Irving Dodge (1886:552–553) recorded the Comanche technique of passing directions from one person to another, indicating how critical natural landmarks were to these early travelers:

All being seated in a circle, a bundle of sticks was produced, marked with notches to mark the days. Commencing with the stick with one notch, an old man drew on the ground with his finger, a rude map illustrating the journey of the first day. The rivers, streams, hills, valleys, ravines, hidden waterholes, were all indicated with reference to permanent and carefully described landmarks. When this was thoroughly understood, the stick representing the next day's march was illustrated in the same way, and so to the end. . . .

A sequence of landmarks is more easily established and remembered than would appear probable to the uninitiated. The general direction is always preserved as far as possible. The first stage of the journey is towards some marked feature of the landscape, on or near that general direction, as a rocky cliff, a prominent knoll, or a gap in a ridge. Arriving at that point, some other prominent feature is selected, as far ahead as possible, and in the same general direction. The person following the Indian's direction will, on arriving at one landmark, readily recognize the next, and so on in sequence.

Thus, we knew that Indian trails were apt to follow landmarks of this sort.

The Rocks by the River, June 30, 1739

Finally, on the 30th, they found Spanish markings on some rocks on the banks of the last river.

They had made, in their estimation, 155 leagues overland from the Pawnees, travelling almost always to the west. They believe that this river is a branch of the Arkansas River and is the river that they encountered lower down on their return journey the tenth day after leaving Santa Fe.

This section of the abstract contains a copyist's error. The Mallet brothers did not head west from the Pawnees, regardless of whether the Pawnees were in central Nebraska or at the mouth of the Niobrara River. Folmer (1939a) was the first to recognize that they must have traveled generally in a south-westerly direction to reach Santa Fe.

Identifying the rocks by the river where the Mallets saw the Spanish inscriptions proved to be the most difficult part of the whole investigation. It was obviously the key to the central portion of the journey. If I could pin it down, I would be able to trace the Mallets south and west from the Arkansas River. Furthermore, any such Spanish inscriptions would be enormously

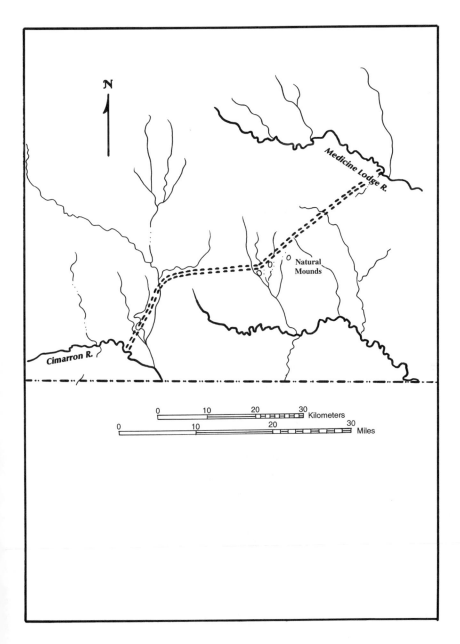

The Mallet route, June 30, 1739.

important. There are records of only three Spanish expeditions to this portion of Kansas prior to 1739: Francisco Vásquez de Coronado in 1541, Leyva and Humaña in 1593, and Juan de Oñate in 1601. Any light the Mallet journal could shed on the routes of any of these expeditions would be of immense historical value.

Unfortunately, all of the clues were misleading. To start with, the Mallets were wrong when they assumed that the river with the inscriptions was identical to one they traveled down on their return the next year (as we shall see in Chapter 8). Furthermore, purportedly Spanish inscriptions popped up all over the place during my research. Early in the investigation, I told Martin Stein of the Kansas State Historical Society about this part of the Mallet journal. It turned out that he not only knew of a spot where a Coronado signature had been found on the Cimarron River but actually had a site record for it. The spot was in the panhandle of Oklahoma, and until I went there, I tried to make it fit with the rest of the Mallet journal. That was difficult, because the Mallets would have to have sped from the Arkansas River crossing to this spot and then to have sauntered along slowly for the next part of their journey. But the Oklahoma inscription site seemed feasible because it fit with my hypothesis (which ultimately proved incorrect) that the Mallets' route cross Raton Pass, in sight of the Spanish Peaks, as this was a possible interpretation of the "Spanish Mountains" mentioned in their abstract.

In 1987 I visited the Oklahoma State Historical Society to pick up more information and talked about the site with Marshall Gettys. He knew more about the inscription, including that it read "Coronatto" rather than "Coronado." He told me that in spite of this apparent error, some people were inclined to accept it as authentic because there was an Italian in Coronado's army, and he might have used this spelling.

I went from Oklahoma City to the panhandle to visit the site. The landowner, Bob Apple, and his wife offered typical western hospitality. When I showed up unannounced at their isolated ranch home, I was immediately invited in and asked to stay for lunch. They discussed the inscription and other finds in the vicinity with me and then gave me directions to the site. It is on a prominent butte overlooking a ford of the Cimarron River. As I climbed up the slope at its base, I spotted numerous flint chips, indications of a prehistoric campsite. The chips were scattered over a wide area, and so were petroglyphs on the rock wall. Many were prehistoric, but there were also some of more recent vintage, including a beer can in the hand of one figure.

The Coronado inscription is in a little nook in the cliff face. It seemed protected enough from the weather to have lasted for centuries, but it had seen rough use in recent years. Someone had filled in the letters with chalk, probably in order to take a clear picture, and another person had later used blue paint for the same purpose. The lettering looked awfully similar to American schoolboy script, and I resolved to try to find examples of Spanish inscriptions from the right time period and of Coronado's signature.

One item that seemed to ring true was an adjacent inscription in block letters that said, "Campo." Andres do Campo was the name of a Portuguese soldier who accompanied Coronado. In 1542 he returned to Kansas with Padre Padilla to bring Christianity to the natives. After Padilla was killed by members of another tribe, Andres do Campo and two Mexican Indians who were in the party walked back to Mexico. The journey took them several years, but their arrival in Panuco on the east coast of Mexico is well documented (Bolton 1964: 339–360).

Here was another false clue.And they kept on accumulating. I spent part of the same afternoon with Mr. and Mrs. Truman Tucker. Truman is the local historian, and we had an enjoyable time discussing the Mallets' possible route and the mystery of the inscription. Mrs. Tucker mentioned that another Coronado inscription had been found at Point of Rocks, near Elkhart, Kansas.

Before checking on that lead, however, I followed up on the Oklahoma site clues in the University of New Mexico library. The early Spanish inscriptions I found were all in Old Spanish script; none looked like the one that said "Coronatto." The famous inscription left by Juan de Oñate at El Morro in New Mexico is a case in point. I also obtained a photocopy of Coronado's

Purported Coronado inscription. This petroglyph on the Cimarron River in western Oklahoma reads "Coronatto 1541." (Photograph by the author.)

signature from a letter he had written to the king of Spain. It, too, was in Old Spanish script. Even inscriptions that were printed rather than in script looked nothing like the Coronado petroglyph (cf. Kessell 1979: 147). At any rate, I thought, I wouldn't be fooled by any more fakes.

A visit to Chris Lintz while I was in Albuquerque clarified matters. Chris, the archaeologist who had recorded the "Coronatto" inscription for the state of Oklahoma, agreed that it was a fake. He even had an explanation for the "Campo" inscription. In the survey he had done in the area, he had turned up several petroglyphs of town names. These had been carved by people who participated in some of the Sunday outings that used to be popular events in the rural countryside. He had seen petroglyphs that said "Boise City" and "Kenton." And about 13 miles north of the "Campo" inscription is the little town of Campo, Colorado. With this information in hand, I had no reason to accept this Coronado inscription.

On my way back to Wichita, I stopped in Elkhart to check on the inscription Mrs. Tucker had told me about. I went first to the newspaper office, figuring that they would have record of it. Indeed they did. After some dusty searching, they produced a photo of the inscription that sent me running back to the car for my copy of Coronado's signature. This one was in Old Spanish script, and it matched my photocopy of Coronado's signature amazingly well. There was no doubt about it; the inscription was in Coronado's hand. I asked dozens of questions in the newspaper office, and finally they sent me over to the bank.

Jack Hayward, the bank president, had been a schoolboy when he was credited with finding the inscription. Mr. Hayward remembered it clearly. In 1941, he was with his family on a picnic when his father found a carving on a piece of the rock face that had been exposed by a recent flood. It consisted of a date, 1541. Later, back at home, Jack remembered why the date had seemed familiar; he and his classmates had studied the Coronado expedition. Word got out around town, and several people went to investigate. When they scraped the sand back from below the date, Coronado's name was uncovered.

Unfortunately, someone destroyed the inscription not too long after it had been found. The local people seemed to think that this had been done during an effort to detach the portion of the rock bearing the inscription, but no one seemed sure. No real experts ever had a chance to see it, but an avocational antiquarian from Oklahoma had pronounced it genuine.

The only suspicion I had involved the date when the inscription had been found. What were the odds that Coronado's signature would resurface precisely on the 400th anniversary of his expedition? I began to check all of the publications regarding his expedition that had been published prior to 1941, looking for any that carried copies of Coronado's signature. I had checked the main ones with negative results when Leo Oliva suggested another source. Leo is an expert on the Santa Fe Trail. We met at a symposium dealing with the trail, and I told him and others about my research on the Mallet brothers. Leo had looked into the Coronado inscription at Point of Rocks, and he told me to consult Paul Jones's 1937 book on Coronado and Quivira.

I did so, and there it was. Or, rather, there they were—three versions of Coronado's signature, published in Kansas in 1937. His signature, like everyone's, varied a bit from document to document. One of them in the Jones book, however, was nearly identical to the eighteen-inch-long inscription in the rock near Elkhart. Like Leo Oliva, I was forced to conclude that the inscription was probably a fake, copied ever so carefully from the book.

Several years later, I gave a presentation on the Mallet brothers at the Santa Fe Trail Symposium in Santa Fe. I mentioned the inscription at Point of Rocks and the false trail it led me down. Afterwards, a member of the audience told me that a friend from Elkhart, now deceased, had explained the hoax to him. He claimed that it had been perpetrated by several members of the local chamber of commerce.

As if two fake Coronado inscriptions were not enough, I soon ran across information about a third. In this case, however, its fraudulent nature had been documented. This one first surfaced in July 1937 (Peterson 1989). It was purportedly found near Oak Mills in Atchison County, in the northeastern corner of Kansas. Carved on a slab of limestone were the words:

AGOSTO EL TRE

1541

TOMO

POR ESPAÑA

QIVER

RANCISCO

Peterson (1989) summarizes the reasons that experts concluded it was a fake: They objected to the form of the letters in the inscription, to the spelling out of (F)rancisco (Señor Vasquez typically abbreviated it), to the misspelling of Quivira, and to the English syntax apparent in "Agosto el Tre[s]" and "por España," both phrases being ungrammatical in Spanish.

Peterson's fine article was nearly the last word on the subject. He documented the aftermath of the reputed discovery and suggested who the culprit might have been. He was unable, however, to determine the whereabouts of the stone. It came as a surprise, therefore, when Betty Romero, director of the Coronado-Quivira Museum in Lyons, Kansas, told me where it was. We were riding on a hay wagon at the 1990 Santa Fe Trail Rendezvous, returning from a trip to see portions of the Fort Hays–Fort Dodge Trail. "I know where that thing is," she said, "it's under my desk at the museum." Later, Peterson (1990) reported the resurfacing of the Coronado stone and, even better, a confession by the perpetrator, who turns out to have been a journalist. It would be nice to have confessions for the other two cases as well.

Once I was set free from spurious clues about Spanish inscriptions, finding the spot where the Mallets reached the river became possible. No longer did I try to make their route reach the Cimarron at Elkhart or in Oklahoma. But reach the Cimarron they did, because the journal says they traveled for five days up the river on which they found the inscriptions. The only river that they could have reached by the 30th of June that is long enough to travel up for five days is the Cimarron.

In 1989 my sons and I tried to find the spot. All of the other evidence that had accumulated to that point suggested that the rocks with the inscriptions were somewhere between Coldwater and Englewood. We checked the river south of the town of Protection. The landscape is incredibly barren there, with scrub grass and sagebrush on sand-dune topography. This eastward extension of the High Plains is sparsely populated and has very few public roads.

We went down to the river on the south side of the bridge on Highway 183 and walked along the stream bank for quite a ways. There were no rocks to be seen, just sand. The boys found the skeleton of a coyote, and we took the skull as a souvenir. We talked to all the landowners and cowboys we could find. All were interested and friendly, and many knew the river. But no one knew of any rocks or inscriptions. Everywhere we could check we found nothing but sand dunes and sagebrush—not a single rock bigger than a pebble. Finally we gave up.

We left for the town of Ulysses and Wagonbed Spring to try to pick up the trail farther west. All along the route, we kept checking creek banks and road cuts looking for signs of rock. There were none in the area where the Mallets were likely to have struck the river, but the evidence from Wagonbed Spring indicated that the Mallets had been through that spot. Indeed, it appeared as though the Mallets reached it after their five days of travel up the Cimarron, which meant that the rocks with the inscriptions had to be near where we had looked.

Eventually, we traveled all the way to Santa Fe and back. We reentered Kansas incredibly tired and spent the night in Liberal. All of us were weary of camping, so for the first time that summer we stayed in a motel. In the morning, we found that a tire on the station wagon had gone flat. More bad luck. It had been bad when we started that trip near Medicine Lodge and it had remained bad until we got to Wagonbed Spring. Things had been great in Oklahoma and New Mexico, but now that we were back in Kansas, the worm seemed to be turning once again.

Though we were all feeling a little apprehensive about the car, we made one last try at finding rocks in the deserted countryside along the Cimarron River. We took the back roads and field trails, hoping that the old Subaru would hold out. Proceeding east from Liberal, we stuck as close to the river as possible, scanning every cut bank and hillside for rocks of any description. Finally, south and west from Ashland, we saw a pickup truck about to enter the road from a field near the river. I casually pulled up without quite blocking off his access to the road. The driver turned out to be Terry Arnold, a contractor from Ashland.

When I explained our search for rocks beside the river, he said there were none. "I know," he added, "because I've canoed the river four or five times in the spring when there's enough water to float a canoe." I explained the problem in more detail and showed him where I had traced the Mallet brothers down past Sun City. I told him that the inscriptions, if they remain, would predate 1739 and might even date to 1541. "I don't know of any inscriptions," he said, "but I do remember seeing some rocks a long time ago. When I was younger, I used to cowboy for the Dunne Ranch, and over at the east end, near the Comanche County line, there are some bluffs. There are some rocks on those bluffs, but I've never seen any inscriptions."

The boys and I drove to Ashland, the county seat. We stopped at the Soil Conservation Service office and picked up a free copy of the *Soil Survey of Clark County* (U.S. Department of Agriculture 1982). Soil survey books are one of the few tangible returns you get for your tax dollars, packed with useful information and aerial photographs at a scale of 1:20,000 (about three inches to the mile). On Sheet 70 of the Clark County book, the aerial showed a line of bluffs about a mile and a half long. We checked the rest of the course of the river on the aerials, but there were no other bluffs, just sand dunes and sagebrush. However, an older, 1938 aerial obtained from the county highway department showed the region with extraordinary clarify. I took slides, and we left. There wasn't enough time left on that trip to visit the bluffs. Still, it was an upbeat ending to another summer in the field.

I went back in September with Mike Berry, a reporter for the *Wichita Eagle-Beacon*, his son, John, and Butch Ireland, a photographer for the paper. The newspaper people were there to do a story on the research. I met the others at the Sitka Social Club, the cultural epicenter of this part of Kansas. We drove to the northern end of the bluffs and began the search. After a few hours, Mr. Ireland had to leave, and the Berrys left after I had found a few isolated flakes. By that time we had covered about half of the bluffs, which

The Cimarron River bluffs in Clark and Comanche Counties, Kansas. The trail used by the Mallets crossed the bluffs in the lower right. (Original photo by the U.S. Department of Agriculture, Soil Conservation Service.)

were very rugged. Shortly after the others left, I found the trail. It was marked by flint chips and artifacts. Toward the south end of the bluffs, each high spot had flakes, but they were thickest on both sides of a straight draw that ended at a ford across the old channel of the Cimarron. The old channel happened to have water in it; the dry ford had been formed by material washing down the draw.

When I got back home and looked at my slide of the old aerial photo, this draw stood out from the rest. The others were all irregular in form, with branches in a dendritic pattern. This one ran at an angle to the others and had no branches. It was, in fact, the old trail, which erosion had deepened. The archaeological material occurred on both sides of the trail.

Despite having found the trail, I found no inscriptions. The rock that outcrops there is soft, and any inscriptions that might have existed would have eroded away. Eventually, I made two subsequent trips to the spot to search again; I don't want another fake Coronado inscription to turn up there.

The Cimarron River, July 1–5, 1739

They ascended the left bank of this river until the fifth of July, when they found a village of the Laitane [Comanche] nation. They made a present to these people and received some venison in return. They made their camp at a distance of 1 league from the Laitanes, as they noticed that these people had some evil purpose in mind.

Finding which river the Mallets ascended should not have been especially difficult. There are only three rivers long enough to allow five days' (i.e., 100 miles) travel upstream from where I had traced the Mallets; the Arkansas, the Cimarron, and the Canadian.

According to the abstract, the Mallets crossed the Arkansas on the 22nd of June. By the 1st of July they had encountered seven more streams. Obviously, the river they now ascended for five days could not have been the

Arkansas. Even if they had looped back to the Arkansas after traveling parallel to it, there simply are not enough tributaries to account for the seven stream crossings recorded in the abstract.

The river in question could not have been the Canadian because the travel times are wrong. If the Mallets had traveled south along the trail to the salt plains, they would have reached the Cimarron River on the 30th of June, at a point some 85 miles below the bluffs. Another day of travel would have taken them to the North Canadian, but by ascending it they would have been heading northwest, considerably out of their way. Still another day of travel would have taken them to the South Canadian, but they would have reached it just

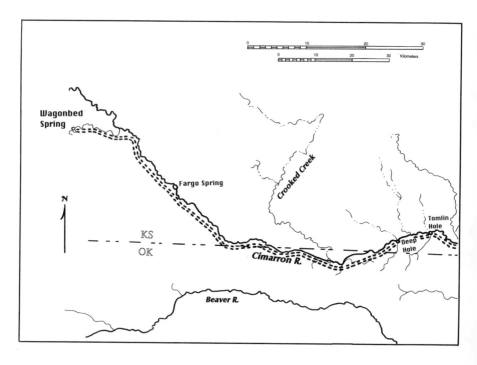

The Mallet route, July 1–5, 1739.

below the point where it makes a series of enormous loops that would have hindered their progress enormously. By process of elimination, then, the river in question must have been the Cimarron.

I wish I had done these calculations before spending the better part of several years searching for the Spanish inscriptions and reading everything I could find on the early history of the counties in south-central Kansas. The reading did not turn up anything on the inscriptions, but it did provide evidence regarding the route that the Mallets did take.

This portion of the Cimarron is dry for parts of the year. Good water sources are rare, and the county histories make specific mention of those that did exist, as early white settlers were as thirsty as their Native American antecedents. One of the good water holes is at the mouth of Snake Creek, a little more than 4 miles west of where the Mallets reached the river. Both Snake Creek and Day Creek flow into the Cimarron here, and the resulting water hole was important enough in the early historic period to have a name: Tomlin Pool. The river bank near it was one of the few spots along this part of the Cimarron to support any trees (Clark County Historical Society n.d.: 1: 31; 3: 14–15; 5: 1–13).

Upstream along the river another 9 miles at the mouth of Clark Creek, also known as Redoubt Creek, was Deep Hole. (The alternate name for the creek derives from a military redoubt constructed in 1871 [Haywood 1986: 26–27]). This important water hole was a stopping place on the road from Fort Dodge to Camp Supply (Haywood 1986: 17–46). This north-south trail crossed the Cimarron just downstream from the pool. About 23 miles north of the crossing the trail forked, and the eastern branch led to the ford of the Arkansas River near the mouth of Mulberry Creek. This is almost certainly the trail Coronado followed northward in his quest for Quivira in 1541.

As one proceeds upstream, other water holes are at the mouth of Crooked Creek in Oklahoma and at Fargo Spring, just downstream from where Highway 83 crosses the river. From there one goes to the junction of the north and south forks of the Cimarron and from there to Wagonbed Spring, south of present Ulysses.

The spring, which no longer flows, is located on the north side of the river, west of the Highway 270 crossing. The Wagonbed Spring Chapter of the Santa Fe Trail Association has marked the spring with a sign. In 1987 I visited the spot with the late Fern Bessire, along with Ginger Anthony and other members of the chapter. I scouted the ground around the spring and saw a few stone flakes that marked an Indian campsite. Fern told me of turquoise beads from another site on a hill to the north, and during another visit Ed Dowell reported finding artifacts on the high ground south of the river.

Wagonbed Spring was known as one of the best water sources in the whole region. It is precisely five days' travel upstream from the bluffs where the Mallets reached the Cimarron, and it provides an explanation for the presence of a Comanche village in 1739. The Mallets positioned themselves a full league from the village in anticipation of trouble.

6.

OKLAHOMA AND NEW MEXICO

Wild Horse Lake, July 6–9, 1739

On the 6th, they left the banks of this stream and upon their leaving, an Arikara Indian who was a captive among the Laitanes told them that this tribe wanted to attack them. They sent him back, saying that they could come and that the French would wait for them. The Laitanes did not make any move, and the slave returned to the French. They asked him if he knew the road to the Spaniards, and he answered that he did, as he had been a slave among them and had been baptized there. They hired him as a guide with the promise to procure his liberty. He consented to this, and that day they made 10 leagues in order to put distance between themselves and the Laitanes.

The Arikara guide appears to have had an incredible streak of bad luck. He must have grown up in one of the villages of his tribe in South Dakota. In this general time period, the Shoshones were raiding the villages along the

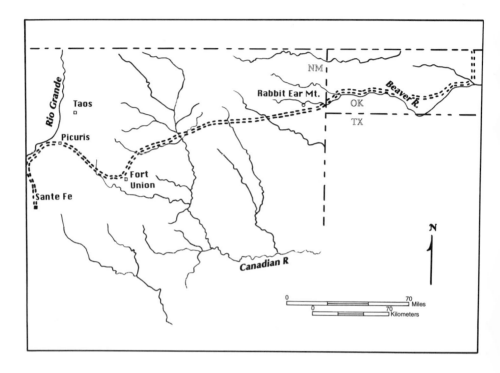

The Mallet route in Oklahoma and New Mexico.

Missouri, killing the men and taking women and children as captives (Smith 1980: 104–110). They transported many of the latter to the Southwest, where they sold them to Spaniards. The Arikara man among the Comanches was probably a boy when he was captured, as the Snakes did not try to enslave grown men. Among the Spaniards, he was baptized in accordance with regulations, as the teaching of Christianity was one of the excuses used for the purchase of captives from Indians. Some time later, and probably while he was still young, he either ran away and was found by the Comanches or was captured by them in one of their raids on Spanish New Mexico. As we shall

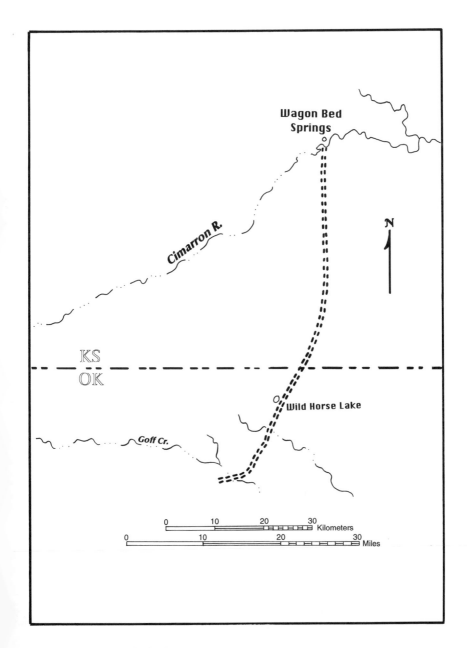

The Mallet route, July 6–9, 1739.

see, there is no clear evidence regarding what happened to him after the Mallets reached Santa Fe.

On what trail did he guide the Mallets away from the Comanche camp? By 1988 I had rejected the hypothesis that the Mallets had proceeded up the Cimarron River from Wagonbed Spring, for reasons that will become apparent later. I had concluded that they must have headed south from the spring, if that is where they had camped, but the prospects of tracing them did not look promising. The only hint of a possible route that I could see on the topographic map was a line of sand dunes aligned north-south that could have provided landmarks. Nothing else in this section of the High Plains could have served as such.

We headed due south, straight through Hugoton, following first the highway, then city streets, then dirt roads. We passed a dried-up playa about a league south of the high ground on the south side of the river. The Mallets could have camped here, but the evidence was not impressive.

The next day we headed toward Goff Creek, named for an old buffalo hunter by Hoodoo Brown, an early figure in the area around Dodge City. Brown joined forces with Goff to hunt buffalo in the Indian country south of the Kansas border, and on the trip, they camped along this creek, where Brown spotted a trail marker.

> About half a mile from this creek was a high, rocky butte with some rocks piled two or three feet high on its top. I knew that Indians had pile rocks up that way, so I went up there to investigate. I looked in between a couple of the rocks and saw twenty-seven little sticks done up in a bundle. I took them down to camp and showed them to Mr. Goff. He said that this was a message for the main band of Indians to pick up, and that it meant that 27 warriors had passed that way (Brown cited in Chrisman 1961: 28).

Goff was probably correct, as there are other references to similar messages elsewhere on the plains (Dodge 1886: 411–412).

I now had evidence for a trail marker at this spot but no proof yet that the Mallets came this way. The mouth of Goff Creek is a short distance from Guymon, Oklahoma. We drove there and stopped at several houses near the creek before we found some people who could help us: Joe Eaton and his wife, Helen Whiting Eaton. The Eatons recognized Brown's description of the isolated hill and gave directions to it. In the course of our conversation, they recommended that we visit the No Man's Land Museum in Goodwell, Oklahoma, and talk with the curator.

With their directions, the boys and I drove to the ranch on which the hill is located. We spotted it from the road and took a picture, but no one was home at the ranch house, so we could not get permission to walk the ground. We moved on to Goodwell and the museum. The curator was out of town, so we talked with her substitute, Becky Hopson. We talked about the Mallets' possible route south from Wagonbed Spring, and she suggested that we visit her father, Roland Hoeme, who farms between Guymon and Ulysses, roughly along the route. She told us that Wild Horse Lake, a large, deep playa on the farm, had Indian camps around its perimeter, but she said her father had modified the basin to make it deeper. We had missed it by only a mile while heading south from Hugoton.

On the way back from Santa Fe, we drove by Wild Horse Lake. Mr. Hoeme was not at the house, but the lake is right beside the road. His daughter said he had modified it "from more or less dish shaped to more or less cup shaped." It was an apt description. The lake has been rimmed with rock, and there is a wooden deck, diving board, the works, all shaded by cottonwood trees that have grown up around the perimeter. It has to be the most impressive swimming pool in the Oklahoma panhandle.

I took a quick picture and we left. But as we did, I marked the spot on the topographic map. In the motel in Liberal that night (we were all tired of camping), I let out a whoop that took the boys' attention away from the cable movie. Wild Horse Lake turns out to be 28 miles south of the playa south of Wagonbed Spring, a perfect match with the distances given in the abstract. The Mallets camped a league from the Comanches (who would have been on the high ground south of the river), then went 10 leagues (27.5 miles) the next day. A route straight south from the playa located a league from this spot would have taken them past the only possible natural landmarks to Wild Horse Lake, at a distance of 28 miles. A continuation of the same route would lead them to Hoodoo Brown's cairn on Goff Creek.

From there, they probably followed a trail that shows up on the General Land Office maps for the area. It heads west to the Beaver River, then continues straight west rather than following the stream. This route provides a shortcut, as the river dips down into Texas before returning to Oklahoma. Becky Hopson provided us with copies of county maps for Texas and Cimarron counties that showed the back roads so that we could follow the trail closely. It leaves the west edge of Goodwell just north of the railroad tracks and strikes the Beaver River at the spot where the Mallets probably camped on the 8th of July. Taking dirt roads, we paralleled the old trail, first to the south and then to the north of it. We could see that the trail headed almost due west, following the highest ground. Eventually we noticed a landmark, just a hint of a dark hill ahead of us. It proved to be a prominent bluff looming over the Beaver River at the end of the cutoff.

We followed the back roads to the highway running southwest from Boise (pronounced "boys") City. It crosses the Beaver in the vicinity where the Mallets would have camped on the 10th. As soon as we rose out of the river valley, we could see the "first Spanish mountain" mentioned in the abstract.

The First Mountain, July 10–12, 1739

On the 10th, they saw the Spanish mountains at a distance of over 10 leagues, and on the 12th, they camped at the first mountain.

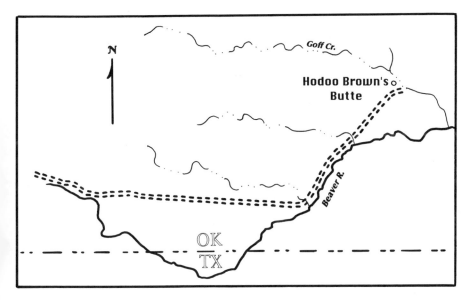

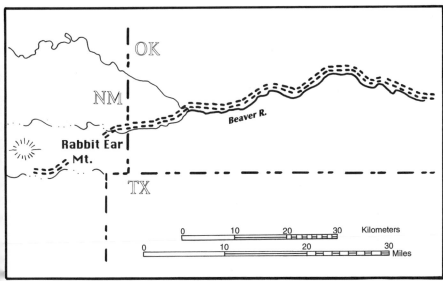

The Mallet route, July 10–12, 1739.

At first I had assumed that this passage referred to the Spanish Peaks. This was an unconscious inference from Folmer's version of the route, which has the Mallets crossing Raton Pass. I had been through the pass many years previously and had been impressed by the spectacular pair of mountains known as the Spanish Peaks. At some point during the investigation, I had passed from wondering if the Spanish Peaks were the Spanish Mountains of the abstract to *assuming* that this was the case.

In 1987, visiting with Bob Apple, landowner of Castle Rock, near Kenton, Oklahoma, I asked which way an eighteenth-century traveler would have gone from there to get to Santa Fe. He was emphatic that one would go south rather than up the river, where the valley closes in on the streambed, making passage difficult. I also asked Truman Tucker, the local amateur historian, how he would get from the vicinity of Kenton to Santa Fe if he were on horseback. He also said it had to be to the south. When I responded that a southerly route wouldn't do if the Mallets were to see the Spanish Peaks, he was kind enough to point out that the Mallets couldn't have seen the Spanish Peaks from the Cimarron, either; there is a mesa in the way.

So, rather than heading up the canyon, I turned south just as night fell. I wondered if it might be impossible to find this portion of the trail and was feeling sorry for myself, but my mood improved as the full moon slowly rose in the east, as big as a basketball and nearly as orange in the dusty atmosphere. I drove the 35 miles to Highway 56, just east of Clayton, seeing only one other vehicle.

The next day I left, driving past the spectacular isolated uplift known as Rabbit Ear Mountain. I went to Albuquerque and eventually on to Santa Fe, hoping to pick up the trail there and backtrack to wherever the first Spanish Mountains might turn out to be. In Santa Fe, I looked up the librarian in the Library of History of the Museum of New Mexico. When I explained my project, he said they had one map in their collection that might prove interesting: the Sectional Map of Colfax and Mora Counties of 1889.

This document is filled with important details, including springs and trails. One, marked "Old Buffalo Trail," runs from Holkeo Creek east-north-east in the general direction of Clayton. Its name probably derives from the fact that it passed Buffalo Spring in the northwestern corner of the Texas panhandle. Another possibility is that the trail was used by *ciboleros*, the bison hunters who hunted seasonally from the Hispanic and Pueblo towns of New Mexico (Kenner 1969: 98–114). Before that, it was probably an Indian trail.

Heading back east from Santa Fe, I drove as close to it as public roads will allow. It took me to Rabbit Ear Mountain once again, and this time I saw the light. Could this be the "first Spanish mountain" of the Mallets? Driving eastward from Rabbit Ear, I alternated between looking at the mountain in my rear-view mirror and reading the odometer. (And they think drunks are a highway hazard.) I was in Oklahoma on the edge of the Canadian River valley, 30 miles from Rabbit Ear, when the peak finally dropped from sight. Thirty miles is nearly 11 leagues, a pretty good match with the "distance of over 10 leagues" of the abstract. It is also the spot to which the boys and I traced the Mallets in 1988.

That year we drove south of the peak to the vicinity of an "Apache Spring" marked on the 1889 map. It appeared to be at the mouth of a canyon, and when we got there, we were fortunate enough to find the landowner, Mr. Bill Waters, and his son repairing fence. Mr. Waters turned out to be interested and knowledgeable. He has helped others search for Apache camps mentioned in some early Spanish records. He told us the canyon was called Apache Canyon and gave us permission to investigate it.

We found a spring and, adjacent to it, a campsite marked by stone chips. We also located a few petroglyphs and bedrock metates (called malpais locally), hollows ground in bedrock in which the Indians ground seeds. One of them still had the grinding stone resting in it. We took some photos but left the grinding stone in place.

Mr. Waters also described the big spring, which is outside the mouth of Apache Canyon and east of the road to Clayton. The artificial bank bulldozed

Apache Canyon, New Mexico. This bedrock grinding slab and hand stone were still in place when we visited this camp on the Mallet route. (Photograph by the author.)

up around it is visible from the road. It yielded 150 gallons per minute and was the town's principal water supply for many years.

The Red River, July 13–14, 1739

On the 13th they stayed at three Laitane lodges, and they made a small present to them. On the 14th, they once again encountered a river, which they named the Red River, but which very likely is another branch of the Arkansas. Twenty-one leagues from here, they found the first Spanish post, which is a mission called Picuris.

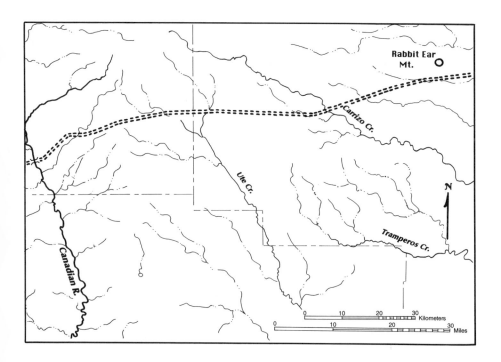

The Mallet route, July 13–14, 1739.

The next day's journey beyond Rabbit Ear Mountain would have taken the Mallets into dry country, a *jornada* (dry stretch) that may have led later wagoneers to shift the route northward. Water can sometimes be had at Carrizo Arroyo and sometimes at the playa lakes south of Sofia. The next watercourse is Ute Creek, which has springs in the vicinity of Point of Rocks, but the Old Buffalo Trail crossed downstream from there. At a point a few miles west of Ute Creek, the Old Buffalo Trail joins the Cimarron Cutoff of the Santa Fe Trailat an early settlement, labeled "Peck" on the map. The Mallets must have put in two long days of travel in this area, as they reached the Canadian River on the 14th.

It is worth considering whether the Old Buffalo Trail might not have been a branch of the Santa Fe Trail for a while after 1822. Josiah Gregg mentions a route that ran south of the Rabbit Ear:

> The first caravan that crossed these plains passed on the south side of these mounds, having abandoned our present route at the "Cold Spring," where we encamped on the night of the 1st of July. Although the route we were travelling swerves somewhat too much to the north, that pursued by the early caravans as stated above, made still a greater circuit to the south, and was by far the most inconvenient (Gregg 1954: 63).

The first caravan to pass that way was William Becknell's in 1822, on his second trip to Santa Fe. It is clear that he was following an Indian trail; the same route appears on the 1807 Pike sketch map, and Pike's map appears to show the Cimarron Cutoff sixteen years before Becknell supposedly pioneered it. The passage from Gregg's book is one of the few clear documentations of the numerous modifications to the old Indian trails necessitated by the arrival of wheeled traffic. It is possible that the shift to the north was generated in part by the scarcity of water along this portion of the older trail.

The Mallets apparently followed the trail that was to become the Cimarron Cutoff to a crossing near Taylor Springs, where there is a rocky ford of the Canadian River. The ford was important not only to the wagon traffic along the Santa Fe Trail but also to the prehistoric inhabitants of the region. Formed by resistant bedrock formations that create shallow spots in a stream, such fords were more a convenience than a necessity to prehistoric foot travelers, but they also were attractive for other reasons (Blakeslee and Rohn 1986: 31–33, 89–97). When the water in a stream flows over a rocky ford, the water moves faster because the same volume must move through a smaller area. The increase in velocity allows the stream to pick up heavier sediment than it carries elsewhere. In effect, a rocky ford acts as a vacuum cleaner, cleaning and deepening the riverbed just upstream. The deep spot will hold water longer than other points along the stream, and during dry seasons this hole will be thick with fish and shellfish and will attract game animals.

The abstract appears to say that the Mallets named this portion of the Canadian the Red River. As we have already seen, this was the name given to the stream by the tribes of the region. The Mallets probably learned it from their Arikara guide. Up to this point, the route through New Mexico is fairly easy to trace out, but from Taylor Springs on the abstract gives confusing information. The first ambiguity is the estimate of the distance from this point to Picuris, given as 21 leagues, or 58 miles. The direct distance is actually 70 miles, and there is no point along the Canadian River that would match the Mallet estimate. By the route followed, the distance is actually 86 miles, which suggests that the problem derives from a transcription error, as 31 leagues (instead of 21) would give 85.25 miles.

This is the place to comment on another proposed route. Faye (1943: 691) places the Comanche village from which they obtained their guide (whom he transforms from a member of the Arikara tribe into a Wichita) on the headwaters of the Arkansas River. His route takes them from the

> northwest fork of the Arkansas and across Raton pass, from the foot of which through a purple plain flows southward the little river of the Jicarilla, which is to become the Canadian Fork of the Arkansas. Down the river a march of twenty-one French post leagues (50 English miles) brought them to the Jicarilla village at the Cimarron confluence twenty Spanish leagues (60 English miles) east of the Taos pueblo. Up the Cimarron brook a strangely easy mountain road led them into a high park, beside its unexpected lake, down along another brook to the torrent that is the Rio Grande, and so to Taos. Thus with flowing water at their hand Frenchmen penetrated into the heart of dry New Mexico (Faye 1943: 691).

This interpretation is based primarily on the idea that the Piquouris of the abstract were actually the Jicarilla: "The name Jicarilla, or Heecah-reeyah in English phonology, becomes Piquouris (Peekwahree) in the report of the brothers Mallet, who, being Canadians, could not recognize aspirates. Perhaps on authority of this report the Picuri (Tegna) tribe occupies the position of the Jicarilla on the map of Coronelli, *Le Nouveau Mexique* (Paris, 1742), in Chalbot op. cit. 18–19" (Faye 1943: 691, n 15).

Faye seems unaware of the existence of Picuris Pueblo and ignores the mention of the missionary who greeted the Mallets at Piquouris. There was no mission among the Jicarilla in 1739. His "Tegna" on the Coronelli map is a misreading of Tegua (i.e., Tiwa), the linguistic group to which the Picuris belong.

The Road to Santa Fe, July 15–22, 1739

> Twenty-one leagues from [the crossing of the Canadian], they found the first Spanish post, which is a mission called Picuris. On the 15th, they encountered three Indians to whom they gave a letter for the commandant of Taos who the next day sent them some mutton and a beautiful loaf of wheat bread. When they arrived at a league from the first post, the commandant and the padre came out to meet them along with the whole population and received them very graciously, even with the ringing of bells, according to their account. The 21st, they left Picuris and arrived at noon at another mission called Sainte Croix, and after dinner they passed another called Le Cañada, and they spent the night at a town called Sainte Marie, where they were pleasantly received by the Spaniards. On the 22nd of July, they arrived in Santa Fe after having traveled 265 leagues from the river of the Panis Maha.

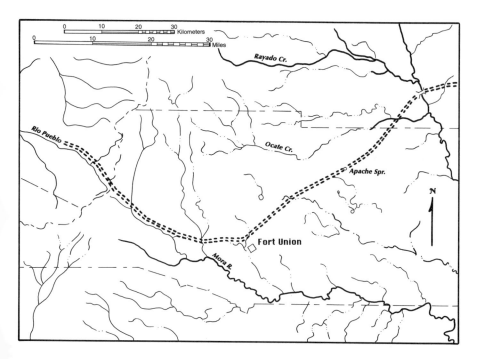

The Mallet route, July 15–18, 1739.

The point at which the Mallets crossed the mountains was not clear to me for a long time. Although I was in the process of criticizing Folmer's version of the route, his idea about where they crossed the mountains had become received knowledge to me. Part of the image had to do with the "first Spanish Mountains" of the journal. These, as I have indicated, I mistook for the Spanish Peaks northeast of Taos, landmarks that dominate the Mountain Branch of the Santa Fe Trail.

Old documents contain evidence that the Spanish Peaks could not have been the Mallets' Spanish Mountains. Pike (Jackson 1966 I: Map 3) indicated that the Spanish Peaks could be seen from the mouth of his first fork of the Arkansas River (the Purgatoire River). It is 108 miles from there to the Spanish Peaks as the crow flies, too great a distance for the Mallets to have crossed in the two days recorded in the abstract of their journal.

Not until my informants in the panhandle of Oklahoma unanimously denied the likelihood that the Mallets would have continued up the river, an argument they based on their knowledge of the landscape, did I begin to consider other possibilities. After talking to them in 1987, I reread the abstract with my blinders removed. It is hard to read the portion quoted above and not realize that the first pueblo the Mallets actually went to was Picuris, not Taos, but I and a lot of other people had managed to do it.

Folmer, of course, had done so. So had Elizabeth John, an excellent historian. She had a better excuse than Folmer, however, as she had the Spanish documents generated by Pierre Mallet's 1750 trip to Santa Fe. In them, he mentions Taos in a context that makes it appear as though it were the first settlement he had encountered in 1739 (see Chapter 8). Whatever the source of the apparent contradiction, the 1740 account, drawn from the Mallet journal, must be given primacy over information recalled more than a decade later.

We have already seen that Picuris lies at the western end of a mountain pass. I learned of its existence in 1987, when I went from Clayton to Albuquerque in order to try to backtrack along the Mallet route. The Coronado Room in the library at the University of New Mexico holds a wealth of historical documents. So does the map room, where I found copies of about a dozen maps that continued pertinent information. One indicated a trail across the mountains directly east of Picuris, and several documents indicated the presence of a pass there.

In 1696, Governor Vargas pursued rebels from Picuris Pueblo across the mountains. His diary describes the trail clearly:

> I followed the road which comes down the river of this pueblo to the east; the river on the right hand. I found the footpath between the

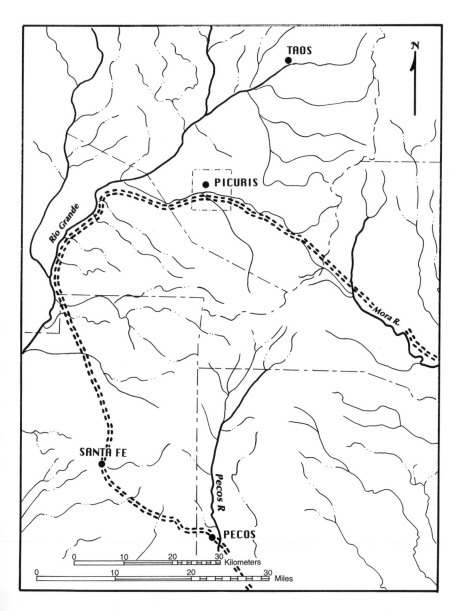

The Mallet route, July 19–22, 1739.

two sierras like a canyon in some places and wholly mountainous, and filled with stones which are in those hills. Having travelled apparently about five long leagues, I found the ranchería which the enemy had attacked first. Further on about two leagues it was recognized that the enemy had been there, because they took the trail from there along the stream (Thomas 1935: 54).

Jean Paëz Hurtado also used the pass in a 1715 expedition against the Faraone Apaches. The Faraones were allied with Pecos Pueblo, and Hurtado used the Picuris pass in the hope that the Indians of Pecos would not be able to warn their friends of the approach of the Spanish army. In this he was unsuccessful, because the Spanish were never able to locate the Faraones, who had apparently fled their usual haunts (Thomas 1935: 80–98).

Another reference comes from Albert Pike, who traveled to Taos in 1831. Referring to a camp at the junction of Cebolla Creek and Mora River, he wrote: "Had [Aaron] Lewis continued up the Demora to the old village [Mora], and thence through the pass of the mountains, he would have found a broken trail, and would have gone in with much more ease" (Pike 1967: 20). Instead, Lewis and his companions headed north to the more southerly of the Taos passes, where they almost perished in the mountains. The following year Pike did take the Picuris pass, traveling from Picuris to his old camp at the mouth of Cebolla Creek in three days (Pike 1967: 35).

There are no entries in the abstract for the period July 16 to July 20, when the Mallets crossed the mountains. Naturally, the reconstruction of this part of the route proved difficult, but there are several implicit hints. The most likely spot for the Frenchmen to have encountered Indians on the 15th is at the crossing of Ocate Creek, 25 miles from the crossing of the Canadian River. Numerous petroglyphs attest to the fact that this was an old Indian crossing (Nancy Robertson, personal communication, 1989).

The Mallets might have stayed at this spot until the Indian messengers dispatched to Taos returned on the next day with the gifts from the commandant.

The trip across the mountains would have been a bit over 40 miles, an impressive distance to cover in one day, but not beyond the capability of Indian runners.

The next day of travel would have taken the Mallets to the region in which Fort Union would later stand. I found their likely route by backtracking from Picuris in 1987. Coming down the mountain pass, the highway runs by the locality known as La Cueva. I stopped there to take pictures of the old mill and to look at the topographic maps of the region. As I did so, I saw a possible direct route. To get to Fort Union from Mora by road, one travels southeast along the river to the vicinity of Watrous before turning north, a distance of some 32 miles. The topographic maps indicated that it might be possible to cut nearly due east from La Cueva and to follow two canyons across a low mesa, reaching the fort in only 20 miles.

I started off in that direction on a dirt road and was soon stopped by a local man who asked if I was lost. When I explained my purpose, he told me that the land in question was on the Salman Ranch and suggested I drive to the ranch headquarters for permission to explore. I started out to do so and was met by David Salman before I could get there. Apparently someone else had seen my car on the road and had phoned him. (In this kind of unpopulated country, everyone keeps an eye on suspicious traffic.) Mr. Salman gave me permission to scout around, and I looked at the land along the west end of the mesa. It was flat and would have provided an easy traverse for men on horseback. An unnamed canyon on the Salman Ranch meets head to head with Higgins Canyon on the other side, so I drove around to Fort Union and the Fort Union Ranch.

The road to the Fort Union Ranch is graveled with huge cobbles, making for a slow and bumpy ride. When I reached the headquarters, the manager was not there, and the young lady who talked to me said that no one else could give permission to be on the land. I learned why the next summer, when I met Rob Carlson and Margaret Ann Gray at a party in Wichita. Rob's in-laws are part-owners of the Fort Union Ranch, and the family story is that their ancestor, Benjamin Franklin Butler, won the ranch in a poker game. His

Higgins Canyon, New Mexico. This photo of the head of the canyon shows the easy passage it provides across a mesa into the La Cueva Valley. (Photograph by the author.)

heirs, some 300 of them, own the ranch in common. The young lady at the headquarters was one of the heirs, vacationing at the ranch after graduating from college.

Rob gave me his father's phone number in California, and he in turn directed me to the manager, Dan Kipp. Several attempts to reach him failed, as he travels frequently between two ranches, and it was not until 1988 that we met. I had gone to Santa Fe to present a talk on the Mallet expedition to the Santa Fe Trail Rendezvous. At the first coffee break, I was standing in line to get a drink, when I noticed the name tag of the person next to me. It was

Dan Kipp. I pulled him aside, and after a very pleasant conversation he gave me permission to explore the ranch.

I went there on my way back to Kansas and explored Higgins Canyon. It is a lovely spot, watered by springs near its head and again at its mouth near the ranch headquarters. I drove along slowly and was able to spot flakes from prehistoric campsites from the car window. When the radiator overheated, I added water from the head spring.

The Mallets could have reached Higgins Canyon on the 17th, as it is about 20 miles south of the Ocate Creek crossing. Another day of travel would have put them on the Mora River, near the present town of the same name. From there, they had two days to cross the mountains by the old trail. Although the linear distance is only 30 miles, the pass is at 8,500 feet above sea level. Hence, two days would be about right for the journey.

The next day, the 21st, they left Picuris for Santa Fe, passing the mission of Sainte Croix, a place called La Cañada, and another called Sainte Marie. They reached Santa Fe the following day. The places named in this entry indicate that the Mallets were led by the old Spanish trail down Embudo Creek to the Rio Grande and then down that stream to the vicinity of modern Española. Apparently they bypassed San Juan Pueblo, as it is not named in the abstract. The Sainte Croix of the abstract is the mission of Santa Cruz de la Cañada. La Cañada was a scattered Spanish settlement near the mission and the second official villa in New Mexico, after Santa Fe. It was founded by Vargas in 1695 with the elaborate title of La Villa Nueva de Santa Cruz de los Españoles Mejicanos del Rey Nuestro Señor Carlos Segundo (Pearce 1965:80). Both the town and the road from it to Santa Fe were described by Lieutenant Peck in 1846:

> Five miles from "San Juan," is the town of "Cañada," a village of 300 or 400 inhabitants, built on a slight roll of land, one mile from the river. At this point the Santa Fe road leaves the river again, and, after crossing an elevated tongue of land, enters the valley of the "Rio

Picuris Pass. This view is of the pass across the Sangre de Cristo Mountain connecting the Mora River valley with the Rio Pueblo leading to Picuris. (Photograph by the author.)

Tezuque." Several settlements of Spaniards and Indians are to be seen along the stream, the principal of which are "Cuyamanque," and "Tezuque," both pueblos. From the village of Tezuque, it is but five miles, over a cedar hill, to the town of "Santa Fé" (Peck in Abert 1848: 62).

Sainte Marie apparently refers to Pojoaque, where the mission was called Nuestra Señora de Guadalupe. Nuestra Señora to a French Catholic would, of course, mean Sainte Marie. Today, State Highway 75 and U.S. 84 approximate the old trail. Picuris to Pojoaque is a long day's journey—some 36 miles.

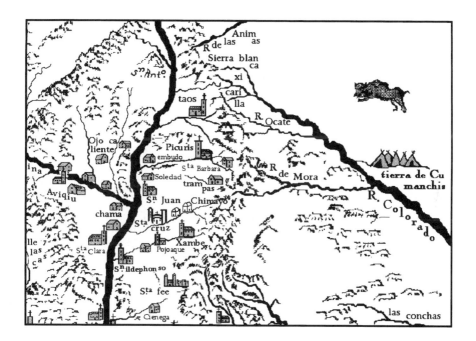

The 1758 Miera y Pacheco map. The original has been lost, but a painstaking reproduction is available (Kessell 1979). (Modified to enhance the clarity of the captions.)

It is safe to assume that the Spanish provided their visitors with fresh horses.
The next day brought them to Santa Fe.

The Mallets estimated the distance they had traveled from the River of the
Panimahas to Santa Fe at 265 leagues. This is about 729 miles, and it provides
a double check on the identity of their Panimaha River. We know the Mallets
left that spot on June 13. If the Panimaha was in fact the Loup River, then they
estimated their rate of travel between the two points as 18.2 miles per day. But
if, as Folmer has it, they intended to indicate the Niobrara River (which they
left on May 29), their estimate of their rate of travel would only have been 13
miles per day, far below the rate indicated in the abstract (Table 1).

Table 1. Correlation of the Abstract with Known Spots

	If the River of the Panimaha is	
	the Niobrara	the Loup
Distances		
Mallet estimate of distance	729 miles	729 miles
Actual distance	1042 miles	806 miles
Error in estimate	313 miles (43%)	77 miles (10%)
Resulting Rate of Travel		
Recorded Departure date	May 29	June 13
Total Days of Travel	55	40
Estimated rate implied	13 mi/day	18 mi/day
Actual Rate	19 mi/day	20 mi/day

If I am correct that the River of the Panimaha was the Loup (See Afterword) the Mallets would have traveled 806 miles to Santa Fe from the spot so named. This gives a discrepancy of 77 miles (about 10 percent) from their estimate of the distance and implies a rate of travel equal to 20 miles per day. But if Folmer had it right, then the distance they actually travelled is 1,042 miles. For this to be correct, they would have to have underestimated the distance traveled by more than 300 miles (43 percent). Clearly, the Loup River provides a far better fit with the Mallet abstract than does the Niobrara. In fact, 28 miles of the 77-mile discrepancy between their estimate and the Loup River–to–Santa Fe distance lies in their underestimate (or a subsequent misrecording or mistranscription) of the distance from the Canadian River to Picuris. This leaves a total error in their estimate of only 49 miles for the rest of a journey of 806 miles spanning 40 days, an average error of only 1 mile per day.

Santa Fe, 1739–1740

One can see in the certificate enclosed herein the manner in which they were received and how they lived there nine months while they awaited the response from the Viceroy of Mexico. It is not surprising that they had to wait for so long because it is 500 leagues by land from Santa Fe to Old Mexico and no more than one caravan makes the journey each year.

Santa Fe, according to their account, is a village built of wood and without any fortification. There are about 800 families, Spanish or mulatto, and in the region roundabout are a number of villages of Indians and residing in each of them is a priest who runs the mission. There are but 80 soldiers in the garrison, a bad gang and poorly armed. There are mines very close by which are not worked at all. There are others in the province which are worked for the royal treasury, the silver from which is transported every year to Old Mexico by caravan.

It would seem, from one of the enclosed letters, that the governors seize for themselves all the merchandise that they desire and control the little commerce that exists, which the priests and others would like to do.

In 1739, Santa Fe was about as far as one could get from Mexico City and still be under its jurisdiction. Communication was usually sent via the annual caravan, which sometimes took longer than the nine months specified in the abstract to go between these two points. The caravan was usually made up of oxcarts and mule-drawn wagons. Horsemen and pack mules often accompanied them, and various servants and poorer folk followed in their dust. In the eighteenth century, this *cordón* between Santa Fe and Chihuahua could include 400 to 500 people.

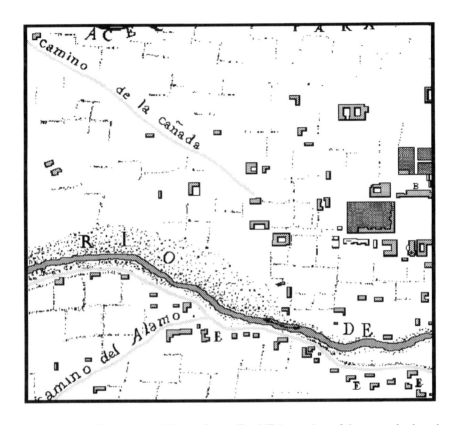

Urrutia's 1766 "Plano de la Villa de Santa Fee." This section of the map depicts the Camino de Cañada, the road into town used by the Mallets in 1739. (Redrawn from a photocopy of the original in the British Library [Add. Ms 17662 M].)

At the core of most early caravans headed north was the mission supply train, which provided the necessities of life to the Franciscans scattered in the New Mexican pueblos. In 1611 it consisted of twenty wagons, each with a capacity of two tons; by 1631 it had grown to thirty-two wagons (Kessell

1979: 118, 147). Private parties carried other goods for the secular side of the colony, and government items included gifts for friendly Indian tribes.

On the way south, the same wagons carried the produce of New Mexicans and the Indians with whom they traded. Bison robes and tanned hides were important in these shipments, which were accompanied by livestock and human slaves being driven to the markets farther south. As the mining frontier of northern New Spain developed, New Mexican traders focused on intermediate points such as Parral and Chihuahua City, reducing their travel time considerably. Eventually, this *camino real* became incorporated into the Santa Fe Trail, as the actual destination of westering traders on that route was often Chihuahua rather than Santa Fe.

When far-flung mission outposts needed to communicate with each other or with Mexico City, they used the *cordillera* method. In this system, each outpost that received a message was responsible for copying it and sending it along to the next mission. (The *patentes*, or directives, cited below were sent by this means.) Men could also be sent by the same system, with each outpost replacing the travelers' horses and signing off on the documents. Pierre Mallet, to his woe, would learn firsthand how the system worked in 1751.

The Mallets' description of the garrison in Santa Fe—"a bad gang and poorly armed"—was right on the money. It omitted only the fact that the soldiers were seldom paid. The Mallets' estimate of 80 men is useful, as the official figures vary considerably. A muster roll of the garrison in 1715 showed 100 names, but a petition filled out only one month later had 150 names (Athearn 1989: 29). Yet a head count in 1723 came up with only 22 men (Athearn 1989: 37).

Poorly paid, and not very often at that, the soldiers seem to have suffered from low morale and sometimes lax discipline. Petitions pleading for the back pay of the soldiers survive in the records of every early governor of the colony (Athearn 1989: 27). In 1704, immediately upon arriving in the colony, Governor Francisco Cuervo issued an order banning the gambling that was rife among the troops. In 1718, Governor Valverde had to bar the men from selling horses from the government herd, and in 1723 Governor Bustamente forbade the selling of their guns (Athearn 1989: 31). Little wonder they were poorly armed.

There were mines in the general vicinity of Santa Fe. It should be noted that the Mallets used the word to mean a lode or claim rather than a working mine. The same usage appears in the 1634 memorial of Fray Benavides (Hodge, Hammond and Rey 1945). In 1717 a resident of Santa Fe, Diego de Quiros, obtained the grant of a mine near the city (Athearn 1989: 21), and in 1846 Lt. J. W. Abert visited one about 40 miles from Santa Fe.

The comment about competition between the governors and the missionaries over trade is also accurate. Both had access to Indian labor for production of goods that could be sent to Mexico, and both sides were active in the native trade fairs. The governors usually had the upper hand, however. One missionary described the situation vividly in 1761, saying the governors were "gorging themselves first with the largest mouthfuls from this table, while the rest eat the crumbs" (cited in Kenner 1969: 38).

The church took a dim view of the extent to which some of the missionaries participated in the trade. In 1738, Custos Fray Juan García issued a *patente* forbidding friars to bear arms or to attend the Indian trade fairs. In 1746, Fray Juan Miguel de Menchero scolded friars for obtaining permission to travel to Sonora to trade. Custos Fray Juan José de Hinojosa forbade the friars in 1770 from employing Indian helpers in weaving *mantas* and the like, even under the pretext of keeping them busy, and in 1781 Custos Bermejo barred them once again from engaging in trade and barter (Chavez 1957: 161–164).

The Land of the Imagination, 1740

The response of the viceroy, according to the report of the Canadians, was to have them stay in New Mexico. They thought that they would be hired to make the discovery of a country that according to

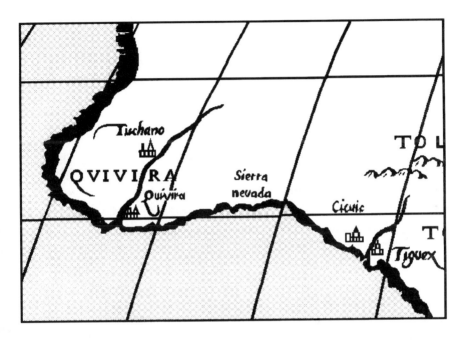

Land of the Imagination. This portion of the Ortelius map of 1570 locates Quivira and other places visited by Coronado on the west coast of the United States. (Redrawn from Wheat 1957: No. #16.)

a tradition of the Indians, whether true or false, lay three months journey overland toward the western coast and where it was said that white men dressed in silk lived in great cities along the edge of the sea. Whatever might be so, they preferred to return and they were allowed to depart with the letters, copies of which are attached.

This most interesting passage documents the persistence of the sort of myth that had brought Spaniards to New Mexico in the first place. Part of the cultural baggage (Brink 1985: 14) derived from the medieval European heritage was belief in "giants, dwarfs, enchanted isles, Amazons, fountains of youth, mystical Seven Cities, [and] El Dorado." (Leonard 1949: 35). The fusion of the old Spanish legend of the Seven Cities of Antillia with native reports of towns of stone to the north of Mexico generated Coronado's expedition in 1541. The disappointing facts he found in Cibola—where there were six, not seven, villages, all utterly devoid of the fabled wealth—only slowed him down for a bit.

When a Plains Indian known as the Turk claimed that some people far to the east had metal, Coronado doubled the amount of ground he covered. The Spaniards showed this man a gold ring, and he called it *acochis*. Eager to find the pot at the end of the rainbow, the Europeans never stopped to consider just what the Turk meant. They assumed *acochis* meant gold. Unfortunately for them, it was simply a word for metal (Wedel 1982:155).

Even after the expedition to Quivira located only some villages of grass houses and but a single piece of *acochis* (a copper pendant worn by one of the chiefs), the beliefs and the hope did not fade entirely. Coronado himself was disillusioned, but many of his men were not convinced. Some pleaded with him not to go back to Mexico (Hammond and Rey 1940: 306). "They were not satisfied to think that there was no gold," Castañeda wrote, complaining that Coronado had tricked them into agreeing to return (Hammond and Rey 1940: 246). They believed that somewhere a little bit farther out there, or maybe to the northwest rather than to the northeast, the great cities were waiting.

The disappointing results of this first probe to the north were eventually forgotten, and after a time the Spaniards came again. In 1601, when Juan de Oñate had just begun the colonization process in the Rio Grande Valley, he took a side trip back to Quivira. Like Coronado, he found no mineral wealth, but this did not stop his cartographer from labeling the Arkansas River the "Rio del Oro" (Hammond and Rey 1953). Moreover, the Miguel map that derives from the same expedition shows a place called Encuche, near a lagoon where gold could be obtained.

The settlers of New Mexico understood that there were no quick riches to be made there. The fabulous places were still somewhere over the horizon, but not forgotten. The name of the place with the lagoon changed from Encuche to Teguayo, and its location changed from northeast to northwest, but the belief in the gold never wavered.

The hope that there were cities filled with men in silk robes along the edge of the sea was grounded at least in an understanding of geography. China lay somewhere to the west (Asia had been Columbus's original goal), and Quivira might be somewhere in the same direction. In Quivira there were said to be cities. What else would people there wear but silk? The Ortelius map at the beginning of this section is one of several from the sixteenth century that showed Quivira on the coast of California.

I do not mean to pick on the Spaniards. Not all of them believed these tall tales, nor were those who did unique to that culture. Fray Alonso de Posada, for one, doubted the rumors. Citing what the natives had to say about more distant tribes in 1686, he concluded that "there is neither so much gold as is imagined nor so much silver as is said" (cited in Kessell 1979: 208). Even today some people hope to find Montezuma's treasure in New Mexico or Arizona despite the fact that the Aztecs had nothing to do with the pueblo world. Many Frenchmen, too, were believers. Some dreamed of the mountain of emeralds that lay somewhere up the Missouri River. Others fell for Diego de Peñalosa's stories of the lands of Quivira and Teguayo, rich in silver and gold (Faye 1943: 652). Peñalosa, a governor of New Mexico, was tried by the Inquisition for heresy and exiled from New Spain. He later traveled to England and France seeking support for an invasion of one or more of Spain's New World colonies.

The actual border between the realms of Spain and France coincided with the one in myth. Oñate's men had called the Arkansas River the Rio del Oro. Le Page du Pratz, inhabitant of Louisiana, published a map showing a gold mine on that river in what is now Kansas. The map surfaced in nineteenth-century Arkansas and led a group of would-be miners to hire Jesse Chisholm to show them to the spot. He took them to the vicinity of present Wichita, at the mouth of the Little Arkansas, rather than to the mouth of the Walnut, where Oñate had gone (Mead 1896: 90).

Both the Spanish and the French myths probably had their origin in the same fact: There were mines on the Arkansas, just east of where the Walnut River empties into it, in the hills above the villages that Oñate visited in 1601. The natives dug there for chert (flint) with which to make their tools. The stone they took from the ground was yellowish in color, but when they heated it to improve its flaking quality, it turned pink. The Rio del Oro was the Flint River, and the "gold mine" located on the du Pratz map was probably the result of a Frenchman's asking a native where men dug yellow rock from the ground.

The heating of this stone may have been what the Turk tried to convey to Coronado's men when, according to them, he indicated by gestures how the Indians heated the "gold" in Quivira (Wedel 1982: 155). It is certainly conceivable that a later legend had a similar origin. Early in the nineteenth century, New Mexico was afloat with stories about the Cerro Amarillo, which some thought to be a hill of gold. According to one Comanche informant, it lay two weeks' travel east of Pecos or San Miguel (cited in Kessell 1979: 430). A likely source for the rumor is the chert quarry north of the town of Amarillo, where Indians also dug for stone. The Mallets were to pass the spot on their return to the French colonies.

7.

THE RETURN

The Canadian River Trail, May 1–10, 1740

On the 1st of May, the explorers, now numbering seven, as Moreau had married in that country, left Santa Fe to find their way to the Mississippi and to New Orleans by a route other than the one they had taken on the outward journey. The 2nd of May, they arrived at a mission named Pecos, where they stayed two days. They left on the 4th and camped on a river of the same name, and they think that this river might be a branch of the Red River or of the Arkansas. They traveled along it on the 5th and left it on the 6th. On the 7th, they encountered another that flowed in the same direction that they named the River of the Mare. They left this stream to cross overland, following the route they had in mind, and on the 10th, they encountered a third river, which they believe flows into the Red River or into the Arkansas, and which they think is the same branch on which they

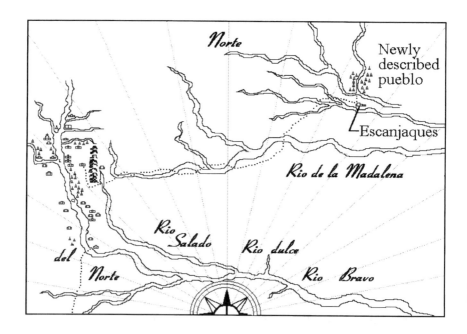

The 1601 Martinez map. This portion of the official map of the Oñate expedition of 1601 shows the route along the Canadian River used by this and many other expeditions, including that of Pierre Mallet in 1750. (Redrawn from a photocopy of the original in Hammond and Rey [1953], with some captions translated.)

found higher up the Spanish inscriptions when they were en route to Santa Fe. They were then 35 or 40 leagues from that capital and they estimate that one could ascend to that place and then return in order to perfect their exploration.

There were two routes from Santa Fe to Pecos. One became a segment of the Santa Fe Trail in later years. It ran through Glorietta Pass, and today's Interstate 25 follows it pretty closely. The other route was a shortcut, an old

Indian footpath that led more directly from Santa Fe to Pecos across the mountains (Vargas in AGI, Guad., 139). It was passable on horseback, and this trail was taken by Lt. J. W. Abert in 1846 (Abert 1848: 45).

It took the Mallet party to Pecos Pueblo, now a National Historic Landmark. The old wheel ruts of the Santa Fe Trail can still be seen south of the ruins of the mission there (Simmons 1988: 94). The Mallets may have used their two days at Pecos to obtain information from the natives about an appropriate route. They went eastward, down the Pecos River. Their first camp probably was where San Miguel now stands, about 20 miles downstream. The Pecos River flows into the Rio Grande, not the Red or the Arkansas, as the Mallets guessed in 1740. It flows southeast where they followed it, which may explain their error. The fact that they stayed with the Pecos for two days suggests that they did not cross it at San Miguel, as many later travelers did, but continued downstream to the vicinity of Villanueva. This route is shown, for instance, on the Gregg map of the Santa Fe Trail (Gregg 1954).

The next river to the east is the Gallinas, which must be the Mallets' River of the Mare. It empties into the Pecos above Colonias, not into the Arkansas or the Red. The party was following a trail well documented in later years. It came to be known as the Fort Smith–Santa Fe road, and its creation is usually attributed to Josiah Gregg, who followed it in 1839 and 1840 (Gregg 1954). On his westward trip, however, he had been given at least general directions by a Comanche at the eastern end (Gregg 1954: 232–233) and more specific guidance by Comancheros at the western end (Gregg 1954: 257–260). On his return trip in 1840, he had the services of a Comanche guide (Gregg 1954:316).

Others had used the same general route prior to the Mallets, including Hernando de Alvarado in 1540 (Hammond and Rey 1940), Francisco Vasquez de Coronado in 1541 (Hammond and Rey 1940), Leyva and Humaña in 1593 (Hammond and Rey 1966: 323–326), Vicente de Zaldivar in 1598 (Hammond and Rey 1966: 323–326), Juan de Oñate in 1601

(Hammond and Rey 1953), and Diego Romero in 1660 (Blakeslee 1981). Its use by multitudes of *comancheros* and *ciboleros* is mostly undocumented, but before Josiah Gregg left the Canadian in 1839, heading in the opposite direction, he was following a well-defined wagon trail these earlier travelers had created through decades of use.

It ran almost due east from Anton Chico to the vicinity of present Tucumcari. From a point east of Anton Chico, the Mallet route would have been identical to Gregg's 1840 route, which is carefully recorded (Fulton 1941). From the ford of the Gallinas, the trail ran 15 miles to Los Esteros. The name of this water hole is preserved as Esteros Creek today. Another 15 miles brought Gregg to Cuervito Creek, now Cuervo Creek, north of present Cuervo, and it was another 12 miles to Pajarito Creek, east of Newkirk. Ten miles farther east he reached the Laguna Colorado, and from there it was 15 miles south of east to present Charco Creek southwest of Tucumcari. From this spot, there were several trails, and the Mallets appear to have taken one that brought them to the Canadian River in the vicinity of Ute Lake State Park. They reached this point on the 10th of the month, having averaging about 20 miles per day since leaving Pecos.

The abstract's wording gives the impression that the Mallets did not know whether the Canadian River flowed into the Red or the Arkansas. Yet this is the river down which the Mallets traveled to the Arkansas. Obviously, the person who made the abstract used their journal entry of May 10th, when they did not yet know the course of the river. They may have been confused at that time because both the native and Spanish names for the river meant "Red River."

Their estimate of distance from Santa Fe to this point, some 35 to 40 leagues, matches estimates given in 1750 for the distance from Pecos to the Canadian. The actual distance is 126 miles, a very good fit with the estimate. The distance from Santa Fe, however, is 142 miles.

The Mallets were partly correct with regard to the river of the inscriptions. It was the Cimarron, which, like the Canadian, is a tributary of the

Arkansas. The Cimarron, however, flows into the Arkansas above the point where they reached it later in their return journey. Hence, they would not have seen its mouth during their return journey. They obviously were confused about the geography of the region, and this may have caused Governor Bienville to send Fabry de la Bruyère to make precise observations in 1741.

The Trail of the Pawnees, May 11–13, 1740

On the 11th, 12th and 13th, they followed this river and on the last day, three of the seven men quit their comrades to retake the road of the Pawnees to go to Illinois, which they accomplished according to letters sent later from that post.

The Mallets apparently followed the river quite closely. Traveling a short distance away from it would have put them in some rugged breaks that would have been very difficult to traverse. The return expedition in 1750 also took this route, and Pierre Jofrellon told of crossing and recrossing the river in knee-deep water (Hackett 1941: 356). Such a route is shown on both the Martínez map of the Oñate expedition of 1601 and the 1807 map by Don Pedro Walker (Wheat 1957–1963 II: 272). The journal of the expedition that generated the latter map has not come to light, but the route clearly reaches the Canadian near Tucumcari, crosses the river several times, goes up Alamosa Creek onto the Llano Estacado, and continues to Palo Duro Canyon. The Mallets, however, stayed on the river.

The trail they were following was recorded four decades later by the Long expedition: "167167[A] large and much frequented Indian trace crossing the creek, from the west, and following down along the east bank. This trace consisted of more than twenty parallel paths. . . .We supposed it to be the road leading from the Pawnee Piqua village, on the Red River to Santa Fe" (James 1966 II: 94).

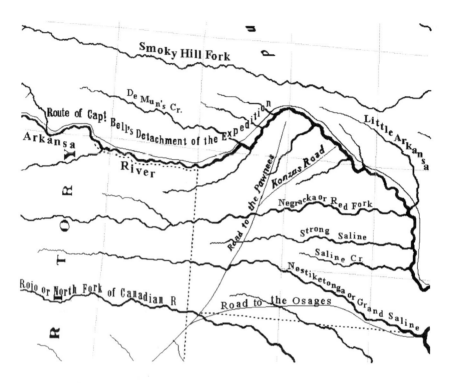

James map of the Long expedition. This section of the map shows the lower portion of the Pawnee Trail. The Konza crossing is probably the same ford of the Arkansas that is shown on the Miguel map (Figure 2). (Redrawn from a photocopy of the original.)

In 1845 another description was penned, this time by Lt. James W. Abert. His exploring party, sent down the Canadian by John Charles Frémont, came upon the trail a short distance west of Ute Creek:

> After a rough march of about five miles, we struck a faint trail, which we followed, and our scrutiny was rewarded by finding a piece of wood bearing evident marks of a knife.... It had no doubt been

fashioned to supply some defective piece of a wagon, or carreta, for the rude workmanship and other marks led us to infer that it was the work of Spanish "ciboleros," who are in the habit of making excursions into the eastern plains for the purpose of procuring supplies of buffalo meat, as well as of trading with the Indians. We drew another favorable inference from the rude fragment; which was, that we were on the most feasible road for descending the Canadian. . . .We crossed the rocky barrier and descended to the plain below, where was the trail on which the wagons or carts had passed. Although faint, it could be distinguished by the color of the grass which grew upon it (Abert 1970: 27).

He noted that he reached Ute Creek at what was called the "Spanish Crossing," marked by deep ruts. Downstream along the Canadian, the trail was marked by numerous broken axletrees and other gear (Abert 1970: 28).

Three days of travel down the Canadian River apparently brought the Mallets to an Indian trail that led north or northeast to the Pawnee country. At their usual rate of travel, three days would have taken them about 60 miles, putting them in Oldham County, Texas, about 36 miles from the present New Mexico line, in the vicinity of the mouth of Rita Blanca Creek. In 1845, Lieutenant Abert found an Indian trail that left the river just downstream from the mouth of this creek, where he had camped on September 7 (Abert 1970: 32). A few miles above the mouth of the Rita Blanca is Los Redos Creek, and by ascending that stream to its very head one comes within 5 miles of a string of playa lakes leading toward present Dumas. At the seventh playa lake, some 13 miles from the first, this possible route joins the Dodge City–Tascosa wagon road. In fact, it is a straight-line extension of the road, which turns south at this playa lake to run toward Tascosa. Although these facts do not prove that an Indian trail existed here, they certainly are suggestive.

The James map of the 1820 Long expedition does show a Pawnee trail in this general vicinity (James 1966). The route runs south and west from a crossing of the Arkansas River to the Canadian somewhere in the Texas panhandle. The Arkansas crossing is below Great Bend and is probably identical with both the Kansas crossing shown on the Nau map of Pike's expedition and the crossing shown on the Miguel map of 1602. The exact route between the Canadian and the Arkansas is very much open to question, as the map is very inaccurate in the region between these rivers. At the Canadian River end, the trail is placed roughly in the position of the Jones and Plummer wagon road, which diverged from the Dodge City–Tascosa road where Beaver, Oklahoma, now stands on the North Canadian (Beaver) River.

James probably got his information about this trail from the guide on Long's expedition, Joseph Bijeau, who had spent at least six years in the region (James 1966 II: 63). It was a bit beyond the point where this path leaves the river that Long and his men realized they had lost the Indian trail along the Canadian, three days after having come upon it (James 1966 II: 97). Three members of the Mallet party left the river after following it for three days to take an Indian trail northeast to Illinois. The similarity in days traveled is not a coincidence; both parties were on the same trail.

What is fascinating about the terse statement in the abstract is that the Mallet explorers were able to recognize that the intersecting trail would lead Bellecourt, Galien, and David back to the Pawnee country. One possible source of this knowledge would have been the Arikara guide, who might still have been with them and who would have known the trails from his time of captivity among the Comanches. This possibility is our only clue as to whether the Mallets were able to keep their bargain and obtain his freedom from the Spanish. The phrasing of the abstract, which says that the three men left their companions to "retake" the road of the Pawnees, certainly suggests that they knew the destination of this particular trail. The most likely source of that knowledge was the Arikara guide.

In 1741, Governor Bienville and the *ordonnateur*, Salmon, wrote that they had received word that these three men had arrived safely in Illinois. The document (if there was one) has not come to light, and there is no direct evidence regarding the route taken by the three men. They could have gone all the way north to the Pawnee villages in Nebraska, then east down the Platte and Missouri to Illinois. A more direct route would have taken them downstream when they reached the Smoky Hill River, along what was later called the Smoky Hill Trail, then downstream along the Kansas River, following Bourgmont's return route in 1724 (Norall 1988: 160–161).

Along the Canadian River, May 14–June 7, 1740

> The other four continued in their resolution to come here. The same day, they encountered eight Laitane men with whom they camped. On the 15th, continuing along the same river, they found a Laitane village where they said they saw a quantity of horses. They spent the night there. The Indians provided them a feast, and they traded horses for some knives and other trinkets. They continued to follow this river until the 22nd, and on that night they lost six horses. From the 22nd until the 30th, they kept at a distance from the river. That day, they encountered two men and three women of the Padokas to whom they offered their hand, but after a bit fear seized the Indians who abandoned the meat they had been carrying and fled with their wives, and it was not possible to make them return.
>
> On the 8th of June, the Canadians returned to the bank of the river which they followed until the 14th.

The Comanche village was more than two days' travel from where the three men headed north. If the latter spot was at the mouth of Rita Blanca Creek, then the village was in the vicinity of Alibates National Monument, a set of ancient quarries where the tribes of the region obtained material to make their chipped-stone implements. Tools of this material are found from the border pueblos of New Mexico to the Wichita villages in Kansas visited by Coronado in 1541. It is a spot where travelers were very apt to find native encampments.

Counting a day for the feasting and trading in the Comanche village, they would have covered about 120 miles before reaching the point where they quit the river and traveled at some distance from it. If the village were, say, at the mouth of Plum Creek, 110 miles would have brought them to a point where other travelers also left the river. At this location, in the vicinity of the Antelope Hills, there was a ford of the Canadian. Just south of the stream is a high divide that separates it from the Washita River. The James map shows a "road to Red River" heading away from the Canadian in this vicinity.

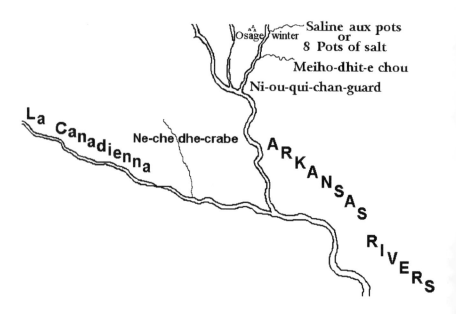

Detail of Lewis and Clark's 1804 map. This is a very early use of the modern name for the Canadian River. (Section of the original redrawn from Moulton [1983: Plate 6].)

This is surely the same trail that later travelers took up the Faux Washita (False Washita, to distinguish it from the Washita River of Texas). Albert Pike heard of this route before he headed west in 1831 (Pike 1967: 6). James R. Mead described a section of it in the northeastern corner of present Caddo County, Oklahoma, as follows: "The gulches originating in this sandstone divide in places only left room for a trail along the summit. This was constantly used by wild animals, and in those narrow passages the rock was worn a foot deep by the countless multitudes if hoofs which had passed along it in past ages" (Mead 1986: 207).

Other evidence for a trail on this divide includes a record of the Kiowa summer encampment on the divide near the head of North Elm Creek in the summer of 1867 (Mooney 1898: 319–320). Archaeological evidence comes in the form of a linear scatter of sites along the crest of the divide discovered by my colleague, David Hughes. David had told me of the finds in 1989, and I replied that they sounded like the kind of site associated with trails. I had marked them on my Oklahoma map, and they turned out to be on the trail when I traced the Mallets' return route in 1991.

Travel is much more difficult on the north side of the Canadian than on the south side because the Cross Timbers reach this far west only on the north. Washington Irving described the Timbers, dense stands of scrub oak, as "forests of cast iron" (1956: 125). In many spots the trees were so thick they had to be cleared with an axe even to make room for a horseman. The prairie that continued for a considerable distance south of the river must have been an inviting route for Native Americans as well as for the Mallets. Abert (1970: 57), who kept to the north bank in 1845, wondered at the absence of trails and Indian camps in a countryside that was so well supplied with game. He probably would have found plenty if he had kept to the south bank.

The four men left in the Mallet party remained away from the river for fifteen or sixteen days of travel. A glance at the map will show why. The Canadian River makes three enormous loops here, and those following the river would be led far out of their way. Once again, I have to marvel at how the Mallets knew this. Perhaps their Comanche hosts provided them with directions. Perhaps they simply were experienced enough at cross-country travel to realize that the divide would provide a more direct route.

Under questioning by his New Mexican captors in 1751, Pierre Mallet testified that when the water became deep enough for boats and their horses gave out, the explorers abandoned their animals and built canoes (Hackett 1931–46 III: 349). This statement suggests that, as the horses weakened, the Mallets' rate of travel dropped below the previous average of about 20 miles per day. Because we do not know how fast they were going, we cannot determine precisely where they returned to the river. Judging from their subsequent travel on the river, and looking at maps of the region, a likely spot is near Purcell, where old Fort Holmes was located. The divide narrows dramatically here, and the increasing density of the Cross Timbers on the south side of the Canadian would have made continued travel on horseback difficult.

Somewhere near where they returned to the river, they met some Padoucas. The little party of two men and three women was at the very northern limit of Apache territory; by this time, most members of this tribe seem to have moved south of the Red River to remove themselves from the danger of Comanche and Wichita attacks. That southward movement brought them into increasing conflict with the Spanish settlements in Texas, generating several decades of warfare with the Spanish around San Antonio (John 1975: 258–275). Indeed, heavy fighting in 1738 may have driven some back north.

After this encounter, the four men continued down the Canadian River, presumably at a fairly slow pace for six days. As we shall see, they probably reached the vicinity of the mouth of Little River in Hughes County, Oklahoma.

On the River, June 15–22, 1740

On the 15th, 16th, 17th, 18th and 19th, they camped and having carefully discussed the course of the river, they resolved to abandon the 18 horses they had and to make elm-bark canoes. They did this although they had but two knives among the four of them. At this point, they had come about 220 leagues by land from Santa Fe.

On the 20th, they embarked in two small canoes and made 6 leagues, as this river does not have a strong current. The 21st, they made the same distance. The 22nd, they saw two beautiful river mouths, which likely could be the Pecos and Mare Rivers, which they had crossed near Santa Fe. Finally, on the 24th, they were agreeably surprised to find themselves at the forks of the Arkansas River. They had made about 42 leagues by canoe. Below the forks, they found an encampment of Canadians who were hunting in order to make salted meat. Because they had nothing left save their arms and a little ammunition, they went hunting with the others and packed a pirogue with salted meat with which they returned to our post on the Arkansas and from there to New Orleans on   1741.

The Mallets estimated the distance from the spot where they launched the canoes to the Forks of the Arkansas at 42 leagues. We know from Pierre Mallet's 1751 description of their return route that they built canoes "as soon as the water became deep enough" (Hackett 1931–1946 III: 349). Such deepening would likely have occurred at or just below the mouth of a significant tributary, and the Little River is at about the right distance from the forks.

They built the canoes in the vicinity of the spot where Fabry de la Bruyère would build his first fortified camp in the winter of 1741–1742. He did so at a point that he estimated to be 42 leagues above the Forks of the Arkansas, precisely the figure given by the Mallets. As he was using boats to ascend the river and ran out of water at this point, there is every reason to believe he was very close to where the Mallets first found sufficient water while descending the river.

The Nau map of the Pike expedition purports to show this point but places it on the Red rather than the Canadian (Blaine 1979: 136). The map reads: "The Acadiens returning from Sta Fee in June 1740 left their horses

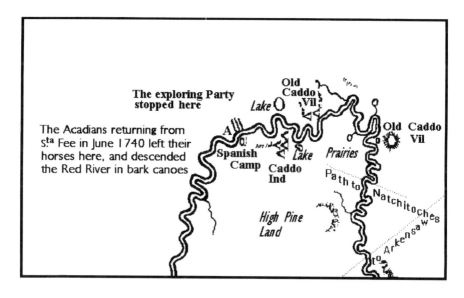

The Red River on the 1810 Pike-Nau map. This detail shows the incorrect placement of the Mallet camp on the Red as opposed to the Canadian River. (Redrawn from the original as published in Jackson [1966: Map 3].)

here and descended the Red River in bark canoes." The Mallets were not, of course, Acadians, as those people had not yet been driven from their homes in Nova Scotia. Fabry de la Bruyère apparently had made a map of the 1741–1742 expedition, and in 1806 it came into the hands of Gen. James Wilkinson, the man behind the Pike expedition (Blaine 1979: 156). He must have passed it on to either Pike or his cartographer, Antoine Nau, who inserted information from it into the Pike map. Interestingly, although he has Fabry's forts of 1741–1742 located correctly on the Canadian River, Nau drew the point where the Mallets built the canoes on the Red River rather than the Canadian. This might be taken as evidence that Wilkinson obtained other documents in addition to the Fabry map, for Fabry knew full well that he was ascending the same river the Mallets had floated down in 1740. The original Mallet journal, from which the surviving abstract was drawn, might have named the river of the descent the "Red River."

The two river mouths mentioned in the abstract must be Gaines Creek and Longtown Creek. The North Canadian also empties into the main stream in this vicinity, but as the Mallets thought that the two rivers might be the Pecos and the Gallinas, which they had crossed after leaving Santa Fe, and as both of those streams flowed to the southeast where the Mallets crossed them, the rivers in question must have come into the Canadian from the south. This gives us not only a clear indication of where they were on the 22nd but also an indication of their rate of travel, which increased to 8 leagues per day downstream from these rivers. Apparently the water from the two streams was enough to increase the current of the Canadian River significantly.

It is clear from the journal entry that the Forks of the Arkansas were familiar to at least some of these Canadians prior to 1739. At least one of the four, all of whom came from Illinois in 1739, had been up the Arkansas River to what is now eastern Oklahoma, presumably on hunting trips. It is likely that they knew some or all of the hunters they met just below the forks in 1740.

There is a minor error in the Margry version of the abstract at this point. He has the Mallets arriving at a *cabane*, or hut of hunters, rather than a *cabannage*, or encampment. The hunters came there to make salted meat to take downstream to the Louisiana colony. The development of this industry is traced by Wedel (1981: 33–49). It began in the context of fur trade with the Wichitas but expanded as the population of Louisiana grew and game there began to be hunted out. Bison meat, tallow, and bear grease all became part of early Louisiana cuisine (Wedel 1981: 38), and the trade centered at the Arkansas Post, an on-again, off-again camp at the mouth of the Arkansas River, made it one of the most profitable to which an officer could be assigned (Faye 1943: 708). Eventually, two Wichita villages on the Arkansas, the Deer Creek and Bryson-Paddock sites, became outposts for the hunting and processing of bison meat. These villages would figure prominently in the expedition of 1750.

The first Frenchmen at the Arkansas Post were six of Henri de Tonty's men, whom he left in 1686. At first it was a commercial operation, but military outposts and missions came and went at the same spot. In 1720, John Law founded a settlement and filled it with German colonists, and the Louisiana officials created a little military post for their defense shortly thereafter (Wedel 1981: 37). In 1725 the German farmers moved closer to New Orleans, and the military post was abandoned for a while, leaving only a handful of traders at the spot. A census taken in 1749 revealed a population composed of three groups (Loudon Papers, 200). First there were the soldiers, some of whom had families. Civilian habitants and their families farmed in the bottoms nearby and raised a little livestock. Finally, there were the hunters and traders, the latter including both bourgeois and their engagés. Both the hunters and the traders were often away from the post, and there was no clear distinction among them. A hunter might trade a few goods with the Indians when the opportunity offered itself, and the traders all knew how to support themselves by hunting.

Faye describes the Arkansas Post as the Mallets would have seen it. It would have looked fairly new, as the commandant had moved it a few years previously to a new location in order to reduce the distance to the mouth of the Arkansas River. It was on the "right bank between the forks and the river mouth, perhaps five English miles or so below the contemporary White River cutoff and about twice that distance from the Mississippi" (Faye 1943: 681). Because it was located on ground that flooded regularly, it was surrounded by a levee that enclosed an area one arpent (three-quarters of an acre) in extent. It probably contained buildings similar to those in its previous location: a log house for the commandant, a powder magazine, also of logs, and a jail and barracks of vertical posts, all with bark roofs (Faye 1943: 674).

To this little post the Mallets came sometime in the summer of 1740. We have no clue regarding how long they remained at the hunting grounds in Oklahoma or how long it took them and their new companions to float down the river to the Arkansas Post. Here they stayed until spring, apparently in no particular hurry to report their discoveries to New Orleans.

8.

THE AFTERMATH, 1741–1756

When the Mallets returned to New Orleans, they carried with them documentation of their success in reaching Santa Fe. It took the form of a letter written for them by Juan Paëz Hurtado, who had been their host in Santa Fe. It was important for the hints it contained that at least this Spanish official would welcome trade with the French. The letter was published in French by Margry (1876–1886 VI: 462–464) and translated by Folmer (1939a: 171). A new translation appears in Appendix A.

In it, Hurtado certifies that eight Frenchmen, including the Mallets, arrived in Santa Fe. He describes how he took them into his home and asserts that they conducted themselves like good Christians the whole time. He mentions that they waited nine months for word from the viceroy but does not describe what that message said. Instead, he advises that the next time they come to Santa Fe the Mallets carry a passport and official permission to open trade. He gives no indication that the viceroy recommended that the Mallets stay in Santa Fe. The viceroy's response must not have been

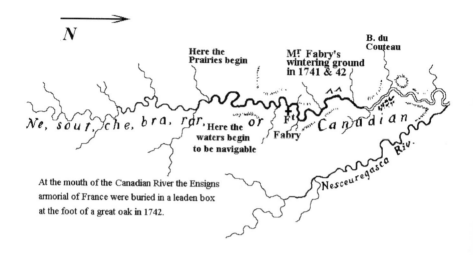

The Canadian River on the 1810 Pike-Nau map. This section depicts the river with data derived from the Fabry expedition. (Redrawn and reoriented from the original as published in Jackson [1966: Map 3].)

worded very strongly, as it would otherwise be unthinkable for the lieutenant governor to suggest (presumably with the governor's blessing) that the Mallets try again.

The other document the Mallets carried with them was a letter from a priest in Santa Fe to one in New Orleans. Margry (1876–1886 VI: 464–465) published the letter in French, and Folmer (1939a: 172) gives a translation. I have retranslated it in Appendix A.

This letter is the only document dating to 1741 that even hints at the presence of Jean-Baptiste Alarie. It says that nine Frenchmen came to Santa Fe but lists only the eight that are common to Bienville's abstract of the journal and Hurtado's letter. To anyone reading the other documents, the mention of nine men would seem like a mistake. One wonders if it was the priest's way of avoiding a lie. In any event, the priest wrote not to recommend the Mallets but to ask for trade goods on credit. He mentioned the silver mines of Chihuahua and said that although he was paid in silver, he had nothing to spend it on in New Mexico. He sent a list of the goods he wanted but, unfortunately, it has not survived.

Like Hurtado's certificate, the letter gives the impression that New Mexicans were anxious for trade with the French. Indeed, this may have been true for the man in the street as well as those high in the provincial hierarchy. Unfortunately for the next Frenchmen to reach Santa Fe, this attitude did not extend as far as Mexico City or Madrid.

The immediate response in New Orleans to the arrival of the Mallets and their two companions, Philippe Robitaille and Michel Beleau, was one of surprise and excitement. In a letter to the crown, Governor Bienville and the *commissaire ordonnateur*, Salmon, briefly summarized previous efforts to reach Santa Fe and reported the anticipated attempt by Fabry de la Bruyère to repeat the exploit. They enclosed the documents the Mallets had carried from Santa Fe. The letter was published by Margry (1876–1886 VI: 466–468), and most of it was translated by Folmer (1939a: 161–162). A new translation is offered in Appendix A.

The fact that the route to Santa Fe lay up the Arkansas River was new and exciting information, as indicated by the underlining in the original (beginning with *that*): "It appears, . . . that a branch of the latter river flows from the Spanish territories and that one may ascend it to within about forty leagues of Santa Fe." The speed with which colonial officials moved to follow up on the discovery reinforces this conclusion; the Mallets arrived in March, and Fabry had his marching orders by June 1.

The letter adds one fact that is omitted from the surviving copy of the abstract of the Mallet journal: the date of the Mallets' arrival in New Orleans. The letter was sent in April, and it reported that the Mallets arrived in March. The detailed portion of the abstract of their journal ended on June 24, 1740, with their arrival at the Forks of the Arkansas. From that point, all it says is that they hunted with some Canadians they found below the forks and loaded a pirogue with salted meat, which they took to the Arkansas Post and from there to New Orleans. The date of their arrival was left blank: "et de la a la nouvelle orleans le _____ 1741." The letter indicates that it had taken them nine months to go from the Forks of the Arkansas to the capital! There is no explanation in any of the documents for this delay.

Within a month of their arrival, André Fabry de la Bruyère, *ecrivain ordinaire* (a clerk or notary) of the navy, volunteered to lead an expedition to follow up on the Mallet discovery (Blaine 1979: 138–139). The letter from Bienville and Salmon to the minister of the navy indicates that Fabry had experience in previous explorations in Louisiana and that he had the qualifications to map the route. In spite of their confidence in him, however, and in spite of the presence of the Mallets and two of their companions, the expedition failed.

Records of the attempt are incomplete. Fabry de la Bruyère apparently wrote a complete account, but, as is the case with the Mallet expedition, all that have survived are excerpts. We do have, however, a copy of the very complete set of orders issued to him by the government. They were published by Margry (1876–1886 VI: 468–471) and are translated in Appendix B.

The orders specified that his party would include himself, one sergeant, one corporal, five soldiers, and seven voyageurs. They instructed him to ascend by the route taken by the Mallets, bypass Santa Fe, and explore toward the western coast of North America. During the expedition he was to make observations appropriate to geography, botany, and the nature of the landscape so that colonial officials would be well informed upon his return. He was told that if he should encounter new Indian nations, he should not only enter into alliances with them on the part of the French colony but also make peace with them on behalf of Spain.

The latter instruction was very likely included in the orders to impress the Spaniards he was actually supposed to visit. But the wording implied that any such visit would be accidental, the result of some emergency. Thus, when he did arrive in Spanish territory, the officials there would have no concrete proof that the government of Louisiana was condoning illegal commerce. The wording was a model of diplomatic tact.

We also have a copy of the letter Fabry was to give to the governor of New Mexico. It was printed by Margry (1876–1886 VI: 471–472) and is translated in Appendix B. It, too, reads as though any direct contact between Fabry and the Spanish would be accidental, and it adds that French officials would return any Spanish deserters to Spanish territory in the hope that such action would be reciprocated. French officialdom had its backside well covered.

The expedition set out from New Orleans in September 1741. It included André Fabry de la Bruyère, commanding, a sergeant named Champart, corporal Alexis Grappe, seven soldiers, and a black man named Pantalon. Accompanying them were the Mallet brothers, Philippe Robitaille, Michael Beleau (La Rose), "their associates," and some hired hands.

Fabry's fragmentary account (Appendix B) begins with the party's arrival at the Arkansas Post, where he had two cattle slaughtered and the meat salted for provisions until they should reach the Forks of the Arkansas. He also purchased five pirogues from the natives. Thus provided, they launched themselves onto the waters of the Arkansas River on October 31, 1741.

After thirty-five days of rowing and poling their boats, they came within 4 leagues of the Forks of the Arkansas. Fabry found this point to be only 145 leagues from the Arkansas Post rather than the 200 or so leagues that hunters had previously claimed. Two days later, on the 7th of December, they reached the forks and entered the stream on their left, now known as the Canadian. They were averaging about 11 miles per day, a good rate considering that they were fighting the current.

Fabry de la Bruyère named the stream they entered for his patron saint, St. André, a clever way of naming it for himself. The name remained in use for a while (Félipe de Sandoval used it in 1750), but according to Faye (1943: 695) the inhabitants of the Arkansas Post soon began to call it the River of the Canadians, a fitting memorial to the Mallets. Unfortunately, Faye does not cite any of the many documents he reviewed to prove his point. Roper (1988) offers a different hypothesis for the origin of the name: the *cañadas* of the sheepherders of the upper Canadian. (Cañadas were routes along which shepherds might legally drive their flocks even though they did not own the land.) Unfortunately for her case, the river appears on the Lewis and Clark map of 1804 as "La Canadienna" (Moulton 1983: Plate 6). The map was based on information collected in St. Louis prior to the expedition's departure, and the French identity of many of the informants is indicated in the spelling not only of this name but of many other place-names as well. Because the name appears at the eastern end of the river and because the map was drawn long before the spread of *pastores* to the Canadian, Faye's interpretation, rather than Roper's, seems correct.

There was enough water in the river to enable Fabry's company to continue an estimated 17 leagues farther, when they reached the mouths of two rivers. These were, apparently, the North Canadian and Gaines Creek (Blaine 1979: 143–144). The waters that these two streams contributed to the Canadian had provided the adequate flow downstream, but upstream the Canadian was temporarily too shallow for the boats. They waited four days, and a storm raised the water enough to allow them to travel for another four days, until Christmas 1741.

Once again they were forced to camp, until January 10 of 1742. Even after the stream rose again, they were bothered repeatedly by shallow water that hindered their progress. By the 15th, they had traveled only 115 miles from the forks, at the maddeningly slow rate of 3 miles per day. On the 15th, they were stranded again, this time at the mouth of Little River in present-day Hughes County, Oklahoma. Their camp was on the left (north) bank, downstream from the mouth of Little River.

Nine days later, fate offered them a way out of their dilemma. A party of 35 Osage warriors visited their camp. The Osages were on an expedition against the Mentos (Wichitas). The Osage war party was on a trail (Blaine 1979: 146–147; Burns 1985: 136) that ran from their villages to the mouth of the Neosho River in northeastern Oklahoma, then to the North Canadian near its mouth, and then along the north bank of the Canadian, crossing the Little River at its mouth. From there, in the vicinity of Fabry's camp, it crossed the Canadian a short distance upstream and ran along the south bank to the vicinity of present Allen. From there it split into two branches. One ran south-southwest to the lower Washita River near present Tishomingo and on to the Red River; the other led southeast along Muddy Boggy Creek, also to the Red.

The Osages told Fabry they had six French traders living in their villages. They discussed the good relationship that existed between the French and the Osages, and the Osage chief gave assurances that his men would offer the Frenchmen no harm. Fabry gave the Osages a gift of powder, balls, and other items. They were not satisfied with this and asked for guns, but Fabry told them they would not get anything more. The Osage chiefs sulked at first, but after consulting among themselves they invited Fabry and Philippe Robitaille, who had served as interpreter, to a feast. The Osages left that morning, promising that if they succeeded in their raid, they would return in six or seven days, bringing slaves.

Some of them returned on the 3rd of February with seven horses, a mule, and two scalps. In the meantime, Fabry had his men build a log enclosure to protect the French from a surprise attack should the Indians return in larger numbers. He told the Osages that he had fortified his position against the Panis Noirs (more Wichitas), who were lurking in the vicinity. The Osages, however, worried that the French expedition was going in search of Panis and Padoucas to create an alliance with them and to trade them guns. Fabry reassured them, saying he and his companions were seeking the "Frenchmen of the West," their brothers of old.

When the Osages asked if they were going to ascend the river, Fabry answered that they would, thinking it would be useless to try to keep the goal a mystery to them, as the Osages probably knew about the Mallets' first expedition. The chief replied that he did not think it possible to take boats up the river, as he had been there more than ten times and had always found it without water.

Fabry, as a result, conferred with his four Canadians and with Sergeant Champart in order to decide whether they should continue upstream or abandon the river route. They said that if the spring flood failed to occur, Fabry would find himself in an embarrassing situation. All were convinced that if the weather did not change, it would be impossible to ascend the river, and they concluded that they should trade for horses with the Osages. The horses could carry most of their goods, lightening the boats; assigning some men to drive the horses would lighten the pirogues even further so that they could be taken up the river even in shallow water.

The Osages had offered to trade the horses previously, but Fabry, who "was of that tribe that made the name of notary proverbial in Louisiana" (Faye 1943: 694), had refused. He had done so even when some of the voyageurs offered to pay for them out of their own pockets. Now, when Fabry approached the Osages again, they had changed their minds; the Osage chief talked to his warriors, but they refused to part with the animals.

In a renewed conference, the Canadians proposed that they follow the trail taken by the Osages to try to get horses from the Mentos, who could not be too far away. Fabry refused. His orders were to ascend the river as far as possible, and because it was only early February, it would be premature to quit the river now. He would wait until Easter for rain, and this would give them time to find some horses.

Fabry wrote to French traders among the Missouris to have them trade for horses for him. He gave the letter to the Osages, who said they could make the journey in seven nights. He wrote that he had the means to pay for the horses and that if some of the traders would bring him the horses before the end of February he would pay 200 francs for their trouble.

When rain finally did come on February 8th, the river proceeded to freeze over. By the end of the month, the river was still too low for easy travel, and no horses had appeared. The little party hauled the boats upstream to a point where they could find bison to hunt. Over the first week in March, they managed only 20 miles or so, and it was not until the 16th that they reached the spot where they had agreed to build their second little fort, on the right (south) bank upstream from the mouth of Sandy Creek.

In the meantime, the Canadians in the group again urged Fabry to let some of them go in search of the Mentos. This time Fabry agreed, and on the 13th Paul Mallet, Philippe Robitaille, Sergeant Champart, and a hired hand called La Grandeur set out on this errand. Fabry gave them a gift for the village chief and a message for him to bring his headmen to a council with Fabry, even suggesting that he hold two of the Frenchmen hostage if he feared the strangers' intentions.

Mallet asked for ten days, and Fabry said he would expect him back in twelve. Fabry told them to go four or five days to the southeast, and, if they did not strike the trail, to head from there to the southwest. The group returned on the 19th, reporting that on the 15th they had seen three signal fires close at hand that they thought must be at the village. In the end, however, they returned before finding the Mentos in order not to cause concern by not making their deadline. Mallet was sure he could find the village if given a second chance.

On the 21st he and his group set out again, with La Rose (Michael Beleau) replacing Philippe Robitaille. While they were gone, the river continued to rise and fall without ever providing enough water for Fabry's party to ascend it. Mallet returned on the 31st with neither horses nor Indians. He reported that when he neared the spot where he had seen the fires, he saw some behind him at no great distance, but he was unable to find the source. He ended up marching a great distance and going without food without finding anything except abandoned villages.

Apparently, the Mentos had retreated from their former location in the face of the Osage attacks and, taking the Frenchmen for another war party, had lit signal fires to warn their comrades. The locations of their villages are not known today. In fact, they are not even discussed in a work that purports to cover these documents (Bell, Jelks and Newcombe 1974: 246–274).

Fabry once again counseled with the four Canadians and the sergeant about what was to be done. Pierre Mallet still held out hope for ascending the river in May, when the elms bloomed, as there would be water enough then. He suggested making canoes from elm bark as the four Canadians had done the previous year. Paul Mallet proposed that they try to obtain horses among the Panis Noirs. (Some maps of the period indicated a place labeled *paniasas* on what appears to be the Neosho River in southern Kansas. Because *paniasas* can be rendered *Panis Noirs* in French, Paul Mallet may have had this destination in mind.) Robitaille and Beleau said they were willing to go either by water or by land, but Sergeant Champart argued that if they had to go by land and on foot, his men could carry only their guns and a few provisions.

Fabry once again found fault with every suggestion made by the more experienced frontiersmen. He was unwilling to wait until May to make canoes because either there would be enough water for the pirogues or they would have to haul both the canoes and the pirogues. He seemed unable to grasp the point that the canoes would be lighter than the pirogues and that dividing the load among more vessels would give all of them a shallower draft. In any case, he was not willing to wait that long.

He also was unwilling to send Paul Mallet to seek the Panis Noirs. If the younger Mallet had not been able to find the Mentos, what chance did he have of locating the Panis Noirs, who were much farther away? Finally, he was unwilling to march overland because they would have to abandon most of the goods they carried in order to do so. Furthermore, he argued, there was no guarantee that they would encounter Indians from whom they could get horses, and soon it would be too hot for the men to march.

Fabry instead proposed to go where he was sure of finding horses: back to the Arkansas Post, where their journey had started. He would try first among the Quapaws, and if they did not have enough he would ask for some from the government herd at the post. With these animals, he would carry trade goods to the Red River and procure still more horses from the Caddos, who were known to have plenty. Heading north from there, he would return to the Canadian and the present camp, which should be no more than about 200 miles from the Caddos.

Fabry took with him Philippe Robitaille, Michel Beleau, Sergeant Champart, La Grandeur, and Pantalon. He left the Mallets in camp as hunters. He left written instructions for the men, exhorting them to keep the peace among themselves and to keep their guard up against Indians. They were to wait for him until the 1st of August. If he had not returned by that time, the corporal was to allow the Mallets to continue the journey if they wished. The soldiers, however, were to return to New Orleans. Some of his own belongings, in case of his death, were to be divided among the Mallets, Robitaille, and Beleau; Corporal Grappe would take the rest to New Orleans.

For their part, the Mallets asserted that they would never go before Governor Bienville again if the expedition failed to reach Santa Fe. They were going, come hell or low water.

Fabry's trip was a comedy of errors. He left for the Arkansas Post on April 4th, but low water so hindered his progress that he had to return to the camp on the 6th to wait for it to rise. He set out once again to join the rest of his party, which he had left downstream. Taking a second boat so that the load could be divided among the two, he made the Forks of the Arkansas on the 12th.

He arrived at the Arkansas Post on the 26th. Though unable to obtain any horses from the Quapaws, he did manage to get five government steeds. He then took his party in search of the Caddos, but his timing was bad. When he set out on the 1st of May, he encountered the spring rains that the Mallets had predicted. High water forced him to return to the Arkansas Post until the 21st. Meanwhile, the men he had left on the Canadian, including the Mallets, were forced by their orders merely to watch the rising waters rather than use them to get to their destination. They reported that it had been high enough for travel for 40 days. Frustration abounded.

When Fabry's party did reach the south bank of the Red River, between the territories of the Yatasses and the Caddos, the guides could not find a trace of the trail. When Fabry reprimanded them, they grew surly. Finally, after having wasted forty-five days, Fabry was forced once again to return to the Arkansas Post. Three of the five horses had given out, forcing him to cache his own merchandise so that he could continue to carry the government's, and he lost nine trade guns and seven axes. Still, he continued to trade with the Indians, "always with great sweetness and liberality," according to his own description. Two days later he sent out Champart and Robitaille with two hired guides and three other volunteers. The guides promised to deliver them to the Caddo village in eight days, but the sergeant fell ill, and they did not reach the Caddos until July 25th, too late to reach the party still stranded on the Canadian River by August 1st.

Nevertheless, their guides led them from the Caddo village to the Forks of the Arkansas. When they arrived at the Canadian, they separated, Champart heading upstream and Robitaille downstream. Ten leagues below the forks, Robitaille came to the camp of a hunter called Brin-d'amour, where he found Corporal Grappe and the soldiers. Robitaille told them that the horse-supply problem had been solved and that Fabry would soon be there. They therefore hired Brin-d'amour to hunt for them and returned to the fort.

When August 1st had come, however, the Mallets had set out on their own, as permitted by Fabry's orders. They took with them some of the government supplies to give to an unnamed tribe (presumably the Comanches) they had met the year before. With these they intended to obtain the horses they needed. They and a companion named Marcelle made an inventory of what they took and gave it to the corporal. They cached the rest of the goods intended for New Mexico at a distance from the camp and departed.

They never arrived in Santa Fe. Documents from the 1750 expedition indicate that they, too, fell ill, and that they lost the goods they were carrying in the river. Fabry's account mentions that Pierre Mallet was ill even before Fabry headed back down the Arkansas River. The reference to losing the merchandise in the river may derive from the fact that Fabry, with the help of a Canadian hunter, found and emptied the Mallets' cache. When they returned from the Comanches, the Mallets would have found only an empty hole in the river bank, and if there had been any rain in the meantime, they might have thought their cache of goods had been washed away by the river. Judging from the 1750 documents, they made this discovery eighteen months after the expedition began, or six months after Fabry emptied the cache, giving them enough time to have gone to the Comanches and back.

And so the great expectations of 1741 gave way to discord and failure. The Mallets wrote to Governor Bienville complaining about Fabry, saying that he would not trade for horses with the Osages nor let them trade with the Panis in Spanish territory. They added that he would not approve of their making canoes of elm bark and, most damning, that for forty days during his absence the water was high enough to proceed.

When Fabry arrived back at the camp, the news of the departure of the Mallets proved to be the last straw. He found plenty of reasons to turn his back on Santa Fe and head for home. On September 4th he did so, and for the first time he managed a real piece of exploration. Rather than returning down the Canadian, he struck south for the Red River, which turned out to be only 20 leagues distant. Proceeding downstream, he came upon Tawakoni and Kitsai villages after three days of travel. These were bands of Wichitas, possibly the Mentos that Paul Mallet had failed to find (cf. Bell, Jelks and Newcombe 1974: 246–274).

Fabry's other contribution was a map that has not yet come to light. Nevertheless, it had an impact. It came into the hands of Gen, James Wilkinson after the Louisiana Purchase, and eventually he gave it either to Zebulon Pike or Antoine Nau, who used it when he compiled his very influential map of the Pike expedition. There is every likelihood that many of the details of the Canadian River on this map are derived from Fabry's chart. The French place-names along it, such as the Trempeuse River, Gros Mern, and Bayou de Couteau, may have been given during this expedition. The two Osage names,

Nesceuregasca for Gaines Creek and *Ne-sour-che-bra-ra* for the Canadian, are later additions.

English captions indicate that Fabry buried the coat of arms of France in a lead box when he laid claim to the Canadian drainage for France. Another incorrectly places the return route of the Mallets along the Red River rather than the Canadian. This information cannot have come from the Fabry map and must derive from a separate written source. Could General Wilkinson have laid his hands on a copy of the Mallet journal? Perhaps this was its fate, as it is not present in the Louisiana archives.

Back in New Orleans in 1742, the *ordonnateur* found that the expedition had cost 22,600 livres and suggested that Fabry should repay 2,026 that he had spent without proper authority (Margry 1876–86 VI: 488–492). Fortunately for Fabry, the minister of the navy saw it differently:

> Although the expedition that the Sieur Fabry undertook in order to penetrate to New Mexico by the overland route did not succeed, it has nevertheless not seemed just to make him liable for any of the disbursements that he made on this account; and the King's intention is that Monsieur Salmon shall provide for the suspended payment of the 2,026 livres that remain to be accounted for. It would be unnecessary, moreover, to inquire the reasons that caused this expedition to fail, but still it seems that the Sieur Fabry's journal will be of value to those who will wish to undertake another such expedition. Since the Canadians with whom he was associated have decided to make a new journey, it is to be hoped that it may not be without success, and I expect you to inform me as to what may be the outcome of it. In addition I find occasion to trust that no disbursement in this direction will be made on the account of His Majesty, who certainly would not approve that any disbursement of any sort should be made without his order" (Faye 1943: 694).

The Mallets, it appears, were already planning another attempt.

The World Stage

England and Spain went to war in 1739 over the issue of the Austrian succession. France entered the conflict in 1744, and English superiority at sea quickly devastated the colonial economy in Louisiana. Few ships made it through with supplies, and the goods necessary for the Indian trade were in very short supply (Wedel 1981: 41–42). The alliance between France and Spain did generate some seaborne trade between the American colonies of the two powers (Lemieux 1990: 31), but with the end of the war in 1748, Spain returned to its usual policy of refusing such exchanges (Faye 1943: 699). Both the opportunity for trade through Indian-dominated territory and the need for a new means of access to the Spanish dominions resulted. The minister of the navy wrote to the new governor, Vaudreuil, in 1750, suggesting that he "favor the trade" with the Spanish by whatever means came to hand (Faye 1943: 699).

The new governor had replaced Bienville in 1743. A native of Canada, Pierre-François Rigaud, the Marquis de Vaudreuil, was another experienced frontier hand. Despite the hardships of the wartime economy, he managed to keep the colony afloat. A firm believer in nepotism, he obtained promotions for a young relative, Louis-Xavier-Martin de Lino de Chalmette, whom he appointed in 1748 to command the Arkansas Post.

The military side of the post was supposed to contain the officer, twenty men, and an interpreter (Faye 1943: 682), but shortly after de Lino's arrival the actual number of troops was twelve. By 1750 it was eight (Hackett 1931–46 III: 320–324). The civilian side of the operation was stronger. Seven families lived at the post in 1749, counting that of the commander. These habitant families comprised fifteen adults, sixteen children, and fourteen black slaves, and they owned three horses, twenty-nine oxen, sixty cows, and twenty-seven pigs. Among them was the family of Paul Mallet, who had a wife, three small daughters, one slave, one ox, and one cow, but no pigs (Faye 1943: 695).

His older brother, Pierre, was not at the post in 1748. He, too, had married and started a family. His wife's name was Marie Louise Dupre (Woods and Nolan 1987: 93). They had two sons, Pierre and Antoine. The date of Pierre's birth was not recorded, but he was baptized on May 10, 1747. He must have been at least a year old, for his younger brother was born only five days later. The latter was baptized on May 19, only a day after the burial of his mother, who died in childbirth. Spanish documents (Hackett 1941 III: 346) indicate that by 1750 Pierre Mallet's residence was in New Orleans and that he was a trader who traveled regularly. Some of his trips took him to the Arkansas Post, the census of which did not credit him with either wife or family. Instead, it described him as a voyageur, a bourgeois who had two engagés on his payroll (Loudon Papers 200).

As such, he was part of the third population at the post, the hunters and Indian traders. Among them were thirty-six voyageurs and some forty-eight engagés. The census does not list families for any of them, even though we know from Spanish documents that at least one was married. Ten bourgeois and 25 engagés were absent from the post against de Lino's orders when he made his count. The absent bourgeois were Brin-d'amour, Pertuy, Michel Lalemant, Bourg, Gagnete, Jofrellon, Boye, Des Catteaux, Bontemps, and Pierre Mallet. Brin-d'amour is the hunter who camped below the forks in the 1741–1742 misadventure. Jofrellon (consistently spelled Jofrion by Mallet, who signed for him in the Spanish documents) and Boye (who signed himself Jean-Baptiste Boiser) would end up as Pierre Mallet's companions in New Mexico in 1750.

Two important things had happened as the war with England wound down. One was the resupply of the colony, which made a renewal of the Indian trade possible. Once again, the French traders had items to exchange for the pelts, meat, and bear fat offered by the Indians.

The other was an alliance between the Wichita bands and the Comanches. Precisely when this bond came into existence is not known, but a great deal of misinformation has been written about the pact. Wedel (1981: 42–44) provides both a succinct summary of the literature and a reasonable interpretation of the documentary evidence. The two tribes cemented their alliance sometime in the mid–1740s, perhaps as a result of the Spanish edict of 1746 prohibiting trade between any inhabitant of New Mexico and the Comanches. Even without this impetus, both groups shared a common enemy: the Apaches (i.e., the Padoucas encountered by the Mallets east of the Comanches and west of Wichita territory). Thus, Governor Thomás Vélez Cachupín of New Mexico wrote of the "Cumanches and the Jumanes, whom the French call Panipiques. They are friends and allies, and carry on a cruel war against the Carlanes and others whom I mention [Palomas, Chilpaines, Pelones, Natagées, and Faraones]" (translated in Hackett 1931–46 III: 325).

The accord allowed the freshly resupplied French traders from the Arkansas Post to penetrate farther west than ever before. From the Wichita villages on the Arkansas River, they were able to head up both the Arkansas and the Canadian deep into the High Plains. Between 1740 and 1748, only one Frenchman had entered the New Mexican colony. He was one Santiago Velo (Jacques Beleau), who reached Pecos Pueblo in 1744. He was interrogated by Governor Codallos y Raball and testified that he had served as a soldier in Illinois (SANM I, no. 1328; SANM II, no. 456). His name resembles that of a member of the 1739 expedition. The Michel Beleau of 1739 was born in Canada, whereas the Jacques Beleau of 1744 was born in Tours, France; thus, it is not likely that they were close relatives.

The lack of Frenchmen on the borders of New Mexico did not last much beyond the end of the war. Early in 1748, Jicarilla visitors told Fray Antonio, the missionary at Taos, that thirty-three Frenchmen had come to their village to trade and that thirty-one had returned east. In 1749, three Frenchmen reached Taos in company with Comanches, and soon two more showed up in the company of a Spaniard. Then, in 1750, four more Frenchmen arrived, this time at Pecos. One of them was Pierre Mallet.

Sometime after he had been reported absent without permission from the Arkansas Post in 1749, Pierre Mallet returned. What he had to tell Ensign de Lino must have excited the commandant, for in the spring of 1750 de Lino accompanied Mallet to New Orleans, introducing him to the new governor (ANC C13A, 34: 315v; ANC C13A, 35: 94, 95v). Mallet discussed with them his previous trip to Santa Fe and some of his more recent activities, declaring that men currently out in the western country owed him money and that he expected to find them either on the plains or in New Mexico. These must have been some of the Frenchmen who arrived in New Mexico in 1749.

The governor had the orders from the ministry to open trade with the Spanish by whatever means he could find, and de Lino had delivered the means to him in the form of Pierre Mallet. The *ordonnateur*, Honoré Michel, agreed that such an expedition was permissible as long as no government funds were involved. Before the ordonnateur could question him, Pierre Mallet was gone, headed to Santa Fe with a supply of trade goods.

Because Mallet had left so abruptly, Michel suspected that the governor had underwritten the expedition for private profit. He complained to the minister of the navy, Rouillé de Jouy, who in turn sent Vaudreuil a stinging rebuke (ANC B, 91: 405–405v). In his reply to the minister (ANC C13A, 35: 94–96v), Vaudreuil issued a partial denial. However, Faye (1943: 700) takes what is *not* said in this letter as a tacit admission that Vaudreuil and/or his family were involved in underwriting Mallet's expedition. Vaudreuil did say that he had given Mallet permission to go to Santa Fe but denied that de Lino had invested in the expedition. Documents at the Spanish end suggested that two New Orleans merchants, Msrs. Duran (Durant?) and Fuiye (Fouille or Fuillet?) might have funded Mallet (Hackett 1931–46: 335). They also indicated that Mallet took few trade goods with him. Ordonnateur Michel may have been mistaken.

But whoever had underwritten the expenses, Pierre Mallet was under way once again.

The seed planted by the Mallets in 1739 was fed by the Comanche-Wichita alliance of circa 1746–1747. The brothers did not fail to nurture it; many of the men who wandered into Santa Fe traced their interest in making the trip directly to the Mallets. The first of these arrived in the spring of 1749, when Louis Febré, Pierre Satren, and Joseph-Michel Raballo showed up in Taos in the company of some Comanches. Their testimony has been translated by Hackett (1931–46 III:299–308) and Wedel (1981: 68–72). They seem to have been typical frontiersmen. Satren was a native of Quebec, a carpenter, forty-two years old and unmarried. He had been a soldier at the Arkansas Post but had deserted within fifteen days of his arrival.

Febré said he was born in New Orleans, and Faye (1943: 697) suggests he might have been a son of a widow LeFebre in New Orleans. He was unmarried and twenty-nine years old, a barber/surgeon by trade. He had served in New Orleans but had deserted and made his way to Michilimacinac and from there to Illinois (which the French sometimes rendered as *Ile Noir* and which is translated in the Spanish document as *la Ysla Negra*).

Raballo testified that he was a native of Fort des Chartres and a carpenter by trade. Twenty-four years old, he had deserted from Fort de Chartres and had made his way to the Arkansas Post, from which he had left with the others for Santa Fe. All three testified that they had left with the intent of going to Santa Fe. Close examination of Satren revealed that he had learned of New Mexico from "other Frenchmen who had been there and returned." The records also mention a Spaniard named Manuel who was married and living in New Orleans who had urged two of them to make the trip.

From the Arkansas Post, the three men had gone upriver to some Wichita villages, which Mildred Wedel (1981) has identified as the Deer Creek and Bryson-Paddock sites in northern Oklahoma. Presumably, Pierre Mallet was referring to these villages when he told Governor Vaudreuil that some men who owed him money had left the Arkansas Post two or three years previously

(1747–1748) and that he thought he would find them on the Oachita River among some Pani Indians. The de Beauvilliers map of 1720 that shows the results of La Harpe's 1719 expedition depicts a River of the Oachitas between the Red River and the Arkansas. Apparently, this is the Canadian River, with the name *Oachitas* reflecting the fact that Wichitas lived on it. The Pani Indians who lived there were Wichitas, and Pierre Mallet would have called them Panis Noirs. Perhaps Governor Vaudreuil had a copy of the map at hand during his discussions with Mallet.

It is also possible that Mallet was referring to the modern Washita River of western Oklahoma, known in the nineteenth century as the Faux Washita to distinguish it from the Washita River of Texas. Review of contemporary documents leaves the impression that there could have been some Wichita settlements on this river in this time period, but there is no clear documentation of any.

The alliance between the Wichitas and Comanches allowed Satren and his companions, led by Wichita guides, to go 150 leagues or so from the Deer Creek and Bryson-Paddock villages to some Comanche camps. They stayed among the Comanche for two months, where they saw the effects of the Wichita-Comanche trade, including five fusils but no powder or balls. From these camps, Comanches took them to Taos.

No details of the route between the Arkansas River villages and Taos are given in any of the documents. A trail used in later years by the Osages would have been one possible route. It crossed the Arkansas at the mouth of Beaver Creek. La Flesche (1932: 112) documents two trails that led to this point, although he misnames the river. From there the trail led up the north side of the Salt Fork of the Arkansas (Mead 1896: 91) and across to the rock-salt source on the Cimarron River (Sibley 1927: 218). One day's journey upstream from this point would have brought them to the spot at which the Mallets reached the Cimarron in 1739. Another possible route would have taken them a day's journey up the Arkansas River to the Osage Trail at present

Oxford, Kansas, and then west on what was later the Overland Branch of the Santa Fe Trail.

In 1750 two other Frenchmen and a Spaniard also reached Taos. The Spaniard, Félipe de Sandoval, had been through a series of adventures extraordinary even for the times (Hackett 1931–46 III: 320–324; Wedel 1981: 72–74). A native of the town of El Puerto de Santa María in Spain, Sandoval had sailed for the New World in 1742, but his ship was seized by an English privateer. He was a prisoner in Jamaica for two years before he escaped on a French ship. He came to Mobile, and from there he worked his way to New Orleans. He was in Louisiana for five years and came to make his living as a hunter at the Arkansas Post.

There he met the Mallets, who enticed him to head for Santa Fe. "They had been in New Mexico in the year 1740, and they facilitated my journey. I, who desired to do the very thing they were persuading me to do, set out on my journey to New Mexico from Los Arcos [the Arkansas Post], accompanied by four Frenchmen, a sergeant, and a German" (Hackett 1931–46 III: 321). This group went upriver to the Wichita villages on the Arkansas in northern Oklahoma. From there they went with twenty Wichitas but did not make contact with the Comanches as they had hoped. Eventually Sandoval obtained a Comanche guide and accompanied him to his homeland. He ended up in a large Comanche camp "at the foot of a mountain, whence issues a river called Case." Faye (1943: 691) argues that this is the Canadian River, but his identification is based on the mistaken assumption that the Piquouris visited by the Mallets were the Jicarilla (see Chapter 6). LeCompte (1986: 76–80), by contrast, suggests that the "Case" is Fountain Creek, a theory that ties in better with some of the other information that was coming into Spanish hands.

While Sandoval was in the Comanche camp, some Frenchmen and a German from Louisiana arrived. Eventually, a Comanche headed toward New Mexico to trade three captives guided him and two French companions to Taos. Apparently he took them by way of the upper Purgatoire River (cf.

Cachupín in Hackett 1931–46 III: 338), over Raton Pass, down the upper Canadian, and then over the mountains to Taos. Thus, these Frenchmen preceded William Becknell by seventy years over some of what became the Mountain Branch of the Santa Fe Trail.

The governor was being swamped with Frenchmen. When Satren, Febré, and Raballo showed up, he asked the viceroy to let them stay in Santa Fe, arguing that their skills in barbering, tailoring, and carpentry were sorely needed there. This permission was granted. But when Sandoval showed up with his two friends, followed shortly by Pierre Mallet and three more men, the governor changed his tune:

> As they have learned the road, I am of the opinion that they will desert frequently. It seems to me less dangerous to these dominions that they should not be sent back from here to their own colonies, with complete information and experience of the lands inspected, in a petulant mood. It would be well if they should settle down in this kingdom, in that of La Vizcaya, or in Sonora, so as not to carry back information to their colonies (Cachupín in Hackett 1941 III: 328).

When this recommendation had been taken to Mexico City, and after due consideration by his counselors, on January 14, 1751, the viceroy ordered that the Frenchmen be sent to Sonora, the province most distant from Louisiana. On February 25, however, before word could be sent to Cachupín, the latter had sent Pierre Mallet and his three companions in a *cordillera* (that is, from post to post) to Mexico City.

Mallet and his friends arrived at Pecos in November 1750, having come by a third route. From New Orleans, they had gone up the Mississippi to the Red River and up that stream to the post at Natchitoches. From there they went to the Spanish settlement at Los Adaes, where they asked permission of the governor to buy horses. He told them they might do so, but not from the soldiers. When the civilians asked too high a price, they went instead to the

Cadohadachos and purchased their pack animals there. From the Cadohadacho village, they went north to the Canadian and followed it at a leisurely pace, "traveling on foot one league a day, and stopping four or five days" (Boiser in Hackett 1931–46 III: 354). They traveled up the Canadian to the portage to Pecos, "crossing it several times, the water being knee deep" (Jofrion in Hackett 1931–46 III: 356). This passage is very reminiscent of the route of the Oñate expedition as depicted on the Martinez map (Wheat 1957: Map 283). From the Canadian, they headed overland to Pecos, essentially retracing the homeward route of 1740. They had come by the later Fort Smith–Santa Fe road.

In 1750 a lone Frenchman, François Charvet (spelled Sarvé in most of the Spanish documents), showed up at San Antonio (Hackett 1931–46 III: 360–362). From there, he went on to the Rio Grande and into Mexico, finally settling as an infantryman in Mexico City, guarding the royal jail. When interrogated in 1751, he said he was from Lyon and that he was originally a silk weaver. He joined the army in France but eventually deserted. In 1736 he enlisted with a Swiss company that was a kind of precursor to the Foreign Legion; any deserter who joined with the intent of serving in New France was given a pardon. As a result, he was shipped to New Orleans and served in Louisiana until 1750.

Then he deserted again, this time from the post at Natchitoches. He went from there to Los Adaes, where he got a passport from the governor of Texas, Don Pedro del Barrio Junco y Esprilla. With that in hand, he went along the Camino Real to San Xavier, San Antonio, and so to the Rio Grande. He said that other French deserters were received kindly in Texas, just as Spanish deserters were allowed to remain in Louisiana (Hackett 1931–46 III: 361). His job at the jail in Mexico City would shortly get him into trouble, as we shall see.

Between the spring of 1749 and November 1750, nine Frenchmen and one Spaniard had entered New Mexico, and at least one Frenchman entered Texas. Of those who arrived in New Mexico, the Spaniard and five Frenchmen came by way of Taos; the others entered through Pecos. All may have used branches of what was later the Santa Fe Trail. The lone Frenchman who went through Texas to Mexico used the Camino Real. Government officials were horrified at the influx.

When Pierre Mallet, Jean-Baptiste Boiser, Pierre Jofrellon, and Jean-Baptiste Rocque showed up at Pecos, the lieutenant governor, Don Bernardo de Bustamente y Tagle, took them briefly to Santa Fe and then sent them on to El Paso, where Governor Cachupín was visiting. There they wrote him a petition, or rather dictated it to a Spaniard who was supposed to know French. The result is a most remarkable document, with French grammar, but written as heard by a Spaniard with only a tenuous knowledge of French. Hackett (1931–46 III: 334–336) offered a translation based on the two translations into Spanish that are in the archives. Another translation, taken directly from the French original, is given in Appendix C.

The document makes clear that Pierre Mallet led the little group of would-be traders. It recalls his previous visit to Santa Fe and mentions the abortive Fabry expedition. It specifies that in 1740 the merchants of Santa Fe encouraged Mallet to return to Louisiana to initiate trade between the two colonies. On this third trip, he said he carried a passport from Governor Vaudreuil and letters from merchants named Duran and Fuiye [Fuillet?] offering to open a line of credit to establish the trade. He told of being robbed by the Comanches and ended by begging the governor to let them return home whether or not he could give permission for the trade. The cool reception had begun to frighten the Frenchmen. Pierre Mallet and Jean-Baptiste Boiser signed for the others, who could not write.

The governor did not wait for the usual caravan to send these men on to the viceroy. Instead, he shipped them in a cordillera to the governor of Nueva Viscaya, asking the latter to send the Frenchmen the rest of the way to Mexico City. He also sent a letter directly to the viceroy, an indication of how urgent a problem he considered Mallet's arrival with what remained of official documents requesting the opening of trade. It certainly contrasts with his

handling of the various hunters and deserters who had arrived on unautho-
rized expeditions in the previous twelve months.

To pay for the transportation of the Mallet party, the governor had their
merchandise appraised and sold at auction. We have the list of the goods and
the appraisal, which was done by Don Bernardo de Miera y Pacheco, who
drafted one of the most important early maps of New Mexico. Several independent lists were made, and Miera's is by far the most critical of the quality of
the goods (Appendix C). No one but Miera made a bid for the goods when
they were auctioned off, so he got them for the appraised price of 420 pesos, 6
reales. One suspects that the auction might have been rigged. The governor
kept 100 pesos to cover the costs of dealing with the Frenchmen in New Mexico and sent the rest on to the governor of Nueva Viscaya as a contribution to
the cost of transporting the Frenchmen to Mexico City. Mallet later complained that his twelve horses were simply taken from him without payment.

In addition, we have the documents from the cordillera, not all of which
are legible. They record the movement of the little party from post to post,
presidio to villa to mine, down the line to Mexico City, where they arrived in
the middle of May 1751. More important, we have the testimony Mallet and
his companions gave in Mexico City, taken in June and July. Hackett (1931–
46 III: 346–360) provides accurate translations of all four depositions, which
are highly repetitive, as precisely the same questions were asked of each man.
For that reason, only a single summary is given here.

When asked about his origins, Pierre Mallet stated that he was forty-seven
years old, a native of Montreal, Canada, now residing in New Orleans, the
capital of Louisiana. He said he had been in Louisiana (which included Illinois) for seventeen years, that his occupation was that of a trader, and that he
made journeys while engaged in this occupation. He testified that he was the
widower of Louisa Deupet [Louise Dupré], but he mentioned no children.

The interrogator then asked him how he came to be a prisoner in Mexico City. Mallet replied that after he and his companions arrived at Pecos,
Lieutenant General Don Bernardo Bustamente arrested them and, after

holding them in Santa Fe for two days, shipped them to El Paso, where the governor happened to be. After keeping them in El Paso for several months, Governor Cachupín sent them under guard to the governor of Nueva Viscaya in the city of Chihuahua, and from there they were passed in a cordillera, "from presidio to presidio and from justice to justice," to Mexico City, arriving on May 17, 1751.

The Mexicans asked next for detailed information about the settlements in Canada and Louisiana and about their defenses. Mallet told them it was about 50 leagues from Montreal to Quebec, where he had visited. He described Quebec as a very large town on the Saint Lawrence River, to which large ships are able to sail. Montreal, according to his account, was also a large place and fortified with artillery. Between the two, scattered along the Saint Lawrence, were smaller French settlements and native villages. He said New Orleans was on the Mississippi River and that large vessels were able to sail directly to it. It was protected by many companies of French and Swiss soldiers, who had a number of cannons. It had a large population, including some 500 families that had arrived just the previous year. He also described the economy of Louisiana, including trade in foodstuffs with the Spanish inhabitants of Pensacola, and mentioned the trade with the Indians, saying the French obtained some 100,000 pounds of furs annually, along with tallow, bear oil, bison meat, and venison.

When asked about the expedition of 1739–1740, Pierre testified that they left from "Misuri," where there was a garrison of French soldiers near where the Missouri River flowed into the Mississippi. He said he had eight companions, so his account includes Jean-Baptiste Alarie, who was absent from all of the French documents of 1740. In fact, he said, two of the nine Frenchmen who came to Santa Fe married there and remained. He had heard that one of them had been executed for "being a sorcerer" but that the other, Juan Alarido, was still living.

He described their route as being through the northern country, an enormous level plain watered by many rivers and streams. He said the land had excellent pasturage and was fertile, supporting deer, buffalo, and birds. This much of his account agrees totally with what Bienville abstracted from his journal. Some of the rest of his testimony does not. For instance, he said the nine of them set out for Santa Fe without any trade goods, whereas the abstract mentions their losing seven horse loads while crossing the River of the Kansas. He said they set out at the insistence of a companion who had lived among the Comanches and had told them that New Mexico lay only eight days from the Missouri. Although someone who had lived among the Comanches prior to 1739 may have given the Mallets information before the expedition, it is very unlikely that such a person actually accompanied them. Otherwise, it is impossible to explain why they ascended the Missouri River as far as they did, as the Comanche country did not lie in that direction.

Mallet also said the expedition encountered no Indian nation except the Comanches, in direct contradiction to the abstract of the journal, with its discussion of Missouris, Kansas, Otos, Panis, Panimahas, and Arikaras. He did mention their confrontation with the Comanches and said he had been told that the tribe consisted of fifty or sixty villages scattered over the plains close to New Mexico.

All of these discrepancies can be accounted for by assuming that during the interrogation Mallet switched from describing the 1739 expedition to speaking about that of 1750. All of the details that do not correspond to Bienville's abstract of the 1739 trip do fit what we know of the 1750 expedition.

Mallet went on to describe his party's arrival and treatment in New Mexico in 1739, saying he and his companions entered at the Pueblo of Taos and went from there to Picuris and by way of Santa Clara to Santa Fe. Once again, there are minor disagreements with the contemporary document, which mentions that messengers were sent to Taos but asserts that the first pueblo visited was Picuris. Further, the abstract speaks of a stop at Sainte Marie (probably Pojoaque), whereas this testimony mentions Santa Clara instead. Perhaps Mallet misremembered, or perhaps he remembered a stop not mentioned in the abstract of the journal. Santa Clara is on the west side of the Rio Grande between Picuris and Santa Fe, and it is possible that the Mallets and their Spanish guides stopped there in 1739.

Mallet said they stayed in Santa Fe for nine months, supporting themselves by hunting some of the time and depending on the hospitality of the residents the rest of the time. He said that during those months they traveled though most of the pueblos and that all nine men had the opportunity to marry there.

He described their return route via Pecos to the Canadian (called the Río Roxo or Colorado in the deposition). He said it was 35 leagues from Pecos to the Canadian, which flows toward the French colonies. They followed the river, "and as soon as the water became deep enough, and their horses became tired, they made a canoe from the bark of trees, embarked, and descended the river." He is quoted as saying they went directly to the Mississippi without stopping at the Cadohadacho village or at Natchitoches, which indicates that his Spanish inquisitors were confused about the identity of the river he descended: Both Natchitoches and the Cadohadacho village were on the Red River, but Mallet went down the Canadian. Even Hackett (1931–46 III: 349 n. 78) became confused about the route.

Mallet said that on their arrival in New Orleans, Governor Bienville questioned them about their trip and about conditions in New Mexico. He said that although Governor Mendoza of New Mexico had not discussed with them the possibility of opening trade, the *alcaldes* of the various pueblos they visited told them of the high prices charged for various commodities in New Mexico. He then described the Fabry expedition briefly, saying that it found the river unnavigable and so returned by way of the Arkansas.

In this passage Mallet dropped a minor bombshell, saying that one of the soldiers from the Fabry expedition was a guard in the prison in Mexico City. He said he could not remember the man's name but that he recognized his face. The guard was François Charvet, the deserter from Natchitoches. He, too, was questioned and, as a Frenchman in Spanish territory, ended up as a prisoner inside the cell with Mallet rather than as a guard outside it.

In response to a question about their route from Louisiana in 1750, Mallet stated that they left from Natchitoches, 7 leagues from Los Adaes. He said they went from there to the Cadohadacho village, where they purchased horses, and from there to the Canadian River. From that point, they simply followed the route by which they had descended from Pecos in 1740.

Not until he was questioned about illicit trade between Texas and Louisiana did he mention that he had gone first to Los Adaes to buy horses and that the governor had given him permission to do so as long as he bought from civilians and not from soldiers. He described their encounter with the Comanches, in which their passport and a letter from the commandant at Natchitoches were stolen. Finally, he pointed out that the twelve horses they had when they reached Pecos had been taken from them without compensation.

Mallet's companions, Boiser, Jofrellon, and Rocque, were asked the same set of questions, and apart from a few details cited elsewhere, their replies were the same. None of them had been with Mallet in 1739–1740 or 1740–1741, so all the information they gave was pertinent only to the 1750 expedition.

The government officials now had to decide what to do with the five Frenchmen in their jail in Mexico City. The previous order to send them from Santa Fe to Sonora had been sent too late, and now they were in Mexico City. In August 1751, the *auditor* and the *fiscal* considered the case. The fiscal cited laws stating that government officials should seek out all foreigners present in their jurisdictions without license from the Spanish government and send them to the *Casa de Contratación* and that all of their goods should be confiscated. He noted that even those serving as soldiers were not exempt, so François Charvet had to be jailed as well. Soon, however, Charvet was able to produce a certificate of naturalization, and he was released.

Only two more Frenchmen made it to Santa Fe in the 1750s. They were Jean Chapuis and Louis Feuilly (Xanxapij and Luis Fxuij to one of the Spanish scribes), who arrived in Taos late in the summer of 1752 carrying a passport from the commandant of Illinois. Their goods were confiscated and sold at auction, and, like Mallet and his companions, they were sent to Mexico City. From there they were shipped to prison in Spain.

The eventual outcome of all of the intrusions was an official complaint from the Spanish government to the French ambassador. He relayed it to Paris, and in 1755 the minister of the navy, Jean-Baptiste Marchault d'Aronville, forwarded it, along with some recommendations, to the new governor of Louisiana, Louis Billouart de Kelérec. He made it very clear that no French traders should give the slightest hint of having any governmental backing. Spain was to be given no more grounds for complaint (ANC B, 101: 245–245v). The governor responded by enlisting the help of the Quapaws and Choctaws in preventing French deserters from leaving the colony. No more Frenchmen made the trip to New Mexico while France retained title to Louisiana. An era had come to an end.

9.

EPILOGUE

The documentary record ends with Pierre Mallet's being sent to the Casa de Contratación in Mexico City while the viceroy ponders what to do with him and his companions. The viceroy originally had ordered the Frenchmen sent to Sonora, as far from the French colonies as possible in northern New Spain. Now they were even farther from home, in Mexico City. Therefore, he might not have kept the previous order in effect. To date, no one has found the records indicating what might have happened to the Frenchmen other than Francois Charvet. They simply disappeared.

The record of Paul Mallet ends with the census of the Arkansas Post in 1749. At that time, he was married, but none of the children born to him by that date would carry on the family name; all three were girls. For that reason, I wasn't too hopeful of a connection when I ran across the Mallet name in modern times.

In 1989 the anthropology department at Wichita State University was having a party. Jim Thomas, one of my colleagues, invited my fiancée, Joy, and

I to go with him and his wife, Janie, to dance to a zydeco band after the party. It turned out to be Terrence Simeon and the Mallet Playboys. Jim noticed the name and asked me if there was any chance that they were somehow related to Paul and Pierre Mallet. I didn't think so, but it was worth a shot. The band was from Louisiana, so the next day I looked up Mallet in the zip code directory. There was no listing for a post office in any such place, and a search of a map of Louisiana also turned up nothing. It appeared to be a dead end.

Then, a few months later, Joy and I went to Oklahoma City. She attended a conference of the Association of American Cultures, while I spent some time looking at General Land Office maps at the state library. One evening there was a dance, and the band was Terrence Simeon and the Mallet Playboys. This time I went straight to the source: I caught the band while they were rehearsing and talked to Terrence Simeon.

"Oh, no," he said, "there's no town there; it's just a place with that name." A little more questioning revealed that it was in St. Anne's Parish. I wrote a letter addressed to the parish priest. Eventually, I got a reply from Father David A. Hamm, S.T. He told me that he, too, was interested in the origin of the name. He said it apparently derived from a land grant or concession made prior to the establishment of church records in the late eighteenth century. There was a Bois Mallet and a Bayou Mallet. He suggested I write to a member of the family, Monsignor Charles Mallet of St. John Berchmans Church in Cankton, Louisiana.

Eventually, Joy and I were able to visit in person with Monsignor Mallet in 1990 when I was New Orleans attending a meeting of the American Anthropological Association. Monsignor Mallet drove into town to meet us, and we spent a delightful evening in his company learning what he knew of the history of the Mallet clan.

The Mallet family is an ancient one that can trace its roots back to the tenth century. It came originally from Normandy, and the founder of the English branch of the family was allied with William the Conqueror. William gave him lands near the Welsh border with the understanding that he would provide defense against attacks from that quarter. His descendants included three signers of the Magna Carta, and the estate was saved from King John's vengeance after he was restored to the throne only because John, who was godfather to one of the Mallet children, did not want his godchild to become landless. The family retains an estate in Somerset to this day.

The French branch of the family also remains prominent. Because the Mallets were Huguenots, they moved to Geneva in 1520. When they later returned to Paris, in 1700, they entered the banking business. They continue in it today, with interests in seven Paris banks. The family estate is near Varangeville, in Normandy.

The American branch of the family is Roman Catholic. Monsignor Mallet has traced this line back to an Antoine Mallet, who was born in the eighteenth century. The Mallets were in Louisiana earlier than that, and they have a tradition that their ancestors did not come from Acadia, as so many did in the latter part of the 1750s. It seemed possible that they were descended from the Mallet brothers, but proof was lacking.

I didn't have much hope of connecting Antoine Mallet with Pierre or Paul when the family living in Louisiana had not been able to do so. Nevertheless, I eventually gave it a try and discovered gold in the Chancery Archives of the Archdiocese of New Orleans. In the course of conversation with Dr. Charles Noland, the archivist, I mentioned Antoine Mallet. He took a moment to look up the name and found that Antoine had been born to Pierre Mallet and Marie Louise Dupre in 1747, the mother dying in childbirth. Dr. Noland was surprised that he had the record, as the birth occurred not in New Orleans but on the German Coast, upriver from the city.

Here I neared the end of the odyssey. The modern Mallet family was indeed descended from one of the brothers who had journeyed to Santa Fe. In 1750, Pierre had told his Spanish interrogators that he was a widower. Now I had learned the cause of his wife's death and had connected Pierre with his living descendants in Louisiana. The fact that the family can now trace its line of descent back to the two brothers from Canada provides a likely explanation for the fact that this branch of the family is Catholic whereas the French and English branches are Protestants; only Catholics were allowed in French Canada after 1625 (Eccles 1972: 26–27).

For a while I had hoped to trace the land grant that Father Hamm had indicated was the source of the place-name, Mallet. Had the brothers received a concession from Governor Bienville as a reward for their epochal journey in 1739–1740? Or had Governor Vaudreuil "invested" in the 1750 venture by giving Pierre a grant? What I really hoped was that the grant was made after 1750 and would show that Pierre had somehow made his way back to Louisiana from Mexico.

I have found no record of a grant from either governor to Pierre or Paul Mallet. The primary place to search for such a record is in the American State Papers, which record land claims prior to the ascendancy of the United States in places once governed by France and Spain. I found several records of people named Mallet who once owned land in the vicinity of Vincennes, but they appeared to be the descendants of another Pierre Mallet, who moved to the area from Detroit.

In the volume dealing with claims in the Western District of Louisiana (American State Papers, 3: 101–102), however, I found several claims involving Pierre's sons. None could be traced to a grant to anyone named Mallet, but the records are not complete. What they do show is that in the 1760s a man named Jacques Courtableau, acting as the guardian of Pierre and Antoine Mallet, purchased land from Louis Pellerin. Pellerin, not the Mallets, had obtained the land in 1764. However, the details of the transaction, which involved Courtableau's giving Pellerin five cows and calves and a three-year-old bull, also had the junior Pierre Mallet trading 20 acres of land to Pellerin for the tract in question. The records do not show the origin of ownership of the land traded by Mallet to Pellerin. In 1813, when these cases were investigated by U.S. commissioners, the 20-acre parcel could be traced back only to the junior Pierre Mallet. How he had obtained it is not stated.

What the land claims records do show is that Pierre Mallet, Senior, was not in Louisiana in the 1760s (the exact date of the land trade is unknown) and that his two sons, who had not yet come of age, were under the guardianship of Louis Courtanbleau. Poor Pierre Mallet, after all of his adventures on the frontier, probably did not survive the jail in Mexico City. His family, however, lives on.

APPENDIX A

DOCUMENTS FROM 1740

Original Abstract of the
1739–1740 Mallet Expedition in French

1739, Mai 29–1749, Juin 24
Extrait du journal de Voyage des frères
Mallet à Santa Fé

Extrait du Journal du voyage fait a Santa Fé Capitale du nouveau Royau-me de Mexique par les deux freres Pierre Et paul Mallet canadiens avec les nom-més La rose, Phillippes, Bellecourt, Petit Jean, Galien, Et moreau.

Pour LIntelligence du chemin que ces Canadiens ent fait pour decouvrir le nouveau mexique il est bon de scavoir quil y a 100 lieües des Illinois aux villages Missouris dans la riviere de ce nom, 80 lieües de la aux Cancés, 100 lieües des Kancés aux otoctatas, Et 60 de la L'Embouchure de la riviere des Panis Maha dans le Missoury. Cette nation est Etablie a LEntrée de la riviere de leur nom, Et c'est de la que les decouvreurs prennent leur point de partance le 29 May 1739.

Tous eux qui avoient tenté jusqu'a present de penetrer jusqu'au nouveau Mexique avoient pensé le trouver aux sources du Missoury, Et a cet Effet ils avoient monté jusqu'aux Ricaras qui sont a plus de 150 lieues des Panis. ces decouvreurs prirent sur la rapport de quelques sauvages une routte toutte differente, Et partant des panis ils traverserent les terres ils retournerent sur leur pas presque paralellement au missoury.

Le 2e Juin ils tomberent sur une riviere quils nommerent le riviere plate, Et voyant quelle neles Ecartoit point de la routte quils avoient En idée ils la suiverent en la remontant a droitte les pace de 28 Lieües et en cet Endroit ils trouverent quelle faisoit fourche avec la riviere des Padokas qui vient sy jetter.

Trois jours apres cest a dire le 13 de Juin ils traverserent a la gauche de lad. riviere Et traversant une langue de terre ils coucherent le 14 de lautre bord de la rivier des côtes qui se jette aussy dans la rivirer platte.

Le 15 Et 16 ils continuerent a couper dans les terres, Et le 17 ils tomberent sur une autre riviere quils nommerent des Cotes blanches ils traverserent dans ces trois jours des pays de plaine, ou ilsne trouverent point des bois seulement pour faire du feu, Et il paroit par leur journal que ces plaines setendent Jusqu'aux montagnes voisines de santa fe.

Le 18 ils coucherent au bord dune autre riviere quils traverserent et quils nommerent la riviere aimable.

Le 19 ils trouverent encore une riviere quils traverserent et quils nommerent la riviere des souces.

Le 20 ils tomberent sur la riviere des Kancés ce qui fait voir approchant la routte quils ont fait partant des Panis. ils la traverserent et y perdirent set chevaux chargés de marchandises. Cette rivière est profonde Et a beaucoup de Courant.

Le 22 ils traverserent Encore une riviere quils nommerent la Riviere a la Fleche.

Les 23 ils traverserent Encore une riviere Et retrouverent ses grandes prairies decouvertes ou ils ne faisoient du feu qu'avec la Boize de vache.

Le 24 ils trouverent encore une riviere et depuis le 26 jusqu'au 30 compris ils en trouverent tous les jours. Enfin le 30 ils trouverent sur des pierres au bord de la derniere riviere des marques Espagnols.

Ils avoient fait alors 155 lieües a leur Estime de Traverse dans les terres depuis le panis, pres-que toujours a Ouest Ils Estiment que cette riviere est une branche de la riviere des Arkansas et la même quils ont trouvé plus bas a leur retour le 10e jour de leur depart de santa fe.

Ils la suiverent en sa gauche jusquau 5 de Juillet quils trouverent un village d'une nation sauvage Laitanes ile firent un present a cette nation et en recurent quelques chevreuils. Ils furent coucher a une lieüe de la, setant apperçu que ces gens la avoient quelque mauvais dessein.

Le 6 Ils s'ecarterent des bords de cette riviere. Et en partant il vient a Eux un sauvage Ricara Esclave chez les Laitanes qui leur dit que cette nation avoit Envie de les defaire. ils le renvoyerent distant quils n'avoient qu'a venir et quils les attendroient. Les laitanes ne firent aucun mouvement Et Esclave etant revenu a Eux ils luy demanderent S'il scavoit le chemin pour aller chez les Espagnols. il leur repondit quil le scavoit ayant este' Escalve chez Eux Et y ayant même eté Baptisé. ils l'engagerent a les guider sur lEsperance de luy procurer la liberté il y consentit Et ce jour la ils firent 10 lieües pour seloigner de cette nation.

Le 10 ils appercurent les montagnes Espagnols a plus de 10 lieües d Eux et le 12 ils coucherent a la premier montagne. le 13 ils coucherent a trois Cabanes Laitanes a qui ils firent un petit present.

Le 14 ils trouverent Encore une riviere quils nommerent la riviere Rouge mais qui vray semblablement est encore une branche de celler des Arkansas. Et la 21 lieües de la ils trouverent le premier poste Espagnol qui est une mission appellée Piquouris.

Le 15 ils avoient trouvée trois Indiens a qui ils avoient donnée une lettre pour le commandant de Taos qui leur avoit Envoyé le leudemain du mouton Et du pain de froment fort beau.

Lors quils furent a une lieüe du premier poste le Commandt Et le Padre vinrent au devant d'eux avec beaucoup de monde on les recut fort bien Et même au bruit des cloches a ce que porte leur Relation.

Le 21 ils partirent des piquouris et arriverent a midy a une autre mission nommé Ste. Croix, lapres diner ils passerent a une autre nommé la Cagnada et ils coucherent a un bourg nommé Ste. Marie ou ils furent bien recu des Espagnols.

Le 22 Juillet ils arriverent a santa fé ayant fait 265 lieües depuis la riviere des panis maha. Ont peut voir dans le certificat cy joint de quelle maniere ils y ont ête recus et y ont vecus pendant les neuf mois quils y ont ête a attendre le reponse du vice roy du Mexique, il nest pas etonnant quils ayent ête si longtemp a attendre parcequil y a 500 lieües par terre de santa fé au vieux Mexique Et il ne part qu'une Caravane tous les ans pour faire ce voyage.

La reponse du Vice Roy etoit selon le rapport de ces Canadiens de tacher de les Engager a rester dans le pays, Et ils pensent qu'on avoit dessein de les Employer a fair la decouverte d'une terre qui suivant la tradition vraye ou fausse des Indiens du pays est a trois mois dans les terres du côté du Ouest ou ils disent quil y a des hommes Blancs retus de soye qui habitent de grandes villes sur le bord de la mer quoy quil en soit ils aimerent mieux s'en retourner Et on les laissa partir avec les Lettres dont copié est cy jointe.

Santa fe suivant leur rapport est une village batie En bois et sans aucune fortification, il peut y avoir 800 familles Espagnoles ou mulatres, Et aux Environs il y a nombre de villages d'Indiens domicilés dans chacun desquels il y a un Padre qui fait la mission. Il ny a que 80 soldats de garrison mauvaise troupe Et mal armée. Il y a des mines fort pres de la, aux qu'elles on ne travaille point, il y en a dautres dans cette province qui sont mises en valeur pour le compte du Roy dEspagne et dont Largent se transporte tous le and au vieux Mexique par la Caravane.

Il paroit par une des lettres cy jointe que les gouverneurs s'emparent des marchandises qui en vienment et fout le peu de commerce quil y a faire ce que les Padres et dautres voudroient bien faire.

La nation Lalitane dont il est parlé dans le Journal n'est pas chretienne comme les autres nations voisines mais Elle est en paix avec les Espagnols. les Canadiens assurent que le peu de marchandises quils y ont distribuée y a fait un grand Effet, Et que cette nation seroit toutte entiere a nous si nous avions quelque Etablissement dans le pays.

Retour

Le premier May 1740 les decouvreurs au nombre de sept le nommé moreau setant marié dans le pays, partirent de santa fé dans le desein de chercher le mississipy et de se rendre a la nouvelle Orleans par une route opposé a celle quils avoient tenue.

Le 2e ils arriverent a une mission nommé pequos ou ils sejournerent deux jours.

Le 4 ils en partirent et vinrent coucher a une riviere de même nom, ils pensent que cette riviere peut estre une branche de la riviere Rouge ou de celle des Arkansas, ils la suivirent le 5 et la quitterent le 6. le 7 ils en rencontrerent une autre courante de même que la première quils nommerent la riviere a la Jument. ils la quitterent pour traverser dans les terres suivant la routte quils avoient en idée, Et le 10 ils rencontrerent une troisieme riviere quils Esti-moient devoir tomber dans la riveire Rouge ou dans celle des Arkansas, et quils croyent estre la même branche ou ils avoient trouve' plus haut en allant a santa fé les premieres marques Espagnoles ils Etoient pour lors a 35 ou 40 lieües de cette capitale et ils estiment qu'on poura remonter jusqua cet endroit lorsquou retournera pour perfectioner leur decouverte.

Le 11, 12 Et 13 ils suiverent cette Riviere ce dernier jour trois des sept prirent le party de quitter leurs camarades pour reprendre la route des panis et se rendre aux Illinois ce quils ont executé suivant les lettres venues en dernier lieu de ce poste. Et les quatre autres persisterent dans la resolution de venir icy. le même jour ile trouverent un party de huit hommes Laitanes avec qui ils Coucherent.

Le 15 en suivant la même riviere ils trouverent un village Laitanes ou ils disent avoir vû une quantité de chevaux, ils y Coucherent, on leur fit festin Et on leur donna des chevaux pour quelques couteaux et autres Bagatelles.

Ils continuerent en suivent la riviere jusqu au 22. la nuit de ce jour ils perdirent six chevaux. depuis le 22 jusqu'au 30 ils prirent un peu plus dans les terres Et a jour ils renconterent deux hommes Et trois femmes Padokas a qui ils donnerent le main mais peu de temp apres la peur prit a ces sauvages qui jetterent la viande dont ils Etoient chargés et se sauverent avec leurs femmes sans quil fut possible de les fair revenir.

Le 8 Juin Ils revinrent sur la bord de la riviere quils suiverent jusqu'au 14. les 15, 16, 17, 18 Et 19 ils sejournerent Et setant bien consultés sur le cours que parroissoit avoir cette riviere ils resolurent d'abandonner 18 chevaux quils avoient

Et de faire des canots d'ecorce d'orme pour sy Embarquer, cela fut Executé quoiquils n'eussent plus que deux couteaux Entre Eux quatre. ils avoient fait alors 220 lieües par terre depuis santafé.

Le 20 ils sembarquerent dans deux petits canots et firent dix lieües, cette riviere n'ayant que peu de courant.

Le 21 ils firent autant de chemin. Le 22 ils virent duex belles Embouchures de riviere qui pouroient bien être les rivieres de pequos, et de la Jument quils avoient traversées pres de Santa fé. Enfin le 24 ils firent agreablement surpris de se trouver a la fourche de la riviere des arkansas. Ils avoient fait alors 42 lieües En canot, ils trouverent au dessous de la fourche un cabanage de canadiens qui Etoient en chasse pour faire des viandes salées. Comme il ne leur restoit plus que leurs armer Et quelque munition Ils le-irent en chasse avec les autres Et chargerent une pirogue de salaison avec quoy ils se rendirent a nôtre fort des arkansas et de la a la nouvelle orleans le   1741.

‡   ‡   ‡   ‡

Copy of a certificate given to seven Frenchmen at Santa Fe by General Jean Paëz Hurtado, *alcalde major* and Captain of War of this capital city of Santa Fe and its jurisdiction, Lieutenant Governor and Captain General of this Kingdom of New Mexico and its provinces.

I myself certify to Captain Don Louis de Saint-Denis, who commands the fort at the mouth of the Red River, and to all other governors and captains, judges and justices of the very Christian King of France, to all military and political officers to whom this may be presented, that on the 24th of July of the past year, 1739, there arrived in this city of Santa Fe eight Frenchmen named Pierre and Paul Mallet, brothers, Phillippe Robitaille, Louis Morin, Michel Beslot, Joseph Bellecourt, and Manuel Gallien, native-born men of Canada in New France, and Jean David of Europe, who were received in my presence by Domingo de Mendoza, Lieutenant-Colonel, Governor and Lieutenant General of this realm, at the gate of the palace, where Paul Mallet entered with the governor and with Sir Santiago Reibaldo, Vicar of this realm. The governor asked them where they came from and to what purpose. Paul answered that they came from New France and that they had come with the intent to initiate a trade with the Spanish of this realm because of the intimate connection that exists between the crowns of France and Spain.

I certify that, with this understood, the lord governor sent their guns to the guards and searched for a place for the Frenchmen to stay, because he had no room at the palace. I took them into my home where I lodged them all, and, a few days later, I sent for their arms and ammunitions and for some old clothes for their use, that they had salvaged from an accident they suffered while crossing a river, where they lost nine horses laden with merchandise and their clothing, the remainder amounting to nearly nothing. According to their report, they were still intent to discover this kingdom and to open communication with the colonies of New Orleans and Canada, and disdainful of all sorts of troubles and of risks from the savage nations that they might encounter, they came to see the Spanish, by whom they were well received, as they were invited by them to dine in their homes and to stay with them, while awaiting the response of the Lord Archbishop, Viceroy of Mexico, Don Juan Antonio Vizarrón, which took nine months.

During this interval, the Mallet brothers, who stayed with me and dined at my table, maintained a very regular and very Christian conduct, and as they intended to return, I recommended that should they obtain a royal patent for trade with this kingdom, they should bring a certificate and passport from their governor, because without these, they would expose themselves to the confiscation of what they carried, which would be regarded as contraband.

Sincerely,
Given at Santa Fe, 30 April, 1740
Signed: Juan Paëz Hurtado

‡   ‡   ‡   ‡

Copy of a letter written to Father de Beaubois by Father Santiago de Rebald, Vicar and Ecclesiastical Judge of New Mexico.

I write to you, sir, on the occasion of the arrival of nine Frenchmen who have come from New France, named Pierre and Paul, brothers, La Rose, Phillippe, Bellecourt, Petit-Jean, Gallien and Moreau, who have communicated to me the desire they have to introduce trade between these provinces, which find themselves completely devoid of money. If they are permitted to execute their plan, one could easily remove this obstacle, as we are not more than 200 leagues from a very rich mine, abundant in silver, called *Chiguagua* [Chihuahua], where the inhabitants of this country often go to trade. And if the people were to see a chance to spend some of this unused silver, it would encourage them to work more mines that they have.

And, as these Frenchmen spoke to me about Your Reverence, and of the great credit you have in the province and city of New Orleans, I write this in

Spanish and not in Latin, not in order to worry you but so that I may inquire of your health, which I pray is perfect, to wish you prosperity, and to offer my services. I occupy here the position of vicar and ecclesiastical judge of the colony.

My Reverend Father, these Frenchmen would have me believe that I could ask you for merchandise that I need for business and to provide for the needs of my family. They say that I could obtain these easily with your help, in light of the credit you have in your community. Therefore, I immediately took advantage of this opportunity to ask that you obtain for me the goods on the enclosed list and to send them, if possible, telling me the price in silver or coins. This I will repay as an honest man and as quickly as I can. And while I am live a country where money hardly ever flows, the salary I earn from my office is paid in silver or in money that I can amass. As for the future, I have four thousand piastres at Chihuahua that I will send for when I receive an answer from Your Reverence and after we agree on prices, so long as I am pleased with the merchandise from your country, but, given what they tell me, I am sure I will be.

Fearing to have troubled you, I am the servant of Your Reverence.

Signed: Santiago de Rebald

‡   ‡   ‡   ‡

Letter to the Minister of the Marine from Bienville and Salmon.

There arrived here last March four Canadians returning from Santa Fe, the capital of the province of New Mexico, where they had gone by land without informing anyone of their intent. We were as surprised as we were satisfied by this discovery, which could offer a very important opportunity for the colony. The Company of the Indies incurred very heavy expenses to obtain knowledge of these Spanish lands. It had a fort constructed on the Missouri, where it had as many as fifty men in garrison, and counted on making it a center for large scale trade. It obtained honors and rewards for Lord Bourgmont, who had undertaken to attempt this discovery and who fell short, as several others had before him.

The most singular thing is that Lord de La Harpe who had tried by way of the Red River and the Arkansas, did not succeed better. It appears, nevertheless, from the journal, an abstract of which is enclosed, *that a branch of the latter river flows from the Spanish territories and that one may ascend it to within about forty leagues of Santa Fe.* It is also possible that there are other branches that approach Santa Fe much more closely. Whether or not this is so, the journey of these Canadians would have been fruitless and no one could have returned to Santa Fe by using their journal, where the routes are not marked, if we had not found someone capable of returning with them in order to make this route known and to make all of the appropriate observations of the country and to lay the foundations of a trade that could become extremely important.

It is true that the trade will pose great difficulties because of the distance in leagues; nevertheless when one can go by water, it will be as easy to make a convoy every year at high water as it is to go to Illinois. As for the rest of the route overland, horses, which are numerous in that country, render the transport of merchandise practical. Anyway, it may be possible to hire Spaniards to come for goods at a point of trade, as it appears (according to one of the enclosed letters) that the people of Santa Fe trade at the mines of Chikagua, at a distance from them of 200 leagues. It is also possible, according to the letter, and the Canadians assure me so, that there are known mines in the vicinity of Santa Fe. They say that the Spaniards showed them one, three-quarters of a league from the city, and that if the Spaniards had a market for the silver they would soon open the mines and put them to good use.

All of these aims, together with those contained in the attached memoir presented us by Lord Fabry, clerk of the Marines here, have made us decide to accept the offer which he makes to go with the Canadians to perfect their discovery; the voyages he has already made in the colony lead us to believe that he will continue to stand up to the strain and risks as he has previously. He is moreover, a person to be emulated, of known talents that predict success not only in this enterprise, but also in all other sorts of affairs where one might employ him. He intends to go to the Arkansas with the next convoy to Illinois, and from there with eight or ten Canadians he will continue the journey to New Mexico, whence he hopes to return in the spring of next year.

We hope that your lord approves the expenditure as suitable for this important discovery and also agree that it bodes well for the balance sheet of the colony.

We are with very profound respect, Your Majesty, your very humble and very obedient servants.

Signed: Bienville
Salmon
At New Orleans, 30 April, 1741

‡   ‡   ‡   ‡

APPENDIX B

DOCUMENTS FROM THE FABRY EXPEDITION

Orders given to Fabry de la Bruyère by Bienville and Salmon.

Jean-Baptiste de Bienville, knight of the Order of St. Louis, Governor for the King in the province of Louisiana; Edmé Gatien Salmon, counsellor to the King, Commissioner of the Marine and Ordonnateur of the said province.

In virtue of the orders of the King, our master, to make discoveries, whenever possible, of the unknown lands and countries situated to the west of this province, to reconnoiter their limits and even to reach the extremities of North America, which is unexplored on the coast that seems to reach toward China and Grand Tartary, we, conforming to the intentions of His Majesty, have ordered and do order Sir Fabry de la Bruyère, one of the royal officers in this province, to go with a detachment composed of a sergeant, a corporal, five soldiers and seven volunteer *voyageurs* to begin the said discoveries in conformity with the following instructions:

First:

He will ascend the St. Louis River [Mississippi] to the mouth of the Arkansas River, and he will ascend that river in the same manner to its forks, after which he will take his route toward the West and the Northwest, by whatever route he deems most practical, concerning the choice of which we defer to Sir Fabry's knowledge and the requirements of the situation.

Second:

He will extend his journey as far as his provisions, ammunition, and the strength of his men will allow, and along his route he will make all observations appropriate to geography, astronomy, botany, and to the knowledge of the location and the quality of the lands he travels through, so that we may be well informed upon his return. He will assess and draw the roads, giving consideration to the distances, in order to provide an approximately correct map.

Third:

If he should encounter any unknown Indian nations, he will propose to them peace and alliance with us, while at the same time keeping on his guard against treason and surprise.

Fourth:

He will inform himself regarding whether these nations are at peace or at war with the Spaniards, and, since we have learned that the Osage, Pawnee and Padouca nations make raids on the flanks of New Mexico, attacking and robbing caravans, he will assemble the chiefs of these nations with whom we are allies, and he will exhort them to cease their raids against the Spanish and will explain to them that the crowns of France and Spain are closely united; and, so that they may obey more readily, he will, in the name of the King, our master, give them presents that we have supplied him for this purpose. All of this is in conformity with the intentions of His Majesty, which have been made clear to us by the letters of His Lord, the Count of Maurepas, Minister of the Marine, dated the tenth of October, 1739, and the twelfth of November, 1740.

If it should happen that on his way out or on his return, he should pass through Spanish territory, or if he should be forced to go there in search of help, he will give to the Governors of His Catholic Majesty the letters we will give him, by which we will ask them, by virtue of the close alliance that exists between our two crowns, to give him aid if he should need it. He will tell them what he has done to pacify the hostile Indian nations mentioned above, and he will offer them, on our part, our good offices and all other kinds of help which they might require of us for the help given and for the good of the service of His Catholic Majesty, and for the tranquility of his colonies bordering on this one.

Finally, not being able to limit the time for his expedition nor to give him more detailed instructions for every instance, we rely on his prudence and on his capacity to deal with unforeseen circumstances not mentioned in this memoir.

Given at New Orleans and sealed with our arms and the countersignatures of our secretaries, the first of June, 1741.

Signed: Bienville and Salmon.

‡   ‡   ‡   ‡

Letter from Msrs Bienville and Salmon to the Governor of Santa Fe.

Sir,

Under the orders of the King, our Master, we have sent Sir Fabry de la Bruyere with a detachment of fifteen men on a journey of discovery of the Sea of the West and of the unknown lands that border this province. As we cannot prevent all of the incidents of a journey that is so long and so perilous, nor to mark precisely the routes that he should take to fulfil his mission, we have the honor of writing this letter to you by which we beseech you to give aid and to provide information that he may need, if he is forced by bad weather, illness or some other similar circumstance to resort to one of the posts of your colony. We hope that, in light of the close alliance that exists between the governments of France and Spain, you will volunteer assistance and protection to this expedition and that if one of those who comprise it should want to desert, which we do not wish to happen, that you will arrest him and return him to Sieur Fabry de la Bruyère, commander of the expedition. We will do the same with the Spanish garrisons from the posts to which we are adjacent, with which we have agreements for the mutual restitution of deserters. We would be much obliged to you in this case for the services that you might offer on this occasion, and we ardently wish to find some fashion to demonstrate the infinite respect with which we have the honor, etc.

Signed: Bienville and Salmon

‡   ‡   ‡   ‡

Extracts of the letters from Bienville and Salmon concerning the Fabry Expedition.

Following the orders of MM. de Bienville and Salmon, Governor and *Commissaire ordonnateur* of the province of Louisiana, Sir André de la Bruyère, *Ecrivain Ordinaire* of the Marine, serving in the said province, left New Orleans in September, 1741, to try to discover the road to Santa Fe in New Mexico, accompanied by Pierre and Paul Mallet, brothers, Philippe Robitaille, and Michel Beleau, Canadian *voyageurs*, and his associates, Sergeant Champart, Corporal Alexis Grappe, soldiers, *engages*, and the man named Pantalon, a negro.

Sir Fabry, having no provisions on his arrival, had two cattle killed and had the meat of one salted for the trip to the Forks of the Arkansas, thinking he could not count on hunting before that point. He obtained, with great difficulty, five pirogues [dugouts] from the savages, in which he left on October 31st, and in 35 days, he reached a point just four leagues from the Forks of the Arkansas, which he places at a distance of 145 leagues, rather than the 200 leagues reported by the hunters. The frequent rains he encountered and the good intelligence of the Canadians and of the soldiers gave him hope of quick success, and he continued his journey and entered on December 7th, the fork from the left, which is the river that is supposed to go up to Santa Fe. There was enough water as far up as the mouths of two rivers, where this river receives water 17 leagues from its own mouth. But on the 13th, the water was not deep enough to continue, and he was forced to camp on the second of the two rivers, which he called the River of the South, until the 21st, when a storm raised the water five feet in the river that goes to the Spanish and to which he gave the name, the River of Saint André. He continued until the 25th, when the water again was inadequate for travel. He could continue on the route only on January 10, 1742, and with great difficulty, as he was obliged to drag the pirogues at several spots.

On the 15th, he arrived at the entrance of a large bayou, at the entrance of which there was hardly six inches of water. He camped on this bayou to wait for the water to rise, having made, in his estimation, 42 leagues from the mouth of the Saint André River.

On the 24th, there arrived at his camp a party of 35 Osages, who were going to fight the *Mentos*, whom these savages also call *Panis*, who were located on this side of the Arkansas River above its forks and about 25 leagues below the *Panis noirs*, whence they moved to the Saint André River where it is still possible to see their old village, and for the last four or five years, to near the *Kadodakious* where they live today.

After the chief of the Osage band had talked from the other side of the bayou and had set up his tent, Sir Fabry crossed over with his men. The Osages told him of the arrival of the Chevalier de Villiers among the Missouris and that the latter have six French traders in their villages. They spoke at length of the good relationship that has been re-established between them and us, asserting that they did not want to do any more harm. They made a fire near our camp and slept.

On the morning of the 25th, Fabry gave the Osages powder, bullets, some knives, etc. They did not seem content with the contents of the gift. They wanted to have guns. When they were told they would not receive anything else, the chiefs, after sulking, consulted among themselves, sent men to plead with Sir Fabry and the one named Philippes, one of the Canadians who acted as interpreter. There was an explanation, but they got nothing more.

They left before noon, promising that if they succeeded, they would be back in six or seven nights and would bring some slaves. Seventeen of them returned on the 3rd of February with seven horses, a mule and two scalps, and said that the rest of the party separated from them on the way to the *Mentos*, and that they had not seen them since. After their departure, Sir Fabry had built a fortification of wood against any surprise and against their coming back in greater numbers. He told them he had entrenched himself against the *Panis noirs* who were lurking in the neighborhood. They seemed to believe him and to approve of this, but they worried about his expedition, imagining that he was looking for the *Panis* and the *Padokas* to make an alliance with them and to trade them guns. He reassured them, and said that he was travelling to see the Frenchmen of the West, our brothers of old. They asked him if he intended to follow the river up; he answered yes, thinking that it was useless to make a mystery of the trip, that they would hear about it among the Missouris, and because they saw with him the Canadians that they knew from their first expedition. The chief told Fabry that he should not think of going up the river, as he had crossed this place more than ten times and he always found it without water. Sir Fabry, not doubting what he said because of his own observations, decided to confer with the four Canadians and the sergeant of the detachment to decide on a solution in case he were forced not to use the river. He pointed out that it had not snowed all winter and that, if the drought continued, they could not count on the spring flood; that if the flood did not occur, as seemed likely, he would be in a quandary. Hence he wanted to have a plan before the departure of the Osages. Everyone agreed that if the weather did not change, it would be impossible to ascend the river and they concluded that it was necessary to trade for the horses of the Osages, which could carry the bulk of the goods, and that with the pirogues lightened, they could go upstream with just a little water and that over half of the group could follow with the laden horses.

He immediately proposed to trade for the horses with the Osage chief, who told him that he would talk with his young men, who replied that they did not want to trade, saying they needed the horses to return home. He conferred again on this problem, and the Canadians proposed to follow the trail of the Osages to search for the nation just attacked, which was located not too far away. The savages had travelled just for two nights from the place they attacked. He [Fabry] presented the risks of approaching an unknown nation which had just been attacked by two or three groups, that it would be necessary to wait for a time. Moreover, if they were to bring many horses, he would not abandon the river, as they proposed, without losing hope of [using] the spring flood. [He said] that he was required by his orders to ascend this river as far as he could, and it being only the beginning of February, it would be acting too precipitately to leave it. He said he wanted to wait for water until Easter, and then it would be time to look for horses. This reasoning was accepted. Nevertheless, in order to have more than one resource, he wrote to the French traders among the Missouris to hire them to trade for horses on his behalf and to bring the animals to him. According to the report of the Osages, they could make the trip in seven nights. He assured them that he had the means to pay for the horses, that if the traders advanced payment in merchandise, he would pay them the price the Missouris demanded, and if two of them would like to come back with the Indians bringing the horses, he would give them 200 Francs for their troubles and that he would wait for them the whole month of February. He gave this letter to the Osage chief, along with powder and bullets for his trip.

The 8th of February, four days after the departure of the Osages, there was a violent storm from the Southeast with rain and hail. The river rose over three feet during the night, but by dawn all the water was already gone. The considerable gradient of this river, which runs completely on a bed of sand, does not help the regulation of the water level. The frost came again and lasted until February 17th after which the weather was warmer and the wind turned from the South, and the ice melted without creating a significant rise because there was no rain. On the 18th, the river rose two feet in the evening, but by morning it was at the same level as before. From the 19th to the 27th, the weather was heavy, but without rain; the 28th the water in the river was six to seven inches higher than usual, and without the many little channels [normally seen].

Because the time for the arrival of the horses had passed, being forced to live on nothing more than lean venison, and the length of time passed in this spot had all undermined the morale of the party, Fabry proposed to drag the pirogues higher up the river to hunt the bison. The departure was fixed for the next day.

The 29th, the pirogues were loaded at the mouth of the bayou. The men were forced into the water to pull the boats, and they could not make more than five quarter leagues in a full day. The first of March, they travelled another one and three quarter leagues in the same manner. On the 2nd they made only a third of a league, it being too cold for the men to remain in the water. On the 3rd, they went three quarters of a league and on the 4th, three quarters. The 5th, they made a league and three quarters, and they had to debark and carry the boats to be able to pass certain places that were entirely without water, but they camped in a warm spot. The 7th, they did not move, as they were too exhausted. They decided to stay in the first spot that seemed good for hunting and to wait there for the water to rise. From the 8th to the 12th, the weather was the coldest they had all winter. During this time, they found their surroundings filled with bears and fat deer, and they decided to camp one league higher in a low spot more convenient for wood.

During their time in this place, the Canadians suggested to Sir Fabry to search for the Mentos. The elder Mallet [Pierre], who appeared to be a resourceful man and the only hunter, was assigned to this mission, and [Fabry] gave him Philippe Champart and an *engagé* named La Grandeur. Mallet asked for ten days to accomplish the mission, and he was given twelve. He was charged with a beautiful present for the chief of the village and was told to hire one of the leaders to join him in order to receive the word of the grand chief of the French and to bring the horses he wanted to trade, and if the Indians showed any sign of reluctance to come, he was to leave two Frenchmen as hostages. With regard to the route, he was told to walk for four or five days to the southeast, and if he could not find the trails to the villages, to strike for the southwest, from whence he could find his way to rejoin the group. All this concluded on March 12th, and on the morning of 13th, they left. At noon, it snowed for the first time that winter. The 14th, it snowed again a bit in the morning. The 15th, in the evening, the river commenced rising from five to six inches until the 16th, when it lowered again. They hastened to embark in order to reach the low spot where they had decided to camp. They were obliged to pull the boats part of the way, and they did not arrive until four hours after noon.

The 17th and 18th, they cut wood to make a log fort and they fortified themselves in a spot where they intended to wait for the *Mentos*, if Mallet could find them.

On the 19th, Mallet returned with his three comrades. He reported that on the fifth day of their march he saw three fires relatively close to him that he did not doubt were made in the village, but those fires seemed to be figments of his imagination. He hesitated to go on because he was not sure of coming back in the span of six days, and that he gave up for fear of creating anxiety on his behalf; but he insisted it was the village and that he could find it if he returned. These assertions comforted Sir Fabry about his having abandoned the mission. He told him that he would leave in two days, but Fabry could not understand any of Mallet's answers on this subject.

On the 21st, Mallet left, and no fixed time for his return was set. La Rose went with him instead of Philippe. After his departure, the weather changed, and it got warmer.

The 25th, Easter Day, the river rose some six inches and lowered an equal amount in the evening. On the 26th and 27th, the weather was still fine, and the river rose and fell as on the 25th. On the 28th, the river stayed low. At this place, the width was 240 paces. All of the water flows in a single channel no more than 20 paces wide, with two feet of water along the outer bank. A pirogue serves as a bridge to cross to the sandbank. It is possible to estimate the level of the water well in certain places where the river has seven to eight channels which meander through the sand.

On the 31st, Mallet returned without horses or Indians. He said that when he arrived near the spot where he had seen the fires, he saw some behind him not too far away. He went over there and found nothing. In the end, he made a long and hungry march but saw nothing but abandoned villages. On the way, he crossed six rivers, one of them large. That was the result and the account he told of his expedition, which greatly disappointed Sir Fabry. He recognized, but a bit late, a principle for assessing explorers, when the problem is to find correctly a place unknown to them. He had given Mallet, at his request, a compass, and which served but to turn him around in the forest a bit more than he should have done, because he did not understand its use.

Sir Fabry assembled the four Canadians and the sergeant. He explained their situation to them: that the shores of this river allow them neither to advance or to retreat, that they had no hope of a rise in the river or that a rise would last long enough to allow them to travel more than three hundred leagues to the portage [to Pecos]. He said they should seek a solution that would allow them to finish the journey, and with their advice, he would decide what to do.

On the next day, the 2nd of April, they got together again. The feeling of the elder Mallet was that there was no reason to abandon the river, that they should wait until May when the elm bark quickens, with canoes made from which they could continue for a while. His brother proposed to seek horses among the *Panis noirs*. Philippe and La Rose said that they would agree to any solution whether by land or by water, and the sergeant said, if it was a question of going by land, that the soldiers would not be able to carry more than their arms and some provisions and that one of them was not in condition to march, but that the rest of the detachment was ready to follow Sir Fabry. Fabry answered that the elder Mallet's proposal to wait until May to build canoes was not agreeable because if the river had water, they could ascend it without the help of canoes, and that if the water did not rise, it would be necessary to drag the canoes as well as the pirogues, because when they went down the river [the previous year] for 40 leagues with two unloaded canoes, they had to drag them in several places. Furthermore he argued that higher up the river where less water would be found, they would have to haul the vessels from morning to night. Even supposing they would not have to haul the boats, it would take more than three months to cover 300 leagues on a river which is a torrent when the water rises and does not keep its water half the time, as Mallet found it low when he embarked on June 20th of the previous year. Besides, Mallet and the others had told him that bark canoes required a great deal of attention, and they would be damaged by exposure to the sun and would be worn out quickly by dragging them across the sand. He argued further that Mallet should realize that soldiers are not accustomed to using such canoes, and they would break one every day; that while sailing in the hot weather, it would be impossible to protect them from the sun; that since they would be obliged to drag the canoes, which was a virtual certainty, the canoes would not last long; that they would find themselves in the prairies where there would be no bark with which to build others, and they would be placed in a very difficult situation. Mallet, unable to respond to all of these objections, saw his proposal rejected.

The suggestion of his brother, Paul, also was not acceptable to Fabry, because since they could not find the *Mentos* who lived only a short distance from camp, it was not reasonable to seek the *Panis noirs* who live six times as far away. With regard to travel afoot, Fabry answered that it would be the last resort, and that then he would have to abandon all that he carried, but when he was given some soldiers, he thought that they could walk for a few leagues, in case they could not find horses among the nations he might have met, but not for as long a distance as they now faced, especially during the hot season; that the Canadians themselves did not make this journey on foot, for they had a number of horses when they left the *Panis Mahas* and they obtained others for their return to the place where they built the canoes.

Fabry decided that there was nothing to do except to send a party to procure horses. He proposed to them to go himself to find them; that to this end he would use empty pirogues to descend to the Arkansas tribe and that if he did not get any from them, where horses are rare, at least he could get some of the King's horses [from the Arkansas Post], which would serve to carry merchandise to the *Kadodaquious*, where he could buy some pack animals at a good price. Then, from the *Kados*, striking north, he could not miss the river they were on. Since that river runs from the south and southwest, at least up to the place they had come, the whole road, that he would take from the south should be shorter than the distance from the mouth of the Arkansas to the *Kados*. He estimated the overland portion of his proposed trip at not more than 70 or 75 leagues. Besides, he could get guides from the *Kados* for the return trip and might be able to pass by way of the *Mentos*, the allies of the *Kados*, if they were found along the way.

Fabry arranged his departure with five men: Philippes, La Rose, Chapart [sic], La Grandeur, and Pantalon. He wanted to bring Pierre Mallet, but, as the latter was an excellent hunter, Fabry left him to feed the men who remained, also fearing that he could not stand the stress of the travel because Mallet was not in good health.

He gave to the *voyageurs* who stayed behind written instructions telling them to keep the peace amongst themselves and to guard themselves well, to wait for him until the first of August at the most, after which, if he had not returned, to decide what was best, adding that if they wanted to continue the journey, not to take the troops with them, but instead to send them back to New Orleans. In this same document, he disposed of some of his property in favor of the two Mallets, Philippes and La Rose, asking that the rest be given to Corporal Alexis Grappe to be transported to New Orleans. He also gave written orders to the corporal to return to the Arkansas Post if he learned that Fabry had been in an accident or if he did not return by the first of August. At this point, the Mallets asserted that if the trip were not successful, they would never again present themselves before Governor Bienville. Fabry made them promise in the presence of all at least to lead the soldiers to a safe spot and to provide them a canoe and food at the Forks of the Arkansas after which they could do as they wished.

After taking all the precautions he judged necessary, Fabry left on April 4th, but the water was so low that he could barely cover a league in three and a half hours, dragging the pirogue the whole way, and this forced him to return to camp to wait for higher water. On the 5th, it rained for the first time since the 8th of February. The water rose a bit during the night, and on the 6th, seeing that it was up three inches, Fabry embarked quickly in another pirogue to rejoin the one he had left further down. He divided the load between both in order to be able to haul them easily and left immediately. It took him six days to reach the forks, where he found the level of the river so low that he took 15 days to go down the river, getting stranded in several spots.

The 26th, he arrived among the Arkansas, where he left Pierre Roussel, a soldier, whose leg was hurting as before, making him unable to walk, and took in his place a man named Bellegarge. During his stay at the post, he gathered with some difficulty five of the King's horses. It was not possible to trade for any with the savages, among whom it was impossible to obtain an appropriate number of horses, and even if he could have gotten some, they would have cost more than slaves. He decided to trade for horses among the *Kados*, after he found two guides who promised to take him there in ten days, which gave him hope that he could rejoin his party at the end of May and could leave immediately for Santa Fe, where he hoped to arrive in less than twenty five days of travel.

He was happy about this decision because he was proud to discover the road to New Spain via the *Kados* and to perfect this discovery on his return, by leaving the river from the edge of the Grand Prairies exactly 30 leagues above the place where he left his people, to cut straight across to the *Kados* and to go to Natchitoches by the usual road, and if the Red River were not fit to descend, to continue by land to the Bayagoulas, where he could embark on the river by November or December, in his estimation.

He counted on leaving the Arkansas Post on the first of May, but the abundant rains that were falling at this time caused a considerable inundation, and he left only on the 4th and was forced to give up on the 5th, unable to cross the low ground. When the roads looked better on the 21st, he set out for the *Kado* village with two Arkansas guides who had previously taken this route, one of whom had been taken captive during a raid.

After they had travelled for seventeen days, on the other side of the Red River, between the lands of the *Yatassés* and those of the *Kados* and had found no trace of the road to the latter, he realized that the guides were leading him astray and that he could not prevent it. When he tried to talk to them and to redress the situation, they became surly. They agreed that, when they crossed the Red River, they were a bit too far south and that he was right in wanting to go west-southwest. Fabry tried everything to persuade them to get back on the road, but in vain. They were so disgusted that, whatever he offered them, they quit after 45 days of travel and in dangerous country. Finally, the French arrived back among the Arkansas on July 5th.

What was even worse for Sir Fabry is that three horses died from fatigue and heat during the journey, and this obliged him to abandon his own merchandise in the forest to save that of the King, and in this way he lost nine trade guns and seven hatchets. Even so, he claimed to have treated the savages with great sweetness and generosity, foreseeing that he would need other guides and that he would have difficulty finding any if the first ones went back unhappy.

This unexpected obstacle did not discourage Fabry [according to his own account]. Two days after his arrival, he sent Champart with one of the Canadians and two good guides, who were joined by three volunteer guides, to report the delay to the party waiting up river, fearing that it might leave on the first of August as per Fabry's instructions. He told Champart and Philippe to hurry, and the savages who were guiding them promised to reach the *Kados* in eight days, whence they would need no more than another eight to go to the French fort, but Champart fell ill on the road. He had 21 abscesses on his knee, and he did not arrive among the *Kados* until the 25th of July. Even though hope was gone that he could reach the fort by the first of August, Champart left from the *Kados*, thinking that the travellers would not be able to travel by river because of low water, and that if they left by land and abandoned all the luggage, he could at least join them at the Forks of the Arkansas, where they could reassemble and could set out again.

But the Mallets, when the time appointed to wait for Fabry neared its end, since they had no news from him, decided to quit the river and continue their trip to Santa Fe on foot. They inventoried Fabry's belongings, and following their orders, gave them to the corporal, who wrote down the inventory. They left all the merchandise, except for some presents for a savage nation they wanted to pass, and sent the troops back to New Orleans.

The Mallets argue it is the fault of Fabry that the enterprise did not attain the success we had desired.

1st. The Mallets say that Fabry did not want to trade for the horses of the Osages, no matter what arguments they made, for he wanted everything or nothing;

2nd. They suggested that one of them go to obtain horses among the *Panis*, but Fabry wouldn't listen,

3rd. They would have built bark canoes with which they would have been able to go up the river, but Fabry would not approve,

4th. While Fabry was absent on his trip to the Arkansas Post and the *Kados*, the river was navigable for a period of forty days.

The first article is treated differently in Fabry's letter, in which he says that he proposed to the Osages to trade for the horses they stole from the *Mentos*, and that the Osages refused. This seems more reasonable than the Mallets' accusation because it Fabry was responsible for obtaining some horses as quickly as possible in order to conveniently search for the nations where he hoped to trade for even more horses. The second point does not appear in this same letter, but a proposal made by the younger Mallet to go to trade among the *Panis noirs* lacked credibility because his brother, in two consecutive attempts, did not find the *Mentos*, who were located much less distantly, which caused Fabry to reject his proposal. The reasons that prevent one from accepting the third article are included in the same letter, and concerning the fourth, it does not accord with the Mallet journal of the previous expedition, in which it seems that the river has been very low and even dry most of the time.

As we have said before, Champart and Philippes left the *Kados* with the guides who were supposed to lead them to the forks. As they approached the Saint Andrés River, they separated, and Philippes arrived on the 12th of August at a spot ten leagues below the Forks at a hut of a hunter named Brin-d'amour. There he found the corporal and the soldiers who had arrived two days previously. Philippes, who brought five horses with him, told the soldiers that Fabry was supposed to arrive soon with the others, and so they all went back to the fort. They hired Brin-d'amour to travel with them to feed them, and when they arrived at the fort, they found Champart who had arrived on the 13th. The soldiers reported the operations and departure of the Mallets with one *engagé*. The corporal showed the spot where he had hidden part of Fabry's goods, which had been returned by the Mallets. But he did not know where they had hidden the King's merchandise and the munitions and merchandise belonging to Sir Fabry and to the two Canadians who were with him. They transported the whole outside the fort, without telling anything to anybody, saying that they would come back with the horses to carry the goods. Champart tried to look for it, and two days later, Brin-d'amour discovered a hiding place in a bayou, one league and a half from the fort, where there was part of the luggage. Champart made an inventory and put the goods in order as much as possible.

While all of this was happening on the Saint André River, Fabry was leaving from the Arkansas Post with new guides, and they arrived among the *Kados* in thirteen and one half days. He was forced to stay for fifteen days to gather thirty horses, a number he estimated to be necessary for the long trip, given that many would die.

He left from the *Kados* on August 16th with the horses he had obtained and he arrived on the Saint André River on the 31st of the same month. There he met Champart and the whole detachment who were descending, having decided to wait at the Forks, where Brin-d'amour could feed them by hunting. They told Fabry everything mentioned above and many other circumstances that are not detailed here.

Sir Fabry was very hurt to see that his expedition had failed while dragging out over an interval of time in which he would have been pleased to finish it—one year of difficulties and constant fatigue. He found himself without guides (in particular Mallet, on whom he was counting), without a hunter to feed his troops, and without ammunition. He had not obtained enough powder for hunting and he had only about 35 pounds of balls in the fort. He also lacked gifts and flags to present to Indian nations. Furthermore, he had two men fall ill at the Forks after they had covered a distance of 50 leagues on foot in nine days. Fabry concluded that while he might be able to continue his travel, he had everything to fear and nothing to hope for from the Spanish governor. That mystery was solved, doubtless, by the Mallets. He took the party to go to the fort to search for the goods, which he found in great disorder. Nevertheless, he saved most of them, the rest having been stolen, hidden, or carried away by the Mallets. He dispensed justice to the soldiers who had made no mistakes and who had conducted themselves throughout with loyalty and uncommon wisdom, who had been strong enough not to steal or to quit with the others who invited them to do so.

Sir Fabry left the fort on September 4th. Because the savages who were with him did not give him the time to send for and bring back the two ill soldiers at the Forks, he sent one of the hired men with old Philippes and Brind'amour, giving them a boat to descend the river via the Arkansas Post.

Leaving the River Saint André, Fabry struck right, to the river of the Natchitoches, in order to explore this part of the colony. He did not go 20 leagues before finding the Red River, three days above the *Tavakavas* and the *Kitsaiches*. He visited these two nations, whence he came via the road of the *Kados* and *Yatassés* to Natchitoches where he returned sixteen horses, the others having died from exhaustion or having been stolen by savages.

APPENDIX C

DOCUMENTS FROM THE 1750 EXPEDITION

Letter of October 2, 1750, from de Rouille, Minister of the Marine, to de Vaudreuil, Governor of Louisiana.

Monsieur,

It has come to my attention that when Sieur Delino, commandant among the Arkansas, proposed establishing trade between that post and the city of Santa Fe, you gave a Monsieur Malet permission to make a trip to that city. You have, however, left me ignorant of this fact, of the reasons that led you to adopt it and of the advantages that you foresee. As soon as you had decided on this course of action, you should have arranged to get permission from His Majesty and ought to have provided the details to me. I presume that it is with an eye to commerce that this expedition has been made, but although you are authorized to promote developments that will allow the colony to carry on trade with the Spanish, you should not take the liberty to permit certain enterprises without first having given a full explanation and without having received permission from the King. Consultation with the *ordonnateur* is required before you do anything of this sort. His Majesty would not miss an occasion to approve your conduct if this were the case.

Someone has also informed me that, without consulting Monsieur Michel, you have permitted a trader in animals to take some from the Natchitoches hills to the Bayagoulas. While Michel himself has not written me about this, I do not doubt the accuracy of what I have learned. By behaving in this fashion, you do not meet the responsibility His Majesty has given you and you should give continual attention to this if you want to maintain the relationship that you have with him.

Permission for this kind of trade as well as that involving the fellow named Mallet having to do with general policy should not be given without the participation of Monsieur Michel. It is not without great pain that I have remarked that there have been other occasions where we have written to you about the rules in this regard. I do not doubt at all the purity of your intentions, but the relations between you and Monsieur Michel are so important in all respects, that I cannot encourage you enough not to do anything that might undermine them. I wish equally for the good of the service and for my personal relationship with you that His Majesty will have every reason to be satisfied with the circumspection that you use in these matters.

I am, sir,
Affé

‡   ‡   ‡   ‡

Letter dictated by Pierre Mallet to be given to Governor Cachupín Monsieur Governor and Captain-General.

Pierre Malet, Jean-Baptiste Boiser, Pierre Jofrellon, Baptiste Rocque, inhabitants and natives of the province of New Orleans place themselves at your lordship's feet. We say:

I, Pierre Mallet, in the year 1740, with eight comrades from the city [sic] of Canada, with the intent to see the country and to provide support for our families, and with New Spain so close, we came from the post of *Ile Noir* [Illinois] in New France, whence we left for Taos in the province of New Mexico and from there to the city and post of Santa Fe, its governor being Don Gaspar Dominque de Mendoça. We stayed there for eight months. The Spaniards were very helpful, and their principal merchants proposed that I go back and get from my governor, Monsieur de Bienville, permission to carry merchandise to them.

This I did, and the governor, in light of what I told him, sent me back to the said province with considerable merchandise, along with my four comrades and ten soldiers that he gave me, a sergeant, an *adjutant de la place*, and a corporal. I carried a passport and a letter for the governor of this kingdom and also one for the merchants of the city of Santa Fe. Thus provided, we left. Then, after eighteen months of travel, we suffered the disgrace of losing all of the merchandise in the Red River. Because of this, we returned to our country, arriving there sick.

But never giving up intent of returning, I went to our new governor, Monsieur de Vaudreuil, who gave permission to return to New Mexico with some merchandise. He gave us a passport and a letter bearing his seal for your lordship and also another for a merchant of the city of Santa Fe, written by Monsieur Duran, a very rich man, and Monsieur Fuillet, also a wealthy man. So that your lordship might give permission to open trade as asked in the letter, the merchants wrote that they were sending invoices with us for all the Spanish might want, which they could provide most readily, even if it came to a half million or more. And if the Spaniards wanted negroes, they would send as many as needed to open the road against any enemies that might be in the vicinity.

For this reason, I started out with my companions and the merchandise. After travelling more than seven months, the misfortune occurred that before reaching the village of Pecos, seven days before our arrival, the Comanche nation with many Indians fell upon us. They opened all our merchandise, taking pieces of wool and calico and all of our papers and letters, which we were unable to retrieve from them. We offered them all that we had for only the letter that we carried to your lordship, of which they gave us only a small piece of the envelope and the letter addressed to Morenne [Moreau?] who lives in the vicinity of the Santa Fe, which cost us a fusil valued at 100 piastres. When we arrived at the village of Pecos, we delivered these papers to your lieutenant, Don Bernar de Bustamente, along with the few items the Comanches had left us and twelve horses. In accordance with the orders that Lieutenant Don Bernardo Bustamente had given us, we have come to this royal post and into the presence of your lordship where we await with hope your orders to us so that we might obey, whether or not you give us permission to open the trade, so that we may return to our governor, Monsieur de Vaudreuil, and so that delay does not cause the loss of our homes and our families. This we beg of you, confident in your lordship, because it has been seven months since we have been gone from our country. So that you believe better, our lord, the truth of what we have said, and of our intentions as faithful Catholics, which we are, we swear to God our Lord and by the sign of the Cross that this is the truth, and we sign this with our names for the others who do not know how.

Signed: Pierre Mallet
Jeanbatis Boiser

‡   ‡   ‡   ‡

Pierre Mallet's goods as listed by Bernardo de Miera y Pacheco:

2	black beaver hats with gold braid
4	pairs of men's Lyon stockings, damaged
12	other pairs of women's in god-awful (*para fé males colores*) colors
2	pieces of ribbon embroidered in pink and green
1	other of solid yellow
47	varas of simple black taffeta
40	more varas of yellow, damaged
6	papers of buttons, artificial gold, 24 doz. ea, and 3 papers of 4 doz.
6	more strips of buttons of false silver, very small
1	piece of heavy nankin, damaged, 35 varas
4	loose mesh sheets of striped Cambric, 40 varas
1/2	vara of striped gauze, damaged
2	sheer stockings of Cambric with 22 Varas both
1/2	of another sheet of silk of combined colors without embroidery, 12 varas
1/2	of another sheet of Cambric without embroidery, 8 varas
37	bales of Brittany, narrow width, 194³/8 varas
38¹/2	varas of same, damaged
6	double platters, damaged, very ordinary
20	other simple ones, damaged
3	measures of thread
156	sewing needles, worn
400	pieces of fusil shot
2	pounds of ordinary powder
27	varas of damaged cambric
1	old cloth hood
1	scarf old and torn
2	old shirt fronts with silver buttons
3	women's blouses of pure Silesian linen, damaged
1	petticoat of old chintz, damaged
1	coat of the same
1	old striped smock
1	women's dressing gown of the same material, old
1	other smock of the same
1	other robe of the same, slightly worn
1	other of white chintz
	some very badly worn overcoats

A list of personal property belonging to Pierre Mallet and his companions compiled by Compañero Joseph Manuel Morales:

One silver horse
a blanket
a [illegible]
A cloth gun sheath
a bison hide overcoat
another [illegible]; didn't come
a flask with a bag and a saddletree, broken
a saddle with 5 saddle blankets and a bridle
a blanket
a bison hide
a whip
a bridle
a spur
a saddletree and saddle blanket
a bag for gunpowder
its contents
a saddle with its saddle blanket
a bridle with a piece of halter
a dark horse
a bison hide
a blanket
a saddle with saddle blanket
a bridle and halter
three firearms, two of which are fusils and one a shotgun
a bag of rope
a small sword of [illegible]
a copper pot
a handmill and three chocolate cups

REFERENCES

Unpublished archival material

Mexico

AGI, Guad., 139
SANM, I, 1328
SANM, II, 456
(photocopies, University of New Mexico, Albuquerque)

France

Archives National, Colonies B 91: 405–405v
Archives National, Colonies B 101: 245–245v
Archives National, Colonies C13A 34: 315v, 35: 94–96v
Archives National, Colonies F3 24: 387–391v
(photocopies in Library of Congress Manuscript Division)

U.S.A.

Census of the Arkansas Post, 1749. Loudon Papers, 200. Huntington Library, San Marino, CA.

General Land Office documents, Ponca, NE, Lincoln, NE, Topeka, KS, Oklahoma City, OK.

J. R. Mead Collection, Special Collections Division, Ablah Library, Wichita State University, Wichita, KS.

Topeka Capital Journal, Kansas State Historical Society, Topeka, KS.

Kingman Public Library, notes on trails, Kingman, KS.

Records of the Superior Council of Louisiana, Nos. 23662 and 25449–3966, Louisiana Historical Museum Library, NewOrleans, LA.

Published Sources

Abert, James W.

1848   Report of Lieut. J. W. Abert of his Examination of New Mexico, 1846-'47. 30th Congress, 1st Session, Executive Document 23. Washington, D.C.: U.S. Government Printing Office.

1970   Through the Country of the Comanches in the fall of the year, 1845. The Journal of ... Lieutenant James W. Abert, edited by John Galvin. San Francisco: Lawton and Alfred Kennedy.

Adams County Weekly Record

1899   Vol. 2, Nos. 33 and 36.

Alvord, Clarence Walworth (ed.)

1907   Cahokia Records, 1778–1790. Collections of the Illinois State Historical Library, Vol. 2. Springfield, IL: Trustees of the Illinois State Historical Library.

Athearn, Frederic J.

1989   A Forgotten Kingdom: The Spanish Frontier in Colorado and New Mexico, 1540–1821. Denver: Bureau of Land Management.

Bell, Robert E., Edward B. Jelks, and W. W. Newcombe

1974   Wichita Indian Archaeology and Ethnohistory, a Pilot Study. New York: Garland Press.

Blaine, Martha R.

1979   "French Efforts to Reach Santa Fe: André Fabry de la Bruyère's Voyage up the Canadian River in 1741–1742." Louisiana History 20: 133–157.

1982   "Mythology and Folklore: Their Possible Use in the Study of Plains Caddoan Origins." Nebraska History 60 (2): 240–248.

Blakeslee, Donald J.

1975   "The Plains Interband Trade System." Ph.D. dissertation, University of Wisconsin-Milwaukee.

1981   "The Origin and Spread of the Calumet Ceremony." American Antiquity 46: 759–768.

1988a   "Tools, Trails and Territories." Paper presented at the Society for American Archaeology, Tucson, Az.

1988b   "The Rattlesnake Creek and Walnut Creek Crossings of the Arkansas River." Wagon Tracks 3: 4–5.

Blakeslee, Donald J., Robert Blasing, and Hector Garcia

1986   Along the Pawnee Trail: Cultural Resource Survey and Testing, Wilson Lake, Kansas. Wichita: Donald J. Blakeslee.

Blakeslee, Donald J., and John O'Shea

1983   The Gorge of the Missouri: An Archaeological Survey of Lewis and Clark Lake, Nebraska and South Dakota. Omaha: U.S. Army Corps of Engineers.

Blakeslee, Donald J., and Arthur H. Rohn

1986   Man and Environment in Northeastern Kansas: The Hillsdale Lake Project. Kansas City: U.S. Army Corps of Engineers.

Blasing, Robert

1986   Personal communication, Wichita, KS.

1991   Personal communication, telephone conversation.

Bodine, John J.

1979   "Taos Pueblo." Handbook of North American Indians, Volume 9: Southwest, 255–267. Washington, D.C.: Smithsonian Institution.

Bolton, Herbert E.

1914   Athanase de Mézières and the Louisiana-Texas Frontier, 1768–1780. Cleveland: Arthur H. Clark.

1964   "French Intrusions into New Mexico, 1749–1752." In Bolton and the Spanish Borderlands, edited by John Francis Bannon, 150–171. Norman: University of Oklahoma Press.

Boone, Nathan

1929   Chronicles of Oklahoma 7: 58–105.

Bray, Robert T.

1978   "European Trade Goods from the Utz Site and the Search for Fort Orleans." Missouri Archaeologist 39: 1–75.

Brink, James Eastgate

1985 "The Function of Myth in the Discovery of the New World." In *Coronado and the Myth of Quivira*, edited by Dianna Everett, 11–22. Canyon, TX: Panhandle-Plains Historical Museum.

Brown, Donald N.

1979 "Picuris Pueblo." Handbook of North American Indians, Volume 9: Southwest, 268–277. Washington, D.C.: Smithsonian Institution.

Bruce, Robert

1932 The Fighting Norths and Pawnee Scouts. New York: Brooklyn Eagle Press.

Burns, Louis F.

1985 A History of the Osage People. Fallbrook, CA: Ciga Press.

Chamberlain, Von Del

1982 When the Stars Came Down to Earth. Los Altos, CA: Ballena Press.

Champe, John L.

1949 "White Cat Village." American Antiquity 14 (4): 285–292.

Chapman, Carl

1959 "The Little Osage and Missouri Indian Village Sites, ca. 1727–1777 A.D." The Missouri Archaeologist 21 (1).

Chávez, Fray Angélico

1954 Origins of New Mexico Families in the Spanish Colonial Period. Santa Fe: Historical Society of New Mexico.

1957 Santa Fe, New Mexico, Archives, 1678–1900. Washington, D.C.: Academy of American Franciscan History.

Chittenden, Hiram M., and Alfred Talbot Richardson

1905 Life, Letters and Travels of Father Pierre-Jean De Smet, S.J., 1801–1873. 4 vols. New York: F. P. Harper.

Chrisman, Harry E.

1961   Lost Trails of the Cimarron. Denver: Sage Books.

Clark County Historical Society

n.d.   "Notes on Early Clark County, Kansas." Clark County Clipper, Ashland, KS. Reprinted from various issues of a newspaper column.

Conrad, Glenn R. (ed.)

1988   A Dictionary of Louisiana Biography. Lafayette: Louisiana Historical Association.

Cook, Warren L.

1973   The Tide of Empire: Spain and the Pacific Northwest, 1543-1819. New Haven: Yale University Press.

Court of Claims, U.S.

1914   Claims, Case 31002, The Omaha Tribe of Indians v. the United States. Washington, D.C.: U.S. Government Printing Office.

Delanglez, Jean, S.J.

1943   "Franquelin, Mapmaker." Mid-America, new series, 14: 29–74.

Dodge, Col. Richard Irving

1886   Our Wild Indians: Thirty-three Years' Personal Experience among the Red Men of the Great West. Hartford, Conn.: A. D. Worthington & Co.

Dorsey, George A.

1904   Mythology of the Wichita. Washington, D.C.: Carnegie Institution.

Eccles, William J.

1969   The Canadian Frontier, 1534–1760. New York: Holt, Rinehart and Winston.

1972   France in America. New York: Harper and Row.

1987   Essays on New France. Toronto: Oxford University Press.

Faye, Stanley

1943 "The Arkansas Post of Louisiana: French Domination." Louisiana Historical Quarterly 26: 633–721.

Fletcher, Alice, and Francis La Flesche

1911 "The Omaha Tribe." Bureau of American Ethnology, Annual Report 27: 17–672.

Folmer, Henry

1939a "The Mallet Expedition of 1739 through Nebraska, Kansas, and Colorado to Santa Fe." Colorado Magazine 16: 163–173.

1939b "French Expansion toward New Mexico in the Eighteenth Century." M.A. Thesis, University of Denver.

1953 Franco-Spanish Rivalry in North America, 1524–1763. Glendale, CA.: Arthur H. Clark.

Ford, Richard I.

1972 "Barter, Gift, or Violence: An Analysis of Tewa Intertribal Exchange." In Social Exchange and Interaction, edited by Edwin N. Wilmsen, 21–45. University of Michigan Museum of Anthropology, Anthropological Papers 46, Ann Arbor.

Fowler, Jacob

1965 The Journal of Jacob Fowler, Narrating an Adventure from Arkansas through the Indian Territory, Oklahoma, Kansas, Colorado, and New Mexico to the Sources of Rio Grande del Norte, 1821–1822, edited by Elliott Coues. Minneapolis: Ross & Haines.

Fulton, Maurice Garland (ed.)

1941 Diary and Letters of Josiah Gregg. Norman: University of Oklahoma Press.

Gilmore, Melvin R.

1932   "Methods of Indian Buffalo Hunts, with the Itinerary of the Last Tribal Hunt of the Omaha." Papers of the Michigan Academy of Science, Arts, and Letters 18: 17–32.

Giraud, Marcel

1991   A History of French Louisiana. Volume 5: The Company of the Indies, 1723–1731. Translated by Brian Pierce. Baton Rouge: Louisiana State University Press.

Grange, Roger T., Jr.

1968   Pawnee and Lower Loup Pottery. Lincoln: Nebraska State Historical Society.

Graves, O.L.

1964   "Archaeological Investigations of Site 14BT420, Barton County, Kansas." Kansas Anthropological Association Newsletter 9: 7.

1965   "Bissell Point Mound, Barton County, Kansas." Kansas Anthropological Association Newsletter 10: 5.

Gregg, Josiah

1954   Commerce of the Prairies. Norman: University of Oklahoma Press.

Gunnerson, James H.

1960   "An Introduction to Plains Apache Archaeology: The Dismal River Aspect." Bureau of American Ethnology Bulletin 173: 131–260.

1968   "Plains Apache Archaeology: A Review." Plains Anthropologist 13: 167–189.

1969   "Apache Archaeology in Northeastern New Mexico." American Antiquity 34: 23–39.

1984   "Documentary Clues and Northeastern New Mexico Archeology." Papers of the Philmont Conference on the Archeology of Northeastern New Mexico. New Mexico Archeological Council Proceedings 6 (1): 43–76.

Hackett, Charles Wilson (ed.)

1941   Revolt of the Pueblo Indians of New Mexico and Otermín's Attempted Reconquest, 1680–1682. Albuquerque: University of New Mexico Press.

1931–   Pichardo's Treatise on the Limits of Louisiana and Texas. Austin: 1946University of Texas Press.

Hammond, George P., and Agapito Rey

1940   Narratives of the Coronado Expedition, 1540–1542. Albuquerque: University of New Mexico Press.

1953   Don Juan Oñate, Colonizer of New Mexico, 1598–1628. Albuquerque: University of New Mexico Press.

1966   The Rediscovery of New Mexico, 1580–1594. Albuquerque: University of New Mexico Press.

Haywood, C. Robert

1986   Trails South: The Wagon-Road Economy in the Dodge City Panhandle Region. Norman: University of Oklahoma Press.

Hodge, Frederick Webb, ed.

1929   "French Intrusion toward New Mexico in 1695." New Mexico Historical Review 4: 72–76.

Hodge, Frederick Webb, George P. Hammond, and Agapito Rey

1945   Fray Alonso de Benavides' Revised Memorial of 1634. Albuquerque: University of New Mexico Press.

Hoijer, Harry

1956   "The Chronology of the Athapaskan Languages." International Journal of American Linguistics 22: 219–232.

1971   "The Position of the Apachean Languages in the Athapaskan Stock." In Apachean Culture History and Ethnology, edited by Keith H. Basso and Morris E. Opler, 3–6. Anthropological Papers of the University of Arizona 21, Tucson.

Holen, Steven R.

1983 "Lower Loup Lithic Procurement Strategy at the Gray Site, 25CX1." M.A. Thesis, Department of Anthropology, University of Nebraska.

Hotz, Gottfried

1970 Indian Skin Paintings from the American Southwest. Translated by Johannes Malthauer. Norman: University of Oklahoma Press.

Howard, Robert P.

1972 Illinois: A History of the Prairie State. Grand Rapids, MI: William B. Eerdmans Publishing Co.

Huse, W.

1896 History of Dixon County, Nebraska. Ponca, Nebraska.

Hyde, George E.

1951 The Pawnee Indians. Denver: University of Denver Press.

1959 Indians of the High Plains. Norman: University of Oklahoma Press.

Hymes, Dell H.

1957 "A Note on Athapaskan Glottochronology." International Journal of American Linguistics 23: 291–297.

Irving, Washington

1956 A Tour on the Prairies. Norman: University of Oklahoma Press.

Jackson, Donald (ed.)

1966 The Journals of Zebulon Pike. Norman: University of Oklahoma Press.

Jackson, Donald, and Mary Lee Spense

1970 The Expeditions of John Charles Frémont. 5 Vols. Urbana: University of Illinois Press.

James, Edwin

1966   Account of an Expedition from Pittsburgh to the Rocky Mountains. Ann Arbor: University Microfilms.

John, Elizabeth

1975   Storms Brewed in Other Men's Worlds. College Station: Texas A&M University Press.

Jones, Paul A.

1937   Coronado and Quivira. Lyons, KS: Lyons Publishing Co.

Kenner, Charles L.

1969   A History of New Mexican-Plains Indian Relations. Norman: University of Oklahoma Press.

Kessell, John

1979   Kiva, Cross and Crown: The Pecos Indians and New Mexico, 1540–1840. Washington, D.C.: National Park Service.

Kingman County 4-H Council

1977   Kingman County: A Township by Township History. Kingman, KS: Cheatum Printing & Litho.

Koontz, John E.

1987   Personal communication, letter of November 30, 1987.

La Flesche, Francis

1932   A Dictionary of the Osage Language. Bureau of American Ethnology Bulletin 109. Washington, D.C.: Government Printing Office.

Le Page du Pratz

1763   The History of Louisiana: or of the Western Parts of Virginia and Carolina; Containing a Description of the Countries that lye on Both Sides of the River Mississippi, with an Account of the Settlements, Inhabitants, Soil, Climate and Products. London: Becket and de Hondt.

LeCompte, Janet

1986 "The French." In A Literature Review and Limited Archaeological Reconnaissance of Cultural Resources on the Banning Lewis Project Area, El Paso County, Colorado, by Jane L. Anderson, Janet LeCompte, and Christoper Lintz. Albuquerque, NM: Pioneer Archaeological Consultants.

Lemieux, Donald J.

1990 "Pierre François de Rigaud, Marquis de Vaudreuil." In The Louisiana Governors, from Iberville to Edwards, edited by Joseph G. Dawson. Baton Rouge: University of Louisiana Press.

Leonard, Irving A.

1949 Books of the Brave: Being an Account of Books and of Men in the Spanish Conquest and Settlement of the Sixteenth Century New World. Cambridge: Harvard University Press.

Loomis, Noel M., and A. P. Nasatir

1967 Pedro Vial and the Roads to Santa Fe. Norman: University of Oklahoma Press.

Ludwickson, John, Donald J. Blakeslee, and John O'Shea

1987 Missouri National Recreational River: Native American Cultural Resources. Wichita State University Publications in Anthropology 3. Wichita, KS: Wichita State University.

Mallam, Clark

1983 A Prehistoric Life Metaphor in South Central Kansas. Lyons, KS: Coronado-Quivira Museum.

Marcy, Captain Randolph B.

1937 Adventure on the Red River, Report on the Exploration of the Red River by Captain Randolph B. Marcy and Captain G. B. McClellan, edited by Grant Foreman. Norman: University of Oklahoma Press.

Margry, Pierre, ed.

1876– Découvertes et établissments des Français dans l'ouest et dans le sud
1886   de l'Amérique Septentrionale. 6 vols. Chicago: Library Resources
        (microfiche).

Mead, J. R.

1896   Trails in Southern Kansas. Transactions of the Kansas State Histori-
        cal Society 5: 88–93.

1986   Hunting and Trading on the Great Plains, 1859–1875, edited by
        Schuyler Jones. Norman: University of Oklahoma Press.

Miller, Wick R.

1986   "Numic Languages." Handbook of North American Indians, Volume
        11: Great Basin, 98–106.

Mooney, James

1898   Calendar History of the Kiowa Indians. Washington, D.C.: Bureau
        of American Ethnology.

1928   "The Aboriginal Population of America North of Mexico." Smithso-
        nian Institution, Miscellaneous Collections 80 (7).

Mott, Mildred

1938   "The Relation of Historic Indian Tribes to Archaeological Manifes-
        tations in Iowa." Iowa Journal of History and Politics 36 (3): 227–
        314.

Moulton, Gary E. (ed.)

1983   The Journals of the Lewis and Clark Expedition. Lincoln: University
        of Nebraska Press.

Munday, Frank J.

1927   The Record of the Pike Expedition. Nebraska History Magazine
        10 (3).

Murray, Charles Augustus

1841   Travels in North America during the Years 1834, 1835 & 1836. 2 vols. London: Samuel Bentley.

Nasatir, A. P.

1952   Before Lewis and Clark: Documents Illustrating the History of the Missouri, 1785–1804. St. Louis: St. Louis Historical Documents Foundation.

Newcomb, W. W., and T. N. Campbell

1982   "Southern Plains Ethnohistory: A Re-examination of the Escan-jaques, Ahijados, and Cuitoas." In Pathways to Plains Prehistory, edited by Don G. Wyckoff and Jack L. Hofman, 29–44. Norman: Oklahoma Anthropological Society, Memoir 3.

Norall, Frank

1988   Bourgmont, Explorer of the Missouri, 1698–1725. Lincoln: University of Nebraska Press.

Opler, Marvin K.

1943   "The Origins of Comanche and Ute." American Anthropologist 45: 155–158.

Opler, Morris E.

1982   The Scott County Pueblo Site in Historical, Archaeological and Ethnological Perspective. In Pathways to Plains Prehistory, ed. by Don G. Wyckoff and Jack L. Hofman, 135–144. Norman: Oklahoma Anthropological Society, Memoir 3.

1983   "The Apachean Culture Pattern and Its Origin." Handbook of North American Indians, Vol. 10: 368–392. Washington, D.C.: Smithsonian Institution.

Osborne, Charles C.

1972 Adams County: The Early Years. In Adams County: The Story, edited by Dorothy Weyer Creigh, 1–5. Hastings, NE: Adams County-Hastings Centennial Commission.

Parks, Douglas R.

1979 "The Northern Caddoan Languages: Their Subgrouping and Time Depths." Nebraska History 60 (2): 197–213.

1989 Personal communication. Letter listing Pawnee names for streams.

Parks, Douglas R., and Waldo Wedel

1985 "Pawnee Geography: Historical and Sacred." Great Plains Quarterly, Summer 1985: 143–176.

Pearce, T. M.

1965 New Mexico Place Names, A Geographical Dictionary. Albuquerque: University of New Mexico Press.

Peters, Emmanuel.

1915 Early History of Webster County. Pamphlet (n.p.).

Peterson, John M.

1989 "The Coronado Stone from Oak Mills, Kansas." The Kansas Anthropologist 10 (1–2): 1–10.

1990 "New Light on the Coronado Stone." The Kansas Anthropologist 11 (2): 28–30.

Pike, Albert

1967 Prose Sketches and Poems written in the Western Country, edited by David Weber. Albuquerque: Calvin Horn.

Richardson, Rupert N.

1933 The Comanche Barrier to South Plains Settlement. Glendale, CA: Arthur H. Clark.

Robertson, Nancy

1989   Personal communication. Conversation at the Santa Fe Trail Symposium, Santa Fe.

Roper, Beryl

1988   "How Did this River come to be Called Canadian?" Panhandle-Plains Historical Review 61: 17–24.

Sánchez, Joseph P.

1987   The Rio Abajo Frontier, 1540–1692: A History of Early Colonial New Mexico. Albuquerque: The Albuquerque Museum.

Sanders, Gwendoline, and Paul Sanders

1968   The Harper County Story. North Newton, KS: Mennonite Press.

Scholes, France V.

1937   "Church and State in New Mexico, 1610–1650." New Mexico Historical Review 11: 9–58, 145–179, 282–293, 297–349; 12: 78–106.

1942   Troublous Times in New Mexico, 1659–1670. Albuquerque: Historical Society of New Mexico.

Schroeder, Albert H.

1979   "Pecos Pueblo." Handbook of North American Indians, Volume 9: Southwest, 430–437. Washington, D.C.: Smithsonian Institution.

Secoy, Frank R.

1951   "The Identity of the Padouca: An Ethnohistoric Analysis." American Anthropologist 53 (4): 525–542.

Shine, Michael A., Monsignor

1924   "In Favor of the Loup Site." Nebraska History 7: 83–87.

Sibley, George C.

1927   "Extracts from the Journal of Major Sibley." Chronicles of Oklahoma 5: 196–220.

Simmons, Marc

1979 "History of Pueblo-Spanish Relations to 1821." In Handbook of North American Indians, Volume 9: Southwest, 178–193. Washington, D.C.: Smithsonian Institution.

1988 "Waystop on the Santa Fe Trail." In Pecos, Gateway to Pueblos and Plains, edited by John V. Bezy and Joseph P. Sánchez, 94–99. Tucson: Southwest Parks and Monuments Association.

Smith, G. Hubert

1974 "Notes on Omaha Ethnohistory, 1763–1820." Plains Anthropologist 18: 257–270.

1980 The Explorations of the Vérendryes in the Northern Plains, 1738–43, edited by W. Raymond Wood. Lincoln: University of Nebraska Press.

Thomas, Alfred Barnaby

1935 After Coronado, Spanish Exploration Northwest of New Mexico, 1696–1727. Norman: University of Oklahoma Press.

Twitchell, Ralph Emerson

1911 Leading Facts of New Mexico History. Cedar Rapids, IA: Torch Press.

1914 Spanish Archives of New Mexico. Cedar Rapids, IA: The Torch Press.

U.S. Department of Agriculture

1982 Soil Survey of Clark County, Kansas. Washington, D.C.: U.S. Government Printing Office.

Vehik, Susan

1986 "Oñate's Expedition to the Southern Plains: Routes, Destinations, and Implications for Late Prehistoric Cultural Adaptations." Plains Anthropologist 31: 13–34.

Villiers, Baron Marc de

1923   "Massacre of the Spanish Expedition of the Missouri (August 11, 1720)." Translated by Addison E. Sheldon. Nebraska History 6: 3–31.

Ware, Eugene F.

1960   The Indian War of 1864. Lincoln: University of Nebraska Press.

Wedel, Mildred Mott

1971   "J.-B. Bénard, Sieur de La Harpe, Visitor to the Wichitas in 1719." Great Plains Journal 10: 37–70.

1973   "The Identity of La Salle's Pana Slave." Plains Anthropologist 18: 203–217.

1981   The Deer Creek Site, Oklahoma: A Wichita Village Sometimes Called Ferdinandina, An Ethnohistorian's View. Norman: Oklahoma Historical Society Series in Anthropology, No. 5.

1982   "The Indian they Called Turko." In Pathways to Plains Prehistory: Anthropological Perspectives of Plains Natives and their Pasts, Edited by Don G. Wyckoff and Jack L. Hofman. Normam: Oklahoma Anthropological Society, Memoir 3.

Wedel, Waldo R.

1936   An Introduction to Pawnee Archaeology. Washington, D.C.: Bureau of American Ethnology, Bulletin 112.

1959   Introduction to Kansas Archaeology. Washington, D.C.: Bureau of American Ethnology, Bulletin 174.

Weltfish, Gene R.

1965   The Lost Universe. Basic Books: New York.

Wheat, Carl Irving

1957–   Mapping the Trans-Mississippi West, 1540–1861. San Francisco:
1963   Institute of Historical Geography.

Wilhelm, Paul, Duke of Württemberg

1973 Travels in North America, 1822–1824, translated by W. Robert Nitske, edited by Savoie Lottinville. Norman: University of Oklahoma Press.

Witty, Thomas A., Jr.

1969 "The Allison Ranch Dig." Kansas Archaeological Association Newsletter 14: 9.

Wood, W. Raymond

1955 "Historical and Archeological Evidence for Arikara Visits to the Central Plains." Plains Anthropologist 4: 27–31.

1983 An Atlas of Early Maps of the American Midwest. Illinois State Museum Papers 18. Springfield: Illinois State Museum.

Woods, Rev. Msgr. Earl C., and Charles E. Nolan

1987 Sacramental Records of the Roman Catholic Church of the Archdiocese of New Orleans, Vol. 1, 1718–1750. New Orleans: Archdiocese of New Orleans.

AFTERWORD

Long after this book was edited, it was too late to add a clarification to the text on page 154. That clarification is presented here. It involves the name *Panimaha* River, which occurs twice in the abstract of the Mallet journal.

The first mention of it occurs at the beginning of the overland trip to Santa Fe. I argued in Chapter 4 that the Mallets had written about the Maha (Omaha) village at the mouth of the Maha River (Bow Creek) but that the person who created the abstract of the journal confused this with references to Panimaha (Skiri Pawnee) villages in several locations, including on the Pani-maha River (Loup River).

The second use of the name *Panimaha* occurs at the end of the journey to Santa Fe. I believe that this use is not in error and that the Mallets intended to describe the distance and duration of travel from the last Pawnee village they had visited. This would have been a Skiri village somewhere on the Loup River—a Panimaha village on the Panimaha River. This identity makes sense of both the duration of their trip, their estimate of the distance involved, and the rate of travel that both figures imply.

INDEX